Arctic
Exploration
&
International
Relations
1900-1932

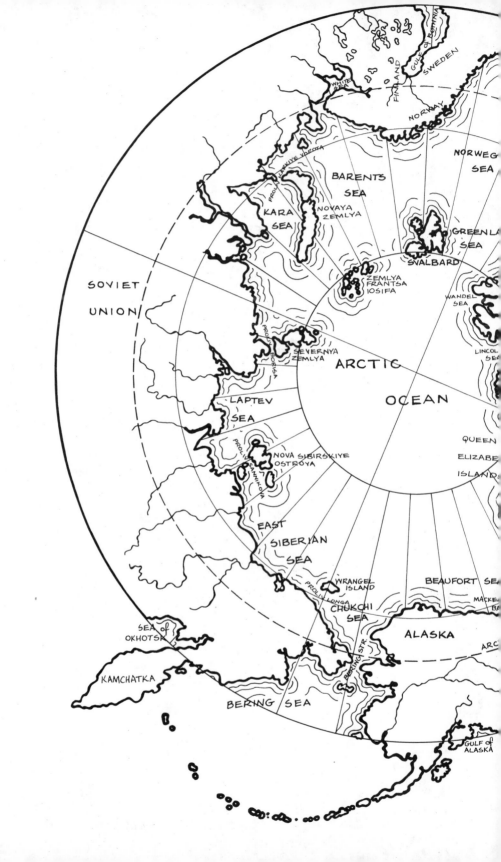

Arctic
Exploration
&
International
Relations
1900-1932

Nancy Fogelson

University of Alaska Press
Fairbanks, 1992

Library of Congress Cataloging-in-Publication Data

Fogelson, Nancy
    Arctic exploration & international relations, 1900-1932 : a period
of expanding national interests / Nancy Fogelson.
      p.   cm.
    Includes bibliographical references and index.
    ISBN 0-912006-61-7 : $15.00
    1. Arctic regions--Discovery and exploration. 2. International
relations. I. Title. II. Title: Arctic exploration and
international relations, 1900-1932.
    G626.F65 1992
    919.8--dc20   92-7321
                                                 CIP

International Standard Book Number: 0-912006-61-7
Library of Congress Catalogue Number: 92-7321

Printed in the United States by Thomson-Shore, Inc.
  on 60# Glatfelter B-16.

This publication was printed on acid free paper that meets the minimum
requirements for the American National Standard for
Information Science—Permanence of Paper for Printed Library
Materials ANSI Z39.48-1984.

Publication coordination and design by Pamela Odom
    with assistance from Deborah Van Stone.
Cartography by Nancy Van Veenen.
Cover design by Dixon Jones, IMPACT/Graphics, Rasmuson Library,
    University of Alaska Fairbanks.

Material in chapter 5 of the present work appeared in a slightly different
version in *Naval History: The Seventh Symposium of the U.S. Naval
Academy*, William B. Cogar, editor. Copyright 1988 by Scholarly Resources
Inc. Reprinted by permission of the publisher, Scholarly Resources Inc.

To Harold
whose steady hand held
the compass all these years.

Contents

Preface

American arctic exploration in the early twentieth century contributed significantly to the development of a global perception leading to the utilization of the Arctic as a strategic frontier after World War II.[1] Between 1900 and 1932, American explorers conducted major geological, geographic, oceanographic, and meteorological studies that provided important information for mining operations, commercial interests engaged in shipping and aviation development, and the establishment of naval and air bases.[2] Because American expeditions were concentrated in the eastern portion of the North American Arctic, an area claimed by Canada, relations between the two countries became strained when the United States ignored Canada's claims and continued to express interest in establishing American bases on islands in dispute. The Canadian government believed that the United States was using exploration to establish an official presence on territory claimed by Canada and to undermine Canadian jurisdiction over arctic islands potentially valuable for economic and military development. Canada was also being pressed from another direction. Scientific expeditions in Greenland and through the North American Arctic by Norwegian explorers, coupled with Norway's annexation of Spitsbergen in 1920 and a dispute with Denmark over claims to Greenland, appeared to be additional threats to Canadian predominance in the Arctic.

The United States also viewed European expeditions with suspicion and considered invoking the Monroe Doctrine against any European country that exhibited an interest in establishing a presence in the North American Arctic. The United States faced the problem of defining the western hemisphere above 70° north latitude as longitudinal lines converged.

By the end of the 1920s, air expeditions sponsored by countries with no arctic borders as well as by those clustered at the arctic perimeter further complicated international relations as countries realized how arctic airways reduced the distance between their countries. Flights conducted from 1927 to 1932 proved the feasibility of northern air routes and verified that no new territorial discoveries were possible. The period of exploration was over; the period of development was about to begin.

An awareness of the strategic and economic importance of the Arctic developed slowly, beginning in the sixteenth century. British expeditions, led by Sir Francis Drake, hoped to find arctic sea lanes, a Northwest Passage, that could be used to counter Spanish control of the seas.[3] Competition for political and economic supremacy continued with the explorers of the eighteenth century, and was still a factor well into the nineteenth century with the expeditions of Sir John Ross, Sir John Franklin, the Hudson's Bay Company, and American explorers such as Elisha Kent Kane, Isaac Hayes, and Charles Francis Hall.[4] Interest and activity in the Arctic broadened in the last twenty years of the decade when Adolphus Washington Greely, Robert E. Peary, and Fridtjof Nansen made major expeditions to Ellesmere Island, Greenland, and across the Polar Sea. Arctic fever intensified in the first decade of the twentieth century and was vividly described in widely publicized tales of the race to reach the North Pole.[5] After World War I, developments in technology contributed to an expansion in arctic exploration.[6] By the 1920s, governments, industries, and scientific societies were engaged in cooperative projects designed to collect scientific data and establish radio posts. Sovereignty became a major issue as the number and scope of expeditions increased and as commanders officially began to represent the interests of their governments.

Questions regarding sovereign rights became even more complex in the late 1920s with the introduction of dirigible and airplane flights across the Arctic. Throughout the 1920s, experiments with aircraft contributed to the application of a new definition of the north polar region as an "Arctic Mediterranean."[7] This area connecting Europe, North America, and Asia became the site for expeditions using both aircraft and traditional ships and sledges led by men less interested in heroic adventure and more concerned with furthering national prestige, collecting scientific data, testing new developments in transportation and communication technology, and locating potentially profitable mineral deposits. While not producing immediate benefits, these enterprises contributed necessary information for the establishment of mining operations, military bases, and polar and Great Circle air routes.[8] Between 1900 and 1932, the collection of scientific data, aviation development, mineral exploitation, and the resolution of diplomatic problems, especially between the United States and Canada, laid the foundation for effective use of the Arctic in World War II and the early years of the Cold War.[9]

The purpose of this study is to examine arctic exploration from 1900 to 1932, the date of the Second International Polar Year, with the intention of describing the impact of explorers' efforts to open the Arctic on international relations in general and on American-Canadian relations in particular. Although numerous disputes arose as nations sponsored expeditions in an apparent effort to establish an official presence on arctic islands, none of the conflicts were major. When aviation technology improved and aircraft were able to fly arctic air routes nonstop, the controversy over expansion subsided. Relations between countries then improved, opening opportunities for cooperation in developing arctic territory for defense and exploitation of oil and mineral deposits.

Few studies of modern arctic exploration have attempted to incorporate either the Arctic or the accomplishments of explorers into the general history of international relations. Neither of the two latest textbooks on American foreign policy, Robert Schulzinger's *American Diplomacy in the Twentieth Century* (second edition, 1984) or Thomas Patterson's *American Foreign Policy* (second edition, 1983) includes a polar perspective or relations with Canada as an important aspect of American diplomatic history. Lawrence P. Kirwan's *A History of Polar Exploration* (1960) and Jeannette Mirsky's *To the Arctic* (1934, reissued 1970), are excellent examples of cohesive narratives that describe arctic exploration as part of national policy, but each covers centuries of exploration, while expeditions after 1920 are examined only briefly. Pierre Berton's *Arctic Grail* adds to the chronicle of attempts to find the North Pole by summarizing the numerous expeditions and ending with the Robert E. Peary claim. Morris Zaslow's *The Opening of the Canadian North, 1870-1914* (1971) succeeded in describing this intricate process for Canada, but the study stops before the introduction of aviation. His second volume, *The Northward Expansion of Canada 1914-1967*, carefully examines the agricultural, administrative, and resource development of the Arctic, analyzing in detail Canadian development in its northern territory. William R. Morrison's *Showing the Flag: The Mounted Police and Canadian Sovereignty in the North 1894-1925* is an in-depth study of the role of the Canadian Mounted Police in establishing policies regarding law and authority in the Canadian Arctic. This is essentially a study of Canadian government policy, and as such provides important background information on the modernization of Ottawa's policy toward developing the north. Richard Diubaldo, in *Stefansson and the Canadian Arctic* (1978), incorporated Stefansson's accomplishments in a broader examination of Canadian politics and is a valuable contribution to the study of arctic affairs, although it deals only peripherally with international relations. *The Circumpolar North*, by Terence Armstrong, George Rogers, and Graham Rowley (1978), is a political and economic geography of the general arctic area and describes in detail the characteristics of each part of the Arctic. However, only one chapter deals with the impact of the Arctic on world affairs, and that concentrates on the present. Shelag Grant's *Sovereignty or Security? Government Policy in the Canadian North 1936-1950* examines the Canadian government's Northwest Territory policies regarding sovereign control and defense from World War II to 1950. An introductory chapter summarizes the period 1867-1930 from the perspective that the area was of little economic, political, or strategic value before World War II. However, the point is made that, after 1920, the Canadian government did exhibit increased interest in the area due to the discovery of oil. *The Age of the Arctic: Hot Conflicts and Cold Realities* (1989), by Gail Osherenko and Oran R. Young, continues the emphasis on political and economic geography, stressing the strategic importance of the Arctic as an international region subject to governments' policies designed to protect both national interests and the environment. Elen C. Signh's *The Spitsbergen (Svalbard) Questions: United States Foreign Policy, 1907-1935* (1980), attempts to put the Arctic in a diplomatic context but concentrates so heavily on the one example of mining operations in Spitsbergen that the development of a foreign policy, including the Arctic, appears to have been singularly concerned with an American coal company. At this time, no study has appeared that examines in detail the relationship between early twentieth century arctic exploration, technological development during this period, and relations among those countries engaged in arctic exploration.

I am most grateful for the help of the many people who made available the material and collections used for this study. Alison Wilson of the Scientific, Economic, and National Resources Branch of the National Archives has been consistently indispensable and knowledgeable about the material and the subject of polar exploration. The staffs of the Bowdoin College Library and the National Archives of Canada were also of tremendous help in completing this project. In addition, the assistance of the staff at the University of Cincinnati Interlibrary Loan Department and their prompt attention to my many requests is greatly appreciated.

Notes to Preface

1. For a description of global perception in relation to the strategic importance of the Arctic, see Alan K. Henrikson, "The Map as an 'Idea': The Role of Cartographic Imagery During the Second World War," *The American Cartographer* 2, 1 (1975): 19-53. For application of a global perspective, see U.S. Air Force Officers Training Corps, *Military Aspects of World Political Geography* (Montgomery, AL: U.S. Air University, September 1954), pp. 143-50. See also William E. Westermeyer and Kurt M. Shushterich, eds., *United States Arctic Interests: The 1980s and 1990s* (New York: Springer-Verlag, 1984).

2. William S. Carlson, *Lifelines Through the Arctic* (New York: Duell, Sloan & Pearce, 1962). J. Anker Nielson, "Our Hibernating Arctic," *Washington Post*, July 11, 1971, pp. 2-3. Blair Bolles, "Arctic Diplomacy," *Foreign Policy Reports* 24, 5 (June 1, 1948): 58-68.

3. With Spain controlling the Magellan Straits at the tip of Argentina, Great Britain hoped to find an alternate route to Asia from England, the shortest being an ice-free passage through the North American archipelago called the Northwest Passage. Derek Wilson, *The World Encompassed: Drake's Great Voyage* (New York: Harper & Row, 1977).

4. Jeannette Mirsky, *To the Arctic* (Chicago: University of Chicago Press, orig. pub. 1934, 1970 ed.), pp. 91-93. Jeannette Mirsky, *Elisha Kent Kane and the Seafaring Frontier* (Boston: Little, Brown & Co., 1954). Raymond H. Fisher, *Bering's Voyages: Whither and Why* (Seattle: University of Washington Press, 1977). Lawrence P. Kirwan, *A History of Polar Exploration* (New York: W. W. Norton & Co., 1960). John E. Caswell, *Arctic Frontiers* (Norman: University of Oklahoma Press, 1956).

5. Between 1900 and 1910, the *Periodical Guide to Literature* and the *New York Times Index* list multiple columns of articles and, in 1909, the entries cover several pages.

6. Lawrence E. Gelfand, *The Inquiry* (New Haven, CT: Yale University Press, 1963), pp. 208-9. Gustav Smedal, *Acquisition of Sovereignty Over Polar Areas* (Oslo: I Kommisjon Has Jacob Dybwad, 1931), pp. 7-9.

7. Vilhjalmur Stefansson, *The Northward Course of Empire* (New York: MacMillan Co., 1924).

8. W. L. G. Joerg, ed., *Problems of Polar Research* (New York: American Geographical Society, 1928).

9. Terence Armstrong, George Rogers, and Graham Rowley, *The Circumpolar North* (London: Methuen & Co., 1978). Central Intelligence Agency, *Polar Regions Atlas* (Washington, D.C.: Government Printing Office, 1978).

Introduction

*Beneath the Surface: A Geographic, Economic
and Political Description of the Arctic*

The Arctic, commonly thought of as the area above the Arctic Circle (66° 33' north latitude), is difficult to define because climate, tree line, ice conditions, and the existence of permafrost and tundra vary widely even at the same latitude. The single characteristic applicable to the entire region is the phenomenon of twenty-four hours of daylight at the summer solstice (June 21) and twenty-four hours of darkness at the winter solstice (December 21) but this in itself provides little guidance. Therefore to comprehend this remote area it is necessary to describe some general features and conditions. The Arctic is made up of a deep ice-covered ocean surrounded by two continental land masses, North America and Eurasia, major islands, Baffin and Greenland, Iceland, and archipelagos north of Eurasia and Canada.[1] The Bering Strait, a narrow funnel-like waterway between Siberia and Alaska, connects the western Arctic Ocean with the Pacific via the Bering Sea, and a wide waterway between Greenland and Spitsbergen connects the eastern Arctic Ocean to the Atlantic. Most arctic land areas consist of lowlands and plateaus although there are mountain ranges in Alaska, western Spitsbergen, eastern Labrador, and eastern Ellesmere and Baffin islands. Greenland, the world's largest island, is covered by an ice sheet which is up to 3 km thick and constitutes the second highest land mass in the northern hemisphere (the highest being the Tibetan Plateau). The surface of arctic land areas is either rock or ice desert or tundra, often underlain with perennially frozen ground or "permafrost."[2] Polygonal cracks sometimes form in the ground as a result of alternate freezing and thawing. Seen from afar, the variety of colorful plants during the short summer months become lost in the vast flat landscape and, in most of the Arctic, tundra

1

and desert regions appear as a monotonous panorama, uniform in color and form.[3]

Arctic climate is complex because it includes large maritime and continental regions. The major climatic differences between Vancouver and Winnipeg at 50° north latitude are comparable to the differences between Anchorage, southern Greenland or Norway and locations in central Canada at Hudsons Bay or central Siberia at Yakutsk. Coastal arctic air is clearest in early spring, but as the temperature rises, warmed air in contact with great expanses of ice and water produces dense fog. Precipitation is slight and variable. The cold dry atmosphere creates a natural environment for preservation. The air is nearly free of bacteria, and caches of food are edible after decades of storage.[4]

A fundamental characteristic of bodies of water located north of the Arctic Circle is ice. Radiation, wind and water currents produce some thawing in the summer but areas affected by thaw are not predictable, and any openings in the ice are limited in area and the length of the time they remain ice-free. Arctic sea ice moves continually because of currents, winds, and tides.[5] It consists of flat ice floes separated by ridges and leads. The ridges are created by compressive forces which force the floes against each other. Openings or leads are created by tensile forces which cause the floes to separate. Those leads may close before freezing or may freeze into thin ice.

The deep arctic basin is surrounded by a continental shelf that changes from a broad smooth northward extension of the Lena Delta north of Eurasia to deep valleys and fjords in the Kara Sea. Although there was still no available description of the shelf north of Greenland in 1928, early in the 1900s Robert E. Peary had described the shelf area north of Ellesmere Island as being uneven and irregularly shaped. The continental shelf surrounding the Canadian archipelago consists of fjords of greater depth and dimension than those found in other areas. The configuration of the continental shelf became a political issue in the twentieth century as countries sought to establish sovereign rights to islands north of Canada. For example, as competition for control over arctic territory and waterways intensified, Canada attempted to protect its interest in these islands by claiming jurisdiction, citing the archipelago's connection to the Canadian mainland via the continental shelf.

A geographic description of the Arctic became available to governments, scientific institutions, and the general public as a result of numerous expeditions. Explorers studying arctic regions in order to obtain accurate geographic data also returned with information of economic value, especially concerning natural resources and the location of fishing grounds. American economic interest in the Arctic had begun early in the nineteenth century when explorers' reports were used in the search for more lucrative fishing and whaling areas.[6] As commerce became more important to the American economy, national interests began to expand from protection of national borders to include protection of sea lanes and potentially profitable fishing grounds.[7] The acquisition of Alaska and Secretary of State William H. Seward's interest in Canada and the Arctic developed from a combination of the idea of "Manifest Destiny," commercial growth, and the association of both with national prestige and power.[8]

Commercial interest in the Arctic expanded at the end of the nineteenth century with the gold rush in the Yukon and Alaska and the discovery of rich coal and iron deposits in Greenland, Canada, and Alaska. The value of the Arctic rapidly became associated with mineral deposits, especially in the 1920s when the first report appeared describing oil in southern Alaska. The news resulted in an "oil rush," and prospectors filed claims on 35,000 acres of potentially valuable oil fields.[9]

The Canadian subsidiary of Standard Oil of New Jersey also located oil deposits in Canada, near the Arctic Circle at Fort Norman. The area was described correctly but prematurely as comparable in value to Mexico and Oklahoma, and predictions were made that within four years exploration would result in profitable oil extraction, and the creation of distribution and storage systems in arctic Canada.[10] The strike encouraged prospectors whose increased claims were more than the government could handle, and the Department of the Interior opened a new office in the Mackenzie district to deal with the increased work load.[11] It was hoped this icebound wealth, locked away by frozen rivers, would become accessible by use of aircraft. Preliminary flights were successful and oil companies began to establish operations, but plans far exceeded the capabilities of aircraft to provide transportation of men and materials or equipment to perform satisfactorily in cold weather.[12]

Standard Oil of California began exploring in Alaska in 1921 when several teams were sent to investigate the area from Nome to Point Barrow. It was acknowledged that transportation could be a problem if oil were found, but the company believed a pipeline could be laid from Point Barrow to Fairbanks where oil could then be shipped out by rail. Each time a new oil site was reported, the find was described with the fanfare of a gold strike and, in July 1921, a report of high-grade oil near Anchorage resulted in a stampede of claim stakers.[13]

American oil companies explored the Asian subarctic as well as the Alaskan and Canadian Arctic in their search for oil fields. In 1921, Sinclair Consolidated Oil Corporation secured an oil lease on Sakhalin Island. Operations were delayed months as the company haggled with the State Department over government protection for its investment, protection the State Department could not guarantee. The central issue was that the United States did not recognize Soviet Russia and therefore could not support a contract between an American national and the Soviet government, especially a contract negotiated over territory also claimed by another country, Japan.[14] The contest over arctic oil rights continued through the middle of the decade. The United States partici-pated in reciprocity treaties with Canada, hoping to protect American drilling interests by stipulating that foreign individuals or governments could only acquire rights to oil lands in the Canadian Arctic if the territory were open to the United States.[15] Efforts to locate new oil fields in Alaska declined when oil was located in California and Oklahoma during the 1920s, but the Arctic remained an area of special interest to the government and industry. Considering the potential value of arctic territory as a mineral reserve and for bases on a transportation route, the government acknowledged the advantage of establishing a political and economic presence in arctic territory outside Alaska.[16]

The political importance of the Arctic is inextricably tied to its economic value and can best be understood by examining conflicting claims to territory. The question of sovereign rights in the Arctic emerged as a major concern after World War I with the introduction of aviation as a means of transportation and exploration. Territorial claims were based on decisions made at the beginning of the century restricting sovereignty to areas settled and/or administered by the claimant. During the 1920s, some attempt was made to allow countries initiating govern-ment-authorized explorations to claim territory discovered as a result of expeditions launched specifically to search for land. The countries involved decided the disadvantages were too great and the idea was never implemented.[17]

American interests in the Arctic extended from Russian Siberia through Alaska and Canada to Greenland where business and government hoped to secure access to natural resources and develop necessary transportation systems, especially air routes.[18] By 1933, American national interests in the Arctic were sufficiently well defined for the government to consider formulating an official policy that would protect the country against foreign claims to or incursion into arctic areas considered within an American geographic sphere. The government realized that new criteria were essential because reliance on the Monroe Doctrine to discourage foreign expansion in the Arctic was of questionable value in an area where converging longitudes nullified the idea of a western hemisphere.[19]

Conflicts among the United States, Canada, and Norway declined in the 1930s when successive flights proved no unclaimed territory existed. Canada settled questions of sovereignty over islands north of the Canadian mainland discovered by the Norwegian Otto Sverdrup, and its claim to the whole archipelago remains unchallenged. The United States continued to develop Alaska, but arctic expeditions were severely curtailed.[20] By 1932, American and Canadian national interests were well defined politically. As economic development slowed under the repercussions of an international depression, government interest in the Arctic declined. World War II once again brought the Arctic into focus, this time as an area of military activity and predictions of strategic value became a reality.

Exploration in the Arctic began with a search for a short route from Europe to Asia. The route did not materialize until the introduction of aviation when not the Arctic itself but the airspace above it became the proverbial Northwest Passage. For centuries men and nations were lured toward the far North. Once they reached the pinnacle of the globe, they reached out beyond its surface, marked paths through the arctic skies, and returned to the ever-present inhospitable wilderness to find neither gold nor glory, but oil.

Notes to Introduction

1. Central Intelligence Agency (CIA), *Polar Regions Atlas* (Washington, D.C.: Government Printing Office, 1978), p. 4. Terence Armstrong, George Rogers, and Graham Rowley, *The Circumpolar North* (London: Methuen & Co., 1978),

p. 6. Otto Nordenskjold and Ludwig Mecking, *The Geography of the Polar Regions* (New York: American Geographical Society, 1928), pp. 108-9. The area identified as arctic is separated from the temperate zone by a subarctic area extending from the tree line through coniferous forests. George Kimble and Dorothy Good, *Geography of the Northlands* (New York: American Geographical Society, 1955), pp. 1-3.

2. Nordenskjold and Mecking, *The Geography of the Polar Regions*, pp. 110-11. Inland ice of any great extent is found primarily in the interior of Greenland whose ice cap, the most spectacular in the Arctic, is characterized by deep fissures and sharp undulations.

3. Kimble and Good, *Geography of the Northlands*, p. 31. Armstrong, Rogers, and Rowley, *The Circumpolar North*, pp. 17-18. CIA, Polar Regions Atlas, p. 11.

4. Nordenskjold and Mecking, *The Geography of the Polar Regions*, pp. 112-14. Kimble and Good, *Geography of the Northlands*, pp. 42, 63. CIA, *Polar Regions Atlas*, pp. 8-9. Armstrong, Rogers, and Rowley, *The Circumpolar North*, p. 8, 16.

5. Nordenskjold and Mecking, *The Geography of the Polar Regions*, pp. 130-33. CIA, *Polar Regions Atlas*, pp. 12-13.

6. Lawrence M. Gould, *The Polar Regions in Relation to Human Affairs* (New York: American Geographical Society, 1958), p. 5. S. W. Boggs, "The Polar Regions," typed ms. State Department Office of the History Advisor, 1933, State Department Records, RG59, 1930-39, 800.014, National Archives, Washington, D.C. [hereafter cited as NA].

7. John E. Sater, *The Arctic Basin* (Washington, D.C.: Arctic Institute of North America, 1968), pp. 9-11.

8. Charles A. Beard, *The Idea of National Interests* (New York: The MacMillan Co., 1934), pp. 28, 51, 62. A similar process occurred in Russia at the same time. C. J. Webster, "The Economic Development of the Soviet Arctic and Subarctic," *The Slavonic and Eastern European Review* (December 1950): 177-211.

9. *New York Times*, July 16, 1920, p. 19.

10. Ibid., October 22, 1920, p. 22.

11. Northwest Territories Council Minutes, 1921, p. 10, M8-11, National Archives of Canada, Ottawa [hereafter cited as NAC].

12. Agnes C. Lairt, "The Sky-Way to the North," *The Independent* (June 11, 1921): 614.

13. *New York Times*, July 13, 1921, p. 17; July 31, 1921, sec. 2, p. 1; Aug. 21, 1921, p. 4.

14. *Foreign Relations of the United States*, 1923, pp. 798-802.

15. U.S. Congress, Senate Document #424, December 6, 1923, 68th Cong., 1st sess. Northern Affairs Program, RG85 v748 f4287, PAC. Philip S. Smith, "A Survey of Oil of Alaska," *Science*, sup. x (February 19, 1926).

16. Boggs, "The Polar Regions."

17. U.S. Navy War College report, "Jurisdiction Over Polar Areas," October 29, 1937, Newport, RI. Norway to State Department, March 1929, State Department Records, RG59 800.014, NA.

18. John Gaddis, *Russia, The Soviet Union and the United States* (New York: Wiley, 1978), pp. 91-93. David A. Shannon, *Twentieth Century America: The Twenties* (Chicago: Rand McNally, 1974), p. 91.

19. Boggs, "The Polar Regions." Lawrence M. Gould, "Strategy and Politics in the Polar Areas," *American Academy of Political Science* (January 1948): 105-14.

20. Richard E. Byrd's Antarctic expeditions in the 1930s were government funded. The decline in arctic exploration may have been because of the certainty that no new land existed combined with the shift of funds to Antarctica.

The First to Go the Farthest

*Nineteenth Century Arctic Exploration
and Manifest Destiny*

Arctic exploration flourished in the nineteenth century. Men who sailed into the unknown and mostly uncharted frozen North sought wealth and glory. Nations that sent them hoped to establish shorter trade routes from the West to Asia, chart ocean tides and the flow of ice, and locate new fishing grounds to satisfy the growing demand for whale products.[1] Great Britain excelled in arctic exploration in the 1800s.[2] British-led voyages were internationally acclaimed and produced a steady accumulation of geographic information about European and Canadian arctic waterways and islands. The expeditions of explorers such as Sir John Ross, the Hudson's Bay Company, and Sir John Franklin demonstrated British proficiency in arctic exploration. However, the tragic death of Franklin and his crew in 1848 marked the decline in large-scale expeditions sponsored by the government and, by the middle of the century individuals and scientific organizations primarily sponsored or funded expeditions.

With the decline in national exploration, Great Britain lost its advantage. Expeditions from Scandinavia and the United States began to compete with those from Great Britain in making discoveries and in acquiring the distinction of having sailed the farthest north.[3] American expeditions began in response to the disappearance of Franklin's ships, but by the end of the century, American arctic exploration had become part of the country's efforts to further commercial opportunities, defend its geographic territory, protect its trade routes, and expand American influence and prestige beyond national borders.[4] The first American expeditions were sent to search for Franklin. Like their European counterparts, they were unsuccessful. As one expedition followed another, the humanitarian motive for finding Franklin gradually was replaced by a personal desire to explore and, by the end of the century, the United States had become as active in arctic exploration as any European nation.[5] Although some explorers hoped to reach the North Pole, the primary purpose of most of this activity was to study natural phenomena.[6] From 1850, when the first expedition sailed to aid Franklin, until 1881, the First International Polar Year, American explorers and scientific organizations contributed information on arctic geography that helped change the popular perception of the Arctic from that of a frozen wasteland to a region potentially rich in natural resources, one that would someday be strategically as well as commercially valuable to the United States.[7]

The nineteenth century was an age of exploration for the United States as well as for European nations.[8] Not only were islands in the major oceans charted, but Antarctica was defined as a continent.[9] The interior of Africa was explored and mapped. The American West was surveyed and its resources catalogued, and the Arctic was subject to an extensive search for riches and trade routes.

After 1840, the purpose of geographic discovery in the United States shifted from simple notation of landmarks and natural wonders to a scientific assessment of basic resources, serious study of primitive cultures, and the application of the engineer's calculations. Much of this investigation had been performed by the U.S. Army through the 1840s, but by the end of the 1850s, the civilian scientist as an expert or specialist in a particular field became the primary agent for scientific investigation. American expansion outside the continent was part of a general westward push, and the exploration of distant lands was closely related to scientific activity in the continental territories.[10] Exploration westward and into the Arctic was an expression of American "Manifest Destiny" to conquer the continent, settle and develop the land, and compete with other countries in the acquisition of scientific knowledge.[11]

American explorers who sailed to the Canadian Arctic to search for Franklin did so out of a combination of a compelling desire for adventure and an equally compelling need to understand the complex natural environment. Sir John Franklin had been one of England's most famous and successful explorers. When his 1845 expedition in search of the Northwest Passage failed to return, all who read of his mysterious disappearance felt the loss. The British government commissioned nine rescue missions between 1847 and 1850, but none was successful.[12]

When English rescue missions failed to locate the men or find any evidence of the ships, Lady Franklin refused to give up the search and, in the spring of 1849, wrote to President Zachary Taylor requesting aid. She appealed for help on humanitarian grounds, but, leaving nothing to chance, reminded Taylor there were possible benefits for the United States from such a mission. She wrote that a Russian relief expedition would be sent out that summer from the Asiatic Bering Strait and went on to describe the possibilities of an international effort to find her husband becoming a "noble spectacle" performed by three great nations "possessed of the widest empires on the face of the globe." Of course she would have preferred that her husband's rescue and the discovery of the Northwest Passage had been accomplished by the British but would rejoice if America were successful. Taylor expressed his sympathy and desire to help, but added he was limited in sending aid because of a lack of ships able to withstand the "perils of a proper exploration" and the lack of congressional appropriations. He could, however, broadcast the announcement of a British reward (£20,000 sterling) among American whalers and seamen and request that Congress consider making an adequate appropriation.[13]

Henry Grinnell, a wealthy American philanthropist and president of the American Geographical Society, on hearing about the renewed interest in rescuing Franklin, offered to finance the expedition. He asked Congress to approve his plan to supply equipment and ships which could then be staffed with navy seamen and officers. Emphasizing that the primary purpose of the expedition was to rescue Franklin and his men, Grinnell added that scientific benefits would accrue from exploring the general area, and that there was also an opportunity for the United States to find and navigate the Northwest Passage. He informed Congress that with the aid of Matthew Fontaine Maury, director of the National Observatory, he had been able to secure two ships outfitted with navigational equipment. He based his request for a navy crew on the belief that the inclusion of military personnel would "give the vessels something like a naval and military discipline" which he felt was essential in order to avoid insubordination.[14]

Henry Clay asked Congress to support the request, although he feared the expedition would not find any of the men alive and doubted any clue would be found. He argued that Congress should accept Grinnell's proposal because "the attempt . . . will be gratifying to the whole world" and "some useful discoveries may be made which will add to the amount of information we already possess."[15] Although Clay was enthusiastic about the expedition, he was cautious with regard to turning it over to Grinnell. He felt it might not be in the best interest of the country. He was hesitant to combine private and government interests in a project such as the one planned because of the possibility of confusion in responsibility occurring by placing U.S. Navy personnel under "control" of a private individual. To avoid losing control of the operation, Clay suggested the government completely fund the expedition and recommended a liberal appropriation to purchase ships. Although Grinnell had offered to place his ships under government control, Clay feared that Grinnell rather than the United States would benefit from the prestige if the proposed expedition were not completely government sponsored. He cautioned Congress to consider the possibility that the United States might look foolish for not having the proper and necessary ships and for having to rely on Grinnell's.[16] After much debate and many objections to the expedition as a "wild goose chase," Clay's recommendation for a completely government-sponsored expedition was rejected, Grinnell's proposal adopted, and the request for 30 seamen and a "few officers" granted.[17]

U.S. Navy Lt. Edwin J. DeHaven, a colleague of Maury's at the Observatory, was chosen to lead the expedition which left May 22, 1850. He had been well trained in navigational skills and shared Maury's view that exploration would contribute to the growth of scientific knowledge rather than simply provide an opportunity to satisfy heroic aspirations. DeHaven's instructions were general enough so that should he decide to try to navigate the Northwest Passage, there would be no reprisals for acting beyond the specifically stated mission of finding Franklin.

The purpose of this expedition is not clear. The possibility of rescuing Franklin was scant. Aside from the rhetoric describing the endeavor as a necessary humanitarian action, instructions regarding the search were vague. In contrast, the less publicized aspect, finding a channel to the Pacific, was well detailed and included directions regarding whom to contact and where, should DeHaven reach the Pacific.[18] Furthermore, he was directed to look for various natural phenomena, one being the existence of open water, an idea based on investigations of winds and ocean currents studied at the National Observatory.[19] DeHaven sighted frost smoke which indicated open water and reinforced the theory that open leads, such as the one sighted, marked the entrance to an open Polar Sea, a theory subsequent expeditions tried to prove.[20] Although DeHaven's expedition did not return with information on Franklin, it did produce valuable coastal charts, hydrographic information, and a detailed description of Grinnell Land.[21]

Elisha Kent Kane, physician on the DeHaven voyage, was the next to attempt to rescue Franklin, again with Grinnell's backing. The expedition, which began in 1853, set a new pattern for polar exploration. Traditional nineteenth century expeditions had employed large crews, more than one ship, and supplies and clothing from the mother country so explorers would not have to resort to what was believed barbarous customs practiced by Eskimos.[22] Kane's expedition was different. He set out in one small, strong, readily maneuverable vessel, the *Advance*. The ship, beset by ice, had to be abandoned and the party traveled 1,200 miles by foot and in a small boat to complete the mission. Kane's party suffered from scurvy, as had nearly all such expeditions. However, the suffering was far less than previous explorers had reported and left no residual effects. Kane's medical training and curiosity had prompted him to experiment with the use of raw seal meat, not as a last resort, but as a staple in the diets of both seamen and officers. Basing his decision on the observation that Eskimos did not suffer from the debilitating and often fatal disease, Kane reasoned that expeditions could remain in the Arctic longer with fewer supplies if Eskimo living habits were studied and used with modifications.[23] This hypothesis became the foundation for Vilhjalmur Stefansson's theory of the Arctic as a friendly environment, capable of providing reasonable living space and supporting development for economic purposes.[24]

Kane, like his predecessors, found no trace of Franklin and it is questionable if he really thought he would. Kane was an extraordinarily inquisitive man with a driving desire for adventure and accomplishment that has been equaled in American arctic exploration only by Robert E. Peary. Kane's expedition, said to have "added more to the knowledge of the Arctic regions than any attempted up to that time," resulted in a survey of Smith Sound, delineation of the northern coast of Greenland, and the discovery and survey of the Humboldt Glacier and the area north to a new land Kane named Washington.[25] The expedition returned in

1853, a huge success. Kane was a hero, the first of what would grow to be an elite cadre of men drawn to the Arctic again and again until either their money or health gave out. In Kane's case, it was his health that failed and his fellow physician and competitor, Dr. Isaac Israel Hayes, continued what by then was becoming a pattern.[26]

Hayes' expedition was supported by the Smithsonian Institute, U.S. Coast and Geodetic Survey, and American Geographical Society.[27] Although he stated that he hoped to find information regarding the Franklin expedition, considerable evidence had been produced showing that the Franklin party had traveled in an opposite direction to the route Hayes had laid out. His repeated insistence that he hoped to return with news of Franklin masked a deeper obsession with besting Kane. Hayes believed that if he could find an open Polar Sea, it could be used as a waterway to reach the North Pole. He also planned to complete a survey of the north coast of Greenland and Grinnell Land and conduct investigations in different branches of natural science.

This ambitious project lacked the humanitarian appeal of previous explorations, and Hayes attracted only a small group of supporters. In an attempt to increase interest, he began to emphasize commercial and nationalistic aspects of his proposal. Hayes noted that the expedition would advance the course of science and add to the credit of the country's "national character." Fund raising was difficult and supporters remained hesitant to commit themselves to the expedition. Grinnell contributed to the venture but with a much smaller amount than he had for either DeHaven or Kane. The venture limped along until March 1860, when the American Geographical Society called a general meeting and Dr. B. A. Gould of Harvard gave a stirring speech which reminded potential backers that "Europe [had] contributed more than her just proportion of geographic expeditions. We Americans now owe it to the world and to ourselves to prosecute these researches."[28]

Hayes sailed on the schooner *United States* in 1860. He reached Smith Sound and attempted to explore the ice cap near Cape Alexander. His observations showed that one discharging glacier had been advancing at the unusually rapid rate of twelve feet a month, information important for fishing and shipping interests whose vessels traveled in the North Atlantic. Aside from this, the rest of his observations and attempts at mapping were too inaccurate to be of much importance.[29] Hayes' efforts were admirable but his reputation as an arctic explorer who had contributed significant information about the Arctic was diminished by his proclivity for exaggeration and flowery prose. His narratives were avidly read, not so much for their geographic or scientific content but as stories of thrilling adventure.

The search for Franklin continued long after there was reasonable hope for finding any of the men alive.[30] Perhaps explorers continued to promote this romantic and humanitarian motive in order to win public support and funding. In the 1860s, Charles Francis Hall, a newspaperman from Cincinnati, set off on the first of two trips he publicized as attempts to find Franklin. Unable to convince the government of the value of his proposals, Hall concentrated on raising money from private sources. In February 1860, he issued a circular stating that the purpose of this, his first expedition, was to search for Franklin and any survivors, complete the history of the Franklin expedition, and "promote and benefit the cause of geography, navigation, natural history, and science."[31] His proposal elicited some support from Grinnell, but interest in Franklin had declined by then. Despite insufficient funding, Hall's voyages were extraordinary. Untrained in arctic or any other kind of exploration, he set out with little equipment and scant knowledge of the Arctic.[32] On his first two trips, 1860-62 and 1864-69, he was able to record valuable information about Eskimos, successfully adopt many of their methods for surviving in the arctic environment, and accurately chart bays, sounds, and islands that had for centuries puzzled more experienced explorers.

Hall hoped to secure government support for a third trip. When results of the first two expeditions reached President Ulysses S. Grant, he agreed to see Hall who then presented his case so convincingly that the President invited him to lecture before Congress. That body responded with an appropriation of $50,000 for this, Hall's last and most successful voyage.[33]

The funding barely covered the cost of supplies and a ship. With little money left for wages for an exploring party, Hall turned to volunteers. The *Polaris* sailed on July 3, 1871, with an international crew. The men were capable, individually experienced in both scientific research and exploration. Each man was accustomed to making decisions and expected others to carry on with the necessary work, a condition that probably worked against any possibility for a harmonious voyage. Hall had been used to being the chief decision maker; the crew believed decisions were a shared responsibility. Hall was irascible and dogmatic, traits not conducive to providing able leadership for a bickering crew divided in its support. Without consulting any of the crew, Hall decided to take advantage of the unusually open water in Kennedy Channel and reached 82°11' north latitude before stopping for the winter, two hundred miles north of where Kane had stopped and fifty miles farther than Hayes. Hall then made a series of sledge trips, bringing back the first data describing the northernmost shore of Ellesmere Island and part of the Polar Basin.[34]

Hall was a "self-made" man, suspicious of anyone he thought might be out to rob him of his due glory. Unfortunately, his abilities as an explorer were overshadowed by his deficiencies as a leader and this, the largest of his expeditions, was the most poorly led. Hall aggravated tensions among the men and when they responded with anger and threats of retribution, Hall expressed fear that he would be murdered. He died on that expedition, probably from accidental food poisoning or a stomach ailment, but charges of foul play led to a lengthy investigation. Although murder charges were dismissed, the story continued to circulate and plague the survivors, and the allegation remained a part of the Hall mythology until publication of his latest biography in 1971.[35]

The mysteries of the Polar Ocean continued to fascinate explorers and the prevalent theory of an open waterway encouraged men to try their luck at navigating this unknown area in the hope of reaching the North Pole. These grandiose schemes, though, were not the only impetus to arctic exploration. From the mid-1800s until the end of the century, increased trading, fishing, and whaling depended on more precise information about the northern Atlantic and Pacific oceans. A lack of adequate maps and sea charts hindered fishermen, who appealed to the government for help.[36] In 1852, Senator William Henry Seward (Republican, NY), then a member of the Committee of Commerce, requested Congressional authorization for the exploration and reconnaissance of whaling routes in the Bering Strait area.[37] Seward argued that the project would promote United States commerce and assure American competitiveness in world trade. His appeal and Maury's report confirming that loss of ships and lives among whalers could be avoided with the proper charts convinced Congress to appropriate $125,000 for the mission.[38] The two-year project, directed by the Secretary of the Navy, was authorized to use one or more naval vessels staffed by army and navy officers.

As Secretary of State, Seward incorporated his interest in the Arctic with his overall philosophy regarding American national interests. The purchase of Alaska in 1867 provided the United States with what he believed could be the keystone in an American defense system which, with the proposed purchase of Greenland, would provide a complete system of bases from which the United States could control the Pacific and Atlantic approaches to North America.[39] Seward also believed that if the United States could acquire Iceland, the presence of a solid American flank on the east of British America would stimulate Canadian desire for annexation by the United States.[40] Seward's vision of the United States expanding through the lower Arctic was linked to his conception of an American empire that included not only Canada, but also Russian Siberia.[41] Seward's dream of an expanding United States with the Arctic as its strategic frontier remained unrealized for almost a hundred years but, as wildly visionary as his schemes may appear, his promotion of Alaska and the general arctic region was an important factor in the increase in American arctic exploration through the rest of the century.

In the 1870s, American expeditions into the Canadian and Russian Arctic gathered data to update ocean charts and improve maps of coastlines. U.S. Army Lt. Frederick Schwatka's 3,000 mile sledge expedition through the Canadian Arctic in 1871 proved that these barren lands could be explored fruitfully without disaster. His route was actually farther south than those of either Kane or Hall, but the detailed maps he produced added precise details about the area that earlier explorations had missed.[42]

In 1879, the *Jeannette*, under the command of Captain George Washington DeLong, was crushed in the ice off the shore of Herald Island as he attempted to duplicate Fridtjof Nansen's historic drift through the polar ice pack in the *Fram* in 1878.[43] The hope had been that, through such a drift, an open waterway would be found and charted. The *Jeannette* got no farther than the eastern edge of Arctic Siberia before it was crushed, but the voyage added important documentation that Wrangel and Herald were true islands and not part of a continental mass leading to the Pole.

The desire to be the first to reach the North Pole still inspired the adventurous, but mapping and exploratory expeditions were becoming more numerous. The geographic and scientific data brought back by these men were examined eagerly by the scientific community, and the leaders of such expeditions began to establish reputations as scientists as well as explorers. The hope of being the first to go the farthest still piqued the imagination of arctic explorers, but there was a new emphasis on mapping land and waterways and contributing to the understanding of natural phenomena.

An important change in the purpose of arctic exploration occurred in 1881. Under the direction of an Austrian explorer and scientist, Karl Weyprecht, the first International Polar Year (IPY) was organized to establish scientific stations in a ring through the Arctic.[44] Weyprecht hoped countries would unite to establish a uniform system of simultaneous observation posts to conduct magnetic and meteorological experiments.[45] The results of these studies of atmospheric change could then be applied to weather conditions in distant regions such as the United States and Europe. A significant characteristic of the plan was that there was to be no special attempt at geographic exploration or any plan to reach the North Pole.[46]

The International Polar Conference began its campaign for the IPY in 1878. Weyprecht described the proposal to the U.S. Army Signal Corps. He believed participation by the corps would be appropriate because of the IPY's emphasis on meteorology and the need for that information by the Weather Bureau, a part of the Signal Corps. Weyprecht suggested that the United States establish a polar station at Point Barrow, Alaska, an area reasonably accessible and suitable for continuous observations.[47] The army and Congress reacted favorably to the proposal. Americans had become more interested in arctic exploration as a result of numerous British, German, and Austrian expeditions which had recently returned from arctic regions with excellent maps and many new discoveries. The climate was right for participation by the United States. An American expedition could contribute valuable scientific studies and promote the country's honor.[48]

Lt. Henry W. Howgate, an officer in the Army Signal Corps, responded to Weyprecht's proposal with a plan to establish a colony as far north as possible, one that could be operated as a scientific station for three years.[49] In 1877, Howgate had sent an expedition to Florence and

Cumberland Gulf to collect provisions for a future colony at Lady Franklin Bay.[50] The site had been selected because of its northerly position and accessible coal seam, making it a logical base camp for the primary objectives of the expedition: to collect meteorological data and reach the North Pole. The ship was disabled while securing provisions and the plan was abandoned.[51] Howgate resubmitted his proposal in 1880, offering his own ship for the purpose of expediting a colonizing effort. The establishment of a polar station was eagerly considered, but Congress expressed concern over using a privately donated vessel. The image of the United States as a naval power was at stake, the same argument raised in 1850, and Congress rejected Howgate's offer.[52]

The Naval Committee of the House of Representatives revised Howgate's proposal, turning the expedition into a completely government funded operation. It justified the expedition by rationalizing that it was constitutional and the results would benefit "mankind" rather than any special interest group. The success of Hall's *Polaris* expedition in obtaining scientific data and charting Robeson's channel, the proposed route, was used to demonstrate that the plan was feasible. The primary purpose of the expedition was defined as reaching the North Pole. Additional instructions were issued for scientific observations, including studies of terrestrial magnetism and meteorology, but these were of secondary importance. Geographic discovery was encouraged as long as it complemented the drive to reach the Pole. The report concluded with a description of economic benefits from reliable sea charts and oceanographic information and noted that "the honor of the American name [was] involved."[53] Congress passed the bill in May 1880, authorizing the President to establish a station at Discovery Harbor in Lady Franklin Bay and to appoint Major Adolphus W. Greely, Fifth Cavalry, commander of the expedition.[54]

The completed plan included provisions for a second polar station at Point Barrow, Alaska, the area recommended by Weyprecht because of its accessibility. The Barrow party, commanded by Lt. P. Henry Ray, U.S. Army, left in July 1881. By October, a well-organized system had been established, including forays into the Alaskan interior and regular hourly observations of magnetic and meteorological conditions. The station was closed in August 1883, the work successfully completed with no casualties.[55]

Major Greely's Lady Franklin Bay expedition left in the summer of 1881. The voyage was uneventful and the easy passage lulled the ship's crew and Greely's party into believing that open water in the Smith Channel was not unusual.[56] Greely and his men erected a sturdy camp which they named Fort Conger. Well provisioned and within sight of a rich coal seam and herds of game, the men could concentrate on their assigned duties, assured that they were safe in the hostile arctic environment. Observations were recorded regularly, and sledging expeditions set out as soon as the dark winter began to wane. The land surveyed and the collection of scientific data exceeded that of any other American expedition. Greely and his crew surveyed the whole of Grinnell Land and compiled a thoroughly detailed report of the area's flora and fauna.[57]

Although the expedition was successful in collecting data, discipline within the party broke down because of constant fighting, apparently exacerbated by Greely's poor leadership. When relief ships, scheduled to arrive in 1882 and 1883, did not appear, Greely made plans to retreat south. The crew had become more difficult to manage and, in August 1883, early ice started to form. Greely's instructions were to retreat by September 1, a somewhat late date, but one which would allow the longest possible time for a relief ship to break through.[58] The camp was abandoned on August 9. Greely's decision to leave early was based on his fear that the newly formed ice would damage his small boat and make retreat extremely hazardous, if not altogether impossible.

There were two possible routes out of Fort Conger, one to Littleton Island off the coast of Greenland and one to Cape Sabine down the coast of Ellesmere. Greely chose Cape Sabine, expecting to find caches of food left by the ships that had evidently been unable to reach Fort Conger. The men encountered severe storms and an ice-filled channel, conditions that made the southward trek almost impossible. Instead of being able to sail straight down the channel, the reverse of their earlier voyage, the small boat was blown farther and farther from the land and was finally caught in the ice. Enough rations had been left at Fort Conger for another winter, but, by the time Greely acknowledged that retreat was impossible, return was also out of the question. Weather conditions had made the channel unnavigable and the men were not provisioned for a return sledge trip so far and so difficult.

The party reached Cape Sabine, but the rations left by the relief ships amounted to only enough for ten days for the twenty-five men. One relief

Kane Basin locating map for 19th century expeditions.

ship had turned back before unloading its emergency supplies, and the second had sunk and its provisions sequestered by the crew. Greely's men were trapped at Cape Sabine until a rescue party reached them in July 1884. Nineteen died of starvation and exposure and one man, kept alive by his companions through the long frightening ordeal, died shortly after the rescue ship sailed for home. The tragedy was attributed to Greely's poor judgment.[59] He clearly shared in the responsibility, but the major fault appeared to lie with the military. The relief expeditions were issued confusing instructions, and jealousy between the army and navy over which branch would be in command resulted in delays that directly contributed to the death of the men.[60]

Greely's records were lost on the return trip but fortunately a copy had been left at Fort Conger. When this set was retrieved and published, the scientific observations and geographic data proved so useful that the material became part of a standard collection used for over fifty years by the military and by scientific organizations. Although Greely's reputation had been badly damaged as a result of the death of so many of his men, he continued his career in the army using what he had learned of the Arctic to promote construction of the Washington-Alaska Military Cable and Telegraph System (WAMCATS) and to encourage men who served under his command to investigate the use of aviation in arctic regions.[61]

Government-sponsored expeditions ceased after the Greely episode and, until the 1920s, further explorations were organized by individuals and scientific societies. Although official involvement in arctic exploration was slight, national interest on a public and scientific level continued to increase. The result of this first IPY had demonstrated that the Arctic was not only a fearsome, cruel place, but also a frontier that could be tamed and subjected to rational study.

Americans historically have thought of their nation as one which developed out of combat with and adaptation to a wilderness frontier, a perception that remained long after the western frontier disappeared. Explorers easily became identified with this wilderness image, and arctic explorers exhibited characteristics of physical bravery and ingenuity which had traditionally been identified with American frontiersmen.[62] In 1920, historian Frederick Jackson Turner described the impact of the American frontier on the colonist as a force which strips off "the garments of civilization and arrays him in the hunting shirt and moccasin." Turner went on to describe this early American as one who "must accept the conditions which [nature] furnished or perish . . . ."[63] Turner's bonding of the early American with nature could readily be applied to arctic explorers who survived by accepting the natural environment in its stark primitiveness, wearing clothing made of seal and caribou skins and existing on raw seal meat. The American continental frontier may have been closed in 1890, but a new frontier was opened in the Arctic and the explorers became the new American frontiersmen.

Although arctic exploration appealed to a sense of adventure and personal desire for glory, it also was a way to advance national prestige.[64] Having achieved what it considered its manifest destiny, namely to develop the contiguous territory between the Atlantic and Pacific coasts, the country was equally convinced it had a mission to explore and open the Arctic. If expeditions had been concerned only with setting records for pushing the farthest north, arctic exploration might be looked at as simply a form of international competition for glory. However, most expeditions in the nineteenth century were designed to collect scientific data and to chart waterways and coastlines. Expanding trade benefitted from the new ocean charts, and fishermen, as vital to the economy as farmers, eagerly followed explorers' descriptions of areas rich in fish, seals, and whales.[65] The political and economic implications of arctic exploration suggest that American expeditions into arctic regions need to be examined as more than a series of heroic adventures.

Notes to Chapter 1

1. Jeannette Mirsky, *To the Arctic* (Chicago: University of Chicago Press, 1970), pp. 3-12. Paul Emile Victor, *Man and the Conquest of the Poles* (London: Hamish Hamilton Ltd., 1964).

2. J. N. L. Baker, *A History of Geographical Discoveries and Exploration* (Boston: Houghton Mifflin Co., 1982), pp. 453-72.

3. J. E. Nourse, USN, *American Exploration in the Ice Zones* (Boston: B. B. Russell, 1884). Angelo Heilprin, *The Arctic Problem* (Philadelphia: 1893), p. 119.

4. Nathan Reingold, *Science in Nineteenth Century America* (New York: Hill & Wang, 1964).

5. John Scott Ketie and O. J. Howarth, *History of Geography* (London: G. P. Putnam's Sons, 1913), pp. 152-60.

6. John E. Caswell, *Arctic Frontiers* (Norman: University of Oklahoma Press, 1956).

7. Mirsky, *To the Arctic.* CIA, *Polar Regions Atlas* (Washington, D.C.: Government Printing Office, 1978). A. Hunter Dupree, *Science in the Federal Government* (Cambridge, MA: Harvard University Press, 1957). John Kirtland Wright, *Geography in the Making: The American Geographical Society 1851-1951* (New York: American Geographical Society, 1952).

8. William H. McNeill, *The Rise of the West* (Chicago: University of Chicago Press, 1963), p. 658. Ray A. Billington, *The Far Western Frontier 1830-1860* (New York: Harper & Bros., 1956), Chap. 7. William H. Goetzman, *Explora-*

tion and Empire (New York: Alfred A. Knopf, 1967), p. 236. Merle Curti, *The Growth of American Thought* (New York: Harper & Row, 1964), pp. 319-22. Lawrence P. Kirwan, *A History of Polar Exploration* (New York: W. W. Norton & Co., 1960), pp. 453-73.

9. Kenneth J. Bertrand, *United States Exploration in Antarctica* (New York: American Geographical Society, 1971).

10. Dupree, *Science in the Federal Government*, pp. 56-69. Goetzman, *Exploration and Empire*, pp. 232, 355.

11. Charles Beard, *The Idea of National Interests* (New York: The MacMillan Co., 1932), pp. 22, 51, 62. Curti, *The Growth of American Thought*, p. 393.

12. Mirsky, *To the Arctic*, pp. 323-33.

13. U.S. Congress, Senate Executive Document #8, Zachary Taylor, "Message from the President of the United States," 31st. Cong., 1st sess., January 4, 1850.

14. Nourse, *American Exploration in the Ice Zones*, pp. 45-46. *Congressional Globe*, April 5, 1850, p. 644.

15. *Congressional Globe*, April 5, 1850, p. 644.

16. Ibid., May 1, 1850, p. 884.

17. Ibid., April 25, 1850, p. 219; May 1, 1850, p. 884.

18. Nourse, *American Exploration in the Ice Zones*, p. 49.

19. William Francis Leigh, *Matthew Fontaine Maury: Scientist of the Sea* (New Brunswick: Rutgers University Press, 1963), p. 539. Dudley W. Knox, *A History of the United States Navy* (New York: Van Rees Press, 1936), p. 182.

20. Samuel Edward Lawson, *Stanford's Compendium of Geography and Travel: North America, Canada and Newfoundland* (London: Edward Stanford, 1897), Chap. 19 Arctic Canada.

21. Nourse, *American Exploration in the Ice Zone*, pp. 43-46. Grinnell Land is the northern part of Ellesmere Island. A long, wide, and deep fjord separates it from the rest of the island at the eastern coast. Before extensive inland exploration, Grinnell Land was thought to be a separate land mass.

22. George W. Corner, *Doctor Kane of the Arctic Seas* (Philadelphia: Temple University Press, 1972), p. 263.

23. Ibid. See also, Jeannette Mirsky, *Elisha Kent Kane and the Seafaring Frontier* (Boston: Little, Brown & Co., 1954). Peter Freuchen, *Arctic Adventure* (New York: Farrar & Rhinehart, 1935), p. 178. Although the theory for avoiding scurvy dated back to Cook's voyages, seamen insisted they could not adopt native customs they considered savage and uncivilized. Kane was the first commander to have any great success in convincing his crew to eat raw meat and fish as a regular part of their provisions.

24. Vilhjalmur Stefansson, *The Friendly Arctic: The Story of Five Years in Polar Regions* (New York: The MacMillan Co., 1922).

25. *Congressional Globe*, March 7, 1856.

26. *Outlook* 130 (March 8, 1922): 368. Corner, *Doctor Kane of the Arctic Seas*. Prescott Holmes, *The Story of Exploration and Adventure in the Frozen Seas* (Philadelphia: Henry Altemus, 1896), p. 130. Kane died February 16, 1857, 37 years old.

27. Nourse, *American Exploration in the Ice Zone*, p. 132.

28. Wright, *Geography in the Making*, pp. 55-58.

29. Mirsky, *To the Arctic*, pp. 161-73. Leslie H. Neatby, *Conquest of the Last Frontier* (New York: H. Wolff, 1966), pp. 69-82. Kirwan, *A History of Exploration*, p. 181.

30. In 1854, Dr. John Rae, representing the Hudson's Bay Company, found an Eskimo who recalled white men who had died of starvation. In 1857, Leopold McClintock, on an expedition commissioned by Lady Franklin, found cairns erected by the Franklin party and confirmed that all had died. His route marked the first successful crossing of the proverbial Northwest Passage.

31. Nourse, *American Exploration in the Ice Zone*, p. 164.

32. Hall conditioned himself for exposure to arctic weather by camping out on Mt. Adams, a Cincinnati hillside.

33. Chauncy C. Loomis, *Weird and Tragic Shores: The Story of Charles Francis Hall, Explorer* (New York: Alfred A. Knopf, 1971), pp. 240-43.

34. Mirsky, *To the Arctic*, pp. 161-68.

35. George M. Robeson, Secretary of the Navy, *Hall's Polaris Expedition: Report to the President of the United States, 1873*, pp. vi-xiii. Loomis, *Weird and Tragic Shores*.

36. "Analysis of the Commerce of the United States With Various Countries of the World," *The Journal of Geography* (September 1906): 330-31.

37. Nourse, *American Exploration in the Ice Zones*, pp. 108-9. *Congressional Globe*, July 27, 1852, p. 1935.

38. *Congressional Globe*, July 29, 1852, pp. 1973-76.

39. Glyndon S. Van Deusen, *William Henry Seward* (New York: Oxford University Press, 1967), pp. 531-35. Morgan R. Sherwood, *Exploration of Alaska 1865-1900* (New Haven: Yale University Press, 1965), p. 4.

40. Van Deusen, *William Henry Seward*, pp. 531-32. Vilhjalmur Stefansson, "U.S. in Relation to Greenland," *Arctic Encyclopedia* (1974) microfilm reel #27.

41. Van Deusen, *William Henry Seward*, p. 535. Thomas A. Bailey, *A Diplomatic History of the American People* (New York: Merideth Corp., 1969), pp. 365-70. William A. Hunt, *Arctic Passage* (New York: Charles A. Scribner's Sons, 1975), p. 174.

42. Box 1, Correspondence, 1884, Donald B. MacMillan Papers [hereafter cited as DBM], Bowdoin College, Brunswick, Maine.

43. Adolphus W. Greely, U.S. Army, "Scientific Results of the Norwegian Polar Expedition 1893-96," *Popular Science Monthly* 57 (August 1900): 420-35. Ben E. Andrews, *The United States in Our Time* (New York: Charles A. Scribner's Sons, 1903), pp. 317-46. The *Jeannette* was equipped by James Gordon Bennett of the *Herald Tribune* (Stanley's patron in the search of Dr. Livingstone). The ship sailed under U.S. Navy orders with a crew that included two American Indians and two Chinese seamen.

44. Adolphus W. Greely, *Three Years of Arctic Service* (New York: Charles A. Scribner's Sons, 1886), p. 20. A. W. Greely, *Handbook of Arctic Discoveries* (Cambridge, MA: John Wilson & Son, 1895), p. 203. Weyprecht's proposal was presented to the German Scientific and Medical Association of Gratz. Bismarck, on hearing of the plan, appointed a scientific commission to study the proposal. The commission reported back that the work would be valuable and

Bismarck made plans for Germany to participate. Julius Payer, *New Lands Within the Arctic Circle* (London: MacMillan & Co., 1876).

45. C. J. Taylor, "First International Polar Year," *Arctic* 34, 4 (December 1981): 370-76.

46. Greely, *Three Years of Arctic Service*, p. 23. Nourse, *American Exploration in the Ice Zones*, pp. 108-9. Payer, *New Lands Within the Arctic Circle*, p. 119. There were 14 stations established, 2 in the Antarctic by France and the rest in the Arctic by Austria, Hungary, Finland, Denmark, Germany, England, Canada, Holland, Russia, Sweden, and the United States. Secondary or auxiliary stations working in cooperation with the polar stations were established in Europe, China, the United States, Latin America, and India. A total of 44 stations participated, manned by 700 men. Only one station suffered any loss of personnel, Lady Franklin Bay under the command of Greely.

47. Winfield S. Schley and J. R. Soley, *The Rescue of Greely* (New York: Charles A. Scribner's Sons, 1885), pp. 11-13. Weyprecht had advised that simultaneous observations be taken at circumpolar stations over a 12 month period. The plan was too extensive to be executed by one country and, therefore, its success depended on international cooperation.

48. Vilhjalmur Stefansson, "U.S. Weather Bureau," *Arctic Encyclopedia* (1974) microfilm reel #10.

49. Schley and Soley, *The Rescue of Greely*, p. 15.

50. Greely, *Three Years of Arctic Service*, p. 21. Henry W. Howgate, "Polar Colonization: The Preliminary Arctic Expedition, 1877," *History: North Pole* 349 (1879): 24-25. Ludwig Kumlien, "Natural History of Arctic America: The Howgate Polar Expedition 1877-78," *Smithsonian Institution Bulletin* vol. 23, art. 5, p. 5.

51. Schley and Soley, *The Rescue of Greely*, p. 14. Howgate, "The North Pole: An Abstract of Arctic Legislation in the Congress of the U.S.," *History: North Pole* (1879): 36-39.

52. *Congressional Record*, April 14, 1880.

53. U.S. Congress, Senate Report #94, 45th Cong. 2nd sess., February 13, 1878. Appropriations for the Lady Franklin Bay Station were $25,000.

54. "United States Arctic Colonization and Exploration in 1881," reprinted from the *Kansas City Review of Science and Industry* (August 1881): 1-21.

Nourse, *American Exploration in the Ice Zones*, pp. 525-66. U.S. Congress, House Report #453, 46th Cong., 2nd sess., March 9, 1880. Donald W. Mitchell, *A History of the Modern American Navy 1883 Through Pearl Harbor* (New York: Alfred A. Knopf, 1946), pp. 310-19. Greely, *Three Years of Arctic Service*, p. 304.

55. Schley and Soley, *The Rescue of Greely*, p. 13.

56. Lt. John W. Danehower, USN, "The Polar Question," *U.S. Naval Institute Proceedings* 11, 4 (1885): 633-99. Description of ice conditions in this area as reported in narratives from 1850 to 1880 indicate heavy ice would be more common.

57. Mirsky, *To the Arctic*, pp. 185-95. Neatby, *Conquest of the Last Frontier*, pp. 167-230. General William Mitchell, U.S. Army, *General Greely: The Story of a Great American* (New York: G. P. Putnam's Sons, 1936), pp. 58-83. Schley and Soley, *The Rescue of Greely*, pp. 22-23.

58. Neatby, *Conquest of the Last Frontier*, p. 186.

59. Schley and Soley, *The Rescue of Greely*. Donald B. MacMillan, *How Peary Reached the Pole* (Boston: Houghton Mifflin Co., 1934), pp. 241-42. Freuchen, *Arctic Adventure*, p. 294. Neatby, *Conquest of the Last Frontier*, p. 229.

60. U.S. Congress, Senate Executive Document #111, 48th Cong., 1st sess., March 1884. U.S. Congress, House Executive Document #56, 48th Cong., 1st sess., January 17, 1884. U.S. Congress, Senate Executive Document #132, 48th Cong., 1st sess., March 17, 1884.

61. Mitchell, *General Greely*, pp. 84-85, 201. Greely, *Three Years of Arctic Service*, vol 1, 2.

62. James Oliver Robertson, *American Myth American Reality* (New York: Hill & Wang, 1980), Chap. 5.

63. Frederick Jackson Turner, *The Frontier in American History* (New York: Holt, Rinehart & Winston, 1962, orig. pub. 1920), pp. 4, 296.

64. Danehower, "The Polar Question," p. 693.

65. Canada, Department of Mines and Technical Surveys, *The Canadian Arctic* (Ottawa, 1951).

2

American Exploration in the Arctic, 1886-1922

A Period of Progress and Modernization

Government-sponsored exploration ceased after the Greely episode and, until the 1920s, expeditions were organized primarily by individuals and scientific societies. From the 1880s through World War I, American arctic expeditions employing the latest technological improvements conducted scientific studies, mapped islands and waterways, and returned with reports of rich mineral deposits and abundant fishing grounds.[1] Expedition leaders were motivated by both a desire for adventure and challenge and the belief that the application of scientific principles could control the forces of nature. American and European exploration during this period reflected this dual motivation as expeditions set out on a race to reach the North Pole, as well as to acquire information about the Arctic, open the region to commercial development, and further national prestige, all goals that reflected a general trend to employ rational means to promote economic and political expansion.[2]

Arctic expeditions had increased dramatically by 1900 as the race to reach the North Pole became an international competition.[3] Reports of the various excursions emphasized improvements in transportation and equipment. Two examples were Russian and German expeditions that experimented with improved designs for icebreakers and submarines, hoping to conquer the ice-blocked waterways and eliminate, as much as possible, dangerous and debilitating sledge treks.[4] Because the results of these experiments demonstrated more theoretical potential than immediate practical use, some explorers continued to rely on traditional means of transportation for getting to and traveling through the Arctic. In 1901, an Italian expedition, using the familiar sailing ship and sledges, succeeded in reaching 86° 33' north latitude, the northernmost point reached by any expedition up to that time. Led by the Duke Luigi Amedeo of the Abruzzi and Umberto Cagni, the voyage in the *Stella Polare* (*Polar Star*) employed the newest information on navigation and geography while carefully avoiding any innovations the men believed were unproven and, therefore, unreliable.[5]

These European expeditions established base camps at Spitsbergen and Franz Josef Land, because these islands were reached relatively easily and were the farthest northern land masses with an available food supply. From there, the explorers hoped to find passable sea lanes leading to the North Pole. Two American expeditions followed this same procedure. Evelyn Briggs Baldwin and Anthony Fiala joined the northward armada in 1901. The press lauded their expedition as an example of American ingenuity, one that carried the most modern supplies, including the newest silk and canvas tents and dehydrated food reputed to be far better than canned provisions and pemmican.[6] The Italian expedition may have carried wine and delicacies to relieve "tired palates," but the Americans, with their fully condensed and dehydrated provisions, were, in the eyes of the press, far more modern and progressive.

William Ziegler, Royal Baking Powder magnate, financed the Baldwin expedition which was directed to "find and plant the American flag at the North Pole."[7] To Ziegler, the United States was in a race against "foreign interests," but he was confident that the country was "great enough and progressive enough" to win.[8] The expedition's two steam whalers and one steam launch sailed for Franz Josef Land. The goal, aside from reaching the Pole, was to make meteorological, magnetic, and astronomical observations and collect samples of flora and fauna.[9] Baldwin and his men left with the good wishes of the press who wrote that it hoped the Americans would "eclipse all others in brilliancy of exploit and results of practical usefulness." When asked about the number of expeditions he might make to the Pole, Baldwin answered, "The more the merrier. If I fail, I fail, and everybody will know it."[10] The expedition did fail, not just once but in two subsequent tries, and everyone did know about it from the press. Baldwin was accorded some praise for returning with a collection of specimens and fossils and for mapping the geological features of approximately 80 square miles of Franz Josef Land, but these accomplishments were not significant enough for Ziegler to provide any further financial support for Baldwin. Fiala, undaunted by what he believed to be a minor setback, continued to promote exploration in the Atlantic Arctic. He attributed previous failures to the American habit of choosing men for arctic exploration who had no training or experience in group relations. The result, he believed, was a breakdown in discipline by midwinter when the men, because of darkness and a lack of nourishment, would "turn green in the face" and those with heart disease, die.[11] According to Fiala's theory, there would be a much greater possibility for success if expeditions were organized using the new theories of personal and group psychology.

In 1906, Walter Wellman, American journalist and explorer, planned an expedition to the North Pole using an airship (dirigible). He became interested in exploring the Arctic by air in 1897 when Salomon Andrée attempted to reach the North Pole in a hot air balloon. When the balloon crashed and the men were presumed dead, Wellman became so discouraged he had insisted that "no one else is likely to try that method."[12] The discouragement did not last long, however, and the desire to be the first to succeed at reaching the North Pole by using new and modern equipment won out over his own warning against balloons. Wellman contracted with the Godard Works at St. Omen, France, to build the airship *America*, described as being "far in advance of anything yet known in aeronautics."[13] The expedition planned to leave from Spitsbergen, but during test flights the dirigible was unable to handle weather conditions. It took three years to correct technical problems, but by then (1909), Robert E. Peary had already claimed the Pole. Wellman had no desire to be second, even with first-class equipment. He abandoned his plans and looked elsewhere for an opportunity for glory and new stories.

These expeditions all returned with valuable information about the Arctic and illustrate the international fervor directed toward reaching the North Pole. A great part of this rush northward was an outgrowth of publicity by the press, national consciousness of the prestige associated with successful exploration, and serious interest in acquiring scientific data. Additional factors that contributed to the proliferation of arctic voyages were Robert Peary's well-publicized yearly treks north.

Peary, the most controversial of all American explorers, was, and continues to be, the subject of intense study by scientists, historians, geographers, and adventure buffs. Peary contributed to the controversy by actively publicizing his expeditions and promoting his maps detailing the geography of Greenland, Ellesmere Island, and the surrounding arctic region, activities he knew were necessary to attract the funds needed for still another expedition. The result was both praise and censure as the press judged him responsible for the deaths of explorers who, following his maps, became lost in mountains or fjords that, according to his reports, should not have been there.[14] Peary's maps and particularly his description of the northern tip of Greenland, when compared to later data, indicate that he had made serious errors identifying sea ice as land ice and mistaking mirages for land masses. Nonetheless, his explorations were heroic in scope and method and the early Greenland expeditions became the model for American explorers for the next thirty years.

Robert Peary obtained his first extended leave of absence from the Navy in 1886 to make his initial voyage to the Arctic. He was obsessed with reaching the North Pole, and each trip was designed to win that prize. This exploration of Greenland, like those to follow, produced important geographic observations (the first detailed report of Greenland's insularity), and prepared him for his assault on the Pole. His next expedition in 1891 was both an attempt to find a passage to the Pole and an effort to chart Greenland's northernmost boundary. By working around the northern extremity, Peary hoped to return with an accurate description of the coastline of Greenland and information about the natural habitat of indigenous Eskimos. He accomplished his goal and successfully crossed the inland ice cap, using a relay system for supplies that was to become his trademark.

On his 1898 expedition, Peary made additional modifications in the procedure that came to be known as the Peary Method for polar exploration, a system based on sending an advance party to establish caches of provisions, marking both the route and location of the caches. He expanded his base camp and established a series of northern supply bases from which parties were then sent to mark trails and build facilities to store food and fuel. With improved organization, Peary was able to complete the arduous trek around the northern coast of Greenland, verifying its insularity, and continue on to the western part of Grinnell Land. There he described new land masses northwest of Greely Fjord and made a complete revision of the map of Hayes Sound, an achievement considered second only to that of reaching the Pole.[15] Peary's route took him to the Fort Conger base established by Greely for the 1881 IPY. Although he found the camp in a shambles, he conducted a thorough search and found a good supply of preserved and edible food and Greely's original records, all in good condition. Peary's report reopened the controversy over Greely's management of the expedition, but the return of the IPY records created even more excitement. The episode still elicited bitter responses, but the value of Greely's data outweighed efforts to revive earlier sensationalism.[16]

Disputes over the validity of Peary's reports were minimized as editors incorporated the results of his expeditions in new editions of geographic atlases, many of which were sold in other countries. Publishers were not alone in recognizing the commercial and prestige value of Peary's work. The War Department, pleased with the success of the United States in arctic regions, acknowledged that the country benefited by the prestige from having Peary's discoveries marked on maps used in many countries, and on his return, the Department congratulated him, expressing its gratitude that the "successful advance [into the Arctic] was led by an American." The expeditions were also seen as a way to test and promote mechanical devices, and engineers experimenting with engines contacted Peary, asking him to consider using experimental models fueled with alcohol for transportation over ice and snow.[17]

Peary continued to stalk the North Pole, convinced it could be reached by way of Smith Sound. The hunt was not just personal; he believed fervently that the Pole "ought to be and must be secured for this country." The Navy agreed, granting him a three-year leave to stage still another attempt to reach his goal. Although the proposed expedition was not funded by the government and no attempt had been made to obtain funding, the Peary Arctic Club felt it was critically important to establish a clearly defined and irrevocable government commitment which remained elusive, but Peary did secure the approval and hearty endorsement of the administration, an accomplishment he described as his "hardest chore."[18]

With this new venture scheduled to begin in April 1894, Peary hoped to win the "last great geographical prize the earth has to offer."[19] Reaching the Pole would be a sign of "man's final physical conquest of the globe," and "our manifest privilege and duty."[20] Numerous expeditions originating in other countries were setting out with the same intention, and the possibility of success by an explorer from another country prompted government representatives to insist that the United States had a patriotic mission to reach the North Pole first. Charles H. Darling, Acting Secretary of the Navy, commented that reaching the Pole should be the main goal of Peary's expedition. Discovery of the North and South Poles was all that was left to complete the mapping of the world and should be done by "our countrymen" as a matter of "national pride."[21]

For this expedition, Peary planned to sail north in a modernized ship equipped with engines twice as powerful as those used earlier, and with sheathing capable of withstanding the northern ice, an American ship that would represent the "exponent of American mechanical ability." Peary may have made numerous organizational modifications and encouraged improvements in ship design, but he eschewed experiments with mechanical transportation for traveling across the ice as not practical at the time and continued to rely on dog-pulled sledges to transport men and supplies. Always looking for ways to make the work of exploration more efficient, Peary redesigned the sledges so that his men could use several lightly packed individual sledges instead of a few packed with heavy loads. He also planned to establish a well-defined communication and supply line connected to a new base approximately one hundred miles nearer to the Pole. Although there is no doubt that these changes were intended to improve his chances of reaching the Pole, Peary had other objectives equal to and perhaps even more important than the Pole. He hoped to complete the geophysical delineation of the unknown arctic regions in the western hemisphere north of the eighty-first parallel.[22]

Whitelaw Reid, impressed with Peary's stature as an explorer whose "experience in the Arctic Regions exceeds that of any other living man," volunteered to help raise funds for the expedition.[23] He appealed to potential contributors by describing Peary's technical competence and suggesting that "to the individual of means, as a business proposition, the financing of such an expedition means an instant and worldwide reputation of the highest character," and an opportunity, if Peary reached the Pole, of being famous long after Carnegie and Rockefeller were forgotten. Peary, the pragmatist, promoted his expedition by tailoring his appeal for funds to individuals and groups. To businessmen, he presented the expedition as a "concrete business proposal" which would return prestige and good public relations for years to come, and to the Navy Department he described the venture as continuing the naval tradition begun by Elisha Kent Kane, the results of which would be a valuable collection of scientific information about the Arctic from Davis Strait to the Bering Sea.[24]

Once again Peary failed to reach his coveted goal, but his efforts and the results of this expedition were notable. He reached 87° north latitude, beating his 1902 record by 3°, and found that the ice drift traveled eastward, opposite to that reported previously by the Norwegian explorer Fridtjof Nansen who had described a westward drift north of the Bering Strait.[25] These observations, important though they were, did not excite readers as much as the report that Peary had discovered a group of islands, "Crocker Land," located in the vicinity of Ellesmere Island.[26] Explorers may have been motivated by scientific inquiry, but news of discoveries sold magazines and newspapers. The press, reporting Peary's discovery of new islands, praised him for his accomplishments as well as for his tenacity, describing him as "the embodiment of the resolute masterly American spirit now revolutionizing the world."[27] Peary himself believed that although the "unfolding of the North" alone would be significant, the United States had a "privilege and duty" to lead the movement to unlock the North and South Poles, the North Pole first because it was our "natural northern boundary." He felt it would be a "splendid feat for this great and wealthy country, if having already girdled the earth, we might reach north and south and plant 'Old Glory' on each Pole."[28]

Peary's exploits were followed closely by President Theodore Roosevelt who believed that the growth of the United States was a result of physical accomplishments and heroic struggles. Roosevelt, a member of the Explorers Club with Peary, had kept up a steady correspondence with him, encouraging and commending Peary for his "admirable work for science," adding that he thought Peary was even more important because of his "admirable work for America [by] setting an example to the young of our day which we need to have set amid the softening tendencies of our time."[29]

Peary agreed that his work in arctic exploration was a national duty. He emphasized the advantages to the United States of developing the Arctic, and the importance of establishing American sovereignty over as much territory as possible. Peary wanted his expeditions remembered for their practical and scientific achievements and resorted to tales of spectacular or adventurous feats only when necessary to raise funds for upcoming expeditions. Employing both his strength as a leader and his ability to delegate responsibility, Peary represented the transition from nineteenth century individualist to twentieth century professional. He conducted his major expeditions by utilizing modern organizational and business procedures but maintained his position as supreme commander. He divided each exploration into projects and assigned specific duties to each man, delegating responsibility for overseeing each project to men who were the equivalent of section managers. While Peary made all major decisions and demanded total loyalty from his men, his last expedition in 1908 was definitely a team effort in which every modern physical and psychological tool was employed to produce an efficient support system. The team cleared the field, but it was Peary's dream and Peary who remains today the individual who won the prize.

On this last expedition, Peary sailed from Sydney, Nova Scotia, in the specially designed ship *S.S. Roosevelt*, with customs clearance for "the Port of North Pole."[30] Supplies had been procured and stored aboard the ship in accordance with specific directions in order to avoid wasted time, space, and motion. Every piece of equipment had its particular storage spot; food was weighed in grams and calories were carefully calculated. Even notebooks had to meet size and weight specifications.[31] The *Roosevelt* was to sail to the northern end of Greenland. Peary planned to establish a base camp there before moving on to Ellesmere Island where he would construct a second base at the beginning of the then familiar path he had begun to call the "American" route.[32]

Other arctic explorers had experimented with using aircraft, submarines, and sledges pulled by a variety of animals, but Peary believed men and Eskimo dogs were the only two "machines" practical for polar exploration. His crew functioned like a well-designed machine. Each man had been instructed in the details of the expedition including specific directions for contingencies, and all adhered faithfully to the minutely detailed plan. Indeed, all had been chosen for their physical fitness and ability to carry out orders. Peary credited the success of this final expedition to a carefully designed, "mathematically calculated plan" that began with a specially built ship capable of maneuvering through the ice farther north than had previously been possible and included the cooperation of Eskimos, earned by "square dealing and generous gifts," and assistants who were "intelligent and civilized."[33]

Peary described this remarkable venture in the usual patriotic and nationalistic terms, expressing "great satisfaction that [the] whole expedition, together with the ship, was American from start to finish." The

Roosevelt had been built with "American timber in an American ship-yard, engined by an American firm with American metal and constructed on American designs." Some allowance had to be made for the captain, "Bob" Bartlett, and the crew who were from Newfoundland, but who were acceptable because they were neighbors and essentially "our first cousins." The expedition, a symbol of American advancement, was made in an "American-built ship," commanded by an American whose goal was to "secure if possible an American trophy."[34]

Peary's insistence that the expedition had been a national effort did not preclude his personal pride in having accomplished what he called his "life work." He recorded in his diary:

> The Pole at last!!! The prize of 3 centuries, my dream and ambition for 23 years. MINE at last. I cannot bring myself to realize it. It all seems so simple and commonplace, as Bartlett said 'just like every day.'
>
> My life work is accomplished. The thing which it was intended from the beginning that I should do, the thing which I believed could be done and that I could do, I have done. I have got the North Pole out of my system. After 23 years of effort, hardships, privations, more or less suffering and some risks, I have won the last great geographical prize, the North Pole, for the credit of the United States, the Service to which I belong, myself and my family.[35]

On his return, Peary telegraphed President William Howard Taft that he had claimed the Pole for the United States and was pleased to present the trophy to the President. Taft answered, thanking Peary for his "interesting and generous offer," adding that although he did "not know exactly what [he] could do with it," he was proud that Peary had added "luster to the name American."[36] Taft may have been nonplussed by Peary's gift, but in his annual message for 1910, he noted that arctic exploration was a complete success for the United States. Peary's "unparalleled accomplishment" in reaching the North Pole had "added to the distinction of our Navy, to which he belongs, and reflects credit upon his country." The official strong praise and clear acceptance of the feat as both Peary's rightful due and American prize, gave notice to other nations that exploring the Arctic was one way of furthering the country's national interests.[37]

Peary's prize was tarnished by the escapades of Dr. Frederick Cook who claimed to have reached the Pole a year before Peary.[38] The meticulous plan, the flag-waving, the extraordinary accomplishment all became mired in bitter controversy in the United States and major European cities.[39] The press alternately praised and scorned Peary as journalists, well-known personalities, and explorers took sides in the dispute which monopolized headlines for over a year.[40] The publicity created as much dissension in Congress as it had with the public and, unfortunately for Peary, a bill to award him the title and salary of a retired Admiral stalled because of debate over whether or not he actually reached the Pole, the role of the Navy and Peary's affiliation with the Service, and, even if these questions were resolved, whether arctic exploration actually constituted either naval or military duty.[41]

When Peary returned from the Arctic in 1910, he was entertained and honored by geographic and scientific societies and government representatives in many European and American cities. At these appearances, Peary formally represented the international community of explorer-scientists and, informally, his country.[42] Praise and awards were numerous. Invited by the Société Normande de Geographie in Rouen, France, to lecture on his discovery of the North Pole, he was honored by the president of the society for contributing to the "everlasting friendly relations existing between the two great Republics." The East Switzerland Geographical Society awarded him a bronze plaque which, because he was unable to attend the ceremony, was sent to the Navy Department. France and Switzerland may have accepted Peary as a representative of the United States, but the Navy Department had deep reservations about Peary's right to represent either his country or the Navy. The award, made in January 1914, was not forwarded to Peary until March, and then only after a prolonged investigation of his service in the Navy.[43]

Peary continued to be fascinated with polar regions even after his success in the Arctic. When he returned from the North Pole, he encouraged his men to continue their work carefully and thoroughly, primarily because of the importance he attached to the results but also because the work would provide valuable experience for a future Antarctic expedition. Peary was in no condition to lead or participate in any such expedition and encouraged Bob Bartlett to take on the chore of leader. He hoped to convince the Peary Arctic Club and National Geographic Society to sponsor jointly the venture which would begin at the Weddell Sea, southeast of Cape Horn, and, if possible, proceed to the South Pole. Peary hoped to include a circuit of Antarctica by ship in order to make scientific observations, take soundings, record the characteristics of the ice, and determine the extent and configuration of the continent.[44] Speaking in Paris at a reception, Peary described the proposed Antarctic expedition as a unique opportunity for the United States "to secure a sphere of influence in the huge region between Cape Horn and the Pole."[45] There was some enthusiasm expressed for the project but there were few contributions and the plan was abandoned.

Unable to continue his career in exploration, Peary turned to aviation, not as an active participant, but promoting the use of aircraft for national defense and exploration. He noted that bay areas in northern Greenland could be accessible by air and that the major industrial nations in North America, Europe, and Asia were connected by a straight line across the North Pole. Aviation could make the potential commercial value of the Arctic a reality. Years of exploring the Arctic and finally reaching the North Pole had convinced Peary "that nothing can stop the ultimate destiny of this country to occupy that portion of the western hemisphere lying between the Panama Canal and the North Pole." Aviation would make it possible to traverse the "ocean of air" free from coasts, mountain ranges, and barriers, where the only limit was "infinite space." Peary promoted the establishment of an air patrol for every sea approach to North America from Greenland to the Spanish Main, and from Columbia to the Bering Strait. He believed the airplane would "complete that close union of all nations in the western hemisphere, which in the near future [would] form a Greater United States of America" stretching from the Arctic Ocean to Cape Horn.[46]

Despite the controversy and lack of congressional support, Peary's arctic expeditions were unique. Beginning with the opening years of the century, explorers had described their expeditions as modern and progressive. However, Peary's last arctic expedition was an unusual blend of traditional adventure and modern industrial and corporate organization. The utilization of precise assembly line procedure, modern technology, and scientific principles which set Peary apart from other explorers of the same period rapidly became a standard component of arctic expeditions.

A less flamboyant figure emerged at this time as one of the new breed of arctic explorers whose accomplishments were measured in terms of technical expertise and the acquisition of scientific and geographic information.[47] Donald B. MacMillan, a member of Peary's 1908 expedition, set off in 1914 to locate the land mass identified by Peary in 1909 as "Crocker Land." MacMillan continued mapping, exploring, and conducting scientific expeditions through the Canadian Arctic and Greenland until his death in 1957.[48] Unlike Peary, MacMillan approached his work in a most matter-of-fact manner. While he too believed in possibilities for economic development in the Arctic and was convinced of the importance of exploration to developments in science and technology, the national chauvinism that infected most explorers was far less evident in MacMillan.[49]

MacMillan's proposal to search for new land north of Alaska coincided with plans made by the American Museum of Natural History to expand its natural history collection. Although "Crocker Land" was only a shadowy existence, the prospect of claiming new land appealed to the Museum, the government, and the general public.[50] The press, intrigued with the idea, reported on every phase of the operation for more than two years. Arctic exploration had become a regular national news item.[51] Working closely with the Museum to develop mutually acceptable goals, MacMillan planned to sail June 1912, and announced that the expedition would ascertain the extent of the continental shelf, map unexplored territory north of Alaska, and investigate mountain peaks sighted by Peary in 1906 from the summit of Cape Thomas Hubbard.[52] The expedition, described as a "distinct credit" to the country and of unusual scientific value, was endorsed by Theodore Roosevelt, the American Geographical Society, Yale University, and the American Museum of Natural History.[53]

MacMillan had remained in continual contact with Peary and had consulted him on expedition details. His plans were similar to Peary's, including caching provisions during the winter in order to be ready for a sledge dash planned for February when daylight returned. However, MacMillan did not just copy Peary's methods; he added innovations of his own. He was the first to use movies to entertain the crew and their Eskimo partners and to record the expedition on film. He was also an enthusiastic believer in the future of radio and brought an expensive wireless outfit, the first used in arctic exploration.[54] The experiments with broadcasting were not entirely satisfactory, but MacMillan's faith was well placed and, by 1920, use of wireless sets began to change the nature of arctic exploration.[55]

MacMillan tended to underestimate the value of the work done on his expeditions. During the "Crocker Land" investigation, he wrote to the head of the American Museum of Natural History that the work was "not at all satisfactory and very disappointing." In 72 days, they covered more than 1,200 miles, a sizeable area, but had to work "with very serious handicaps." There was trouble from the beginning "when [his] chicken hearted captain refused to land" at Cape Sabine for fear of being wedged in the rocks by ice. Separated from Ellesmere by twenty-five miles of water, surging ice floes, and a strong current, they had a most difficult job. MacMillan believed that the conditions they confronted were very similar to those that had caused Greely's men to die of starvation when they found they were unable to make the crossing. MacMillan's party was luckier, and the men were able to make numerous crossings after the first attempt in February failed when the crew came down with mumps and influenza.[56]

Once the crossing was accomplished, the men climbed the Beitstact Glacier to 4,700 feet, a difficult and dangerous feat that took two days to reach the summit, but only twelve hours to descend to the base on the other side of the mountain. At Eureka Sound, they stocked up on meat and relaxed in perfect weather, bright sunshine and no wind, truly the lull before a five-day storm which arrived while they were camped.

After the storm passed, the men set out to search for "Crocker Land." As the coast of Grant Land dropped away, they sighted what appeared to be an "immense land—hills, valley, snow capped peaks, as plain as a land could be." The Eskimos insisted it was nothing but *poojuk* (mist or smoke), but MacMillan continued toward the area until he was finally convinced he was chasing a mirage that changed in extent and appearance as the sun moved toward the south and west.[57] After nine days out, they were 130 miles due northwest from Cape Thomas Hubbard. Tempted by the perfect cloudless weather to go on for another two-day march, MacMillan fortunately turned back just ahead of another severe storm which claimed eight dogs, a sledge, part of their equipment, and a "good man." The Eskimo, Peewahto, died under mysterious circumstances, and the Eskimos persisted in claiming he had been killed by someone in MacMillan's party.[58] MacMillan had no satisfactory explanation and the episode resulted in strained relations with authorities in Greenland and Canada. Even his long friendship with the Eskimos could not overcome their suspicion of his trustworthiness.

The expedition, which lasted 51 months and covered 9,000 miles, discovered coal in By Fjord and on Axel Heiberg and recovered numerous remains from previous explorations which were turned over to museums. It conducted a study of the Smith Sound Eskimos, compiling a dictionary of over 3,000 words and using the new photographic equipment to collect 5,500 photographs and 10,000 feet of motion picture film. The expedition also completed extensive tidal observations and studies in geology, botany, ornithology, and meteorology.[59] The "very disappointing venture" was, in fact, a major accomplishment.

MacMillan's next expeditions in 1921-22 explored Baffin Island to collect botanical and geological specimens and conduct experiments in terrestrial magnetism for the Carnegie Institute. He also hoped to record the movements of glaciers along the coast of Greenland and return with information helpful to scientists who were debating the possibility of an impending ice age measured by the advance of glaciers between 1850 and 1920.[60] In addition, he planned to continue to experiment with the new communications technology by recording the expedition on motion picture film and using short wave radio to transmit and receive messages.[61]

The prospect of voice communication between the United States and the Arctic encouraged thousands of amateur members of the American Radio Relay League who kept their sets tuned, waiting for signals from the expedition. They were not disappointed. There had been some concern among engineers and scientists about the feasibility of transmitting and receiving through the auroral band, but communications were sent during the winter months when the expedition was iced in, the radio functioned well, and broadcasts were picked up all over North America. MacMillan broadcast regularly, and weekly transmissions reached him from WSAZ-Zenith located in the Edgewater Hotel in Atlantic City, New Jersey. Zenith, which had supplied the radio equipment, felt the experiment was successful in providing the necessary information for establishing a communications chain to facilitate future flights. Radio, it was hoped, would reduce the fear of being stranded if a ship were iced in or, during air expeditions, the danger of being isolated in case of a forced landing or crash. If successfully developed, radio could rob arctic exploration of "much of its former terrors."[62]

Advances in radio and aviation technology changed the nature of arctic exploration. Not only had romance and adventure disappeared as motivations for expeditions, but the emphasis on engaging in scientific research for the primary purpose of acquiring knowledge about the North diminished when the government designated isolated arctic islands important to the security of the United States. The north polar area then became an essential link in the general line of defense as aircraft became the "modern eyes of war," guarding the United States from the North Pole to the Panama Canal. The military was skeptical about the possibility of further discoveries and believed that future expeditions should concentrate on acquiring data that would contribute to more rapid improvements in aviation, such as more accurate information on meteorology, oceanography, magnetism, and gravity.[63] The combination of rapid advances in aviation and the application of knowledge of arctic conditions could hasten the production of aircraft with a range of 1,600 to 2,000 miles, capable of using northern routes for defense purposes and to uncover the answers to any remaining riddles about the Arctic. What had begun in 1886 as one man's odyssey had, by 1917, become a national vision.

The adventures of all these explorers, from Baldwin to Peary and MacMillan, were widely publicized. Americans followed both the adventures and underlying conflicts that developed among Canada, Norway, and the United States as each country promoted arctic exploration. There was a general consensus expressed by explorer-writers and journalists that the area explored was a *terra nullius*, a no-man's land, and that while discoveries could and should be claimed for the sponsoring nations, the territory should be kept open to all explorers. Americans enthusiastically supported the move to keep the Arctic an open international arena, one that would be equally available to American explorers and American business. The government sensed that attempts by other countries to divide the area into spheres of influence or national sectors could be disadvantageous to the United States. By encouraging and supporting regular expeditions, the government gave notice that it considered the arctic area important to its national interests, and that it intended to maintain a presence in the region.

Canada watched the parade of expeditions with growing alarm. Claims by Norwegians and expeditions by Danes appeared to be attempts by both countries to expand into territory that Canada claimed lay within its national boundaries. As troublesome as the Scandinavians were, the Americans caused Canada more concern. The combativeness of American rhetoric and the regularity of American expeditions seemed to be a continuation of American territorial and economic expansion, and Canada wondered if it were just coincidental that Peary's major expeditions (1896-1908) had been carried out during the years that the United States acquired an empire that reached into the Caribbean and Pacific, vastly expanding its economic sphere of influence.

Although there is no evidence that the American government seriously considered Canada and Canadian-claimed arctic islands as areas for territorial acquisition, relations between Canada and the United States became more strained as arctic exploration and development increased and Americans expressed their belief that their country would continue to be the economic leader in North America. Peary's march north symbolized the expansion of American economic, cultural, and political influence and, in turn, the Arctic became a natural area toward which an expanding nation could turn.

Notes to Chapter 2

1. F. C. Schrader, *Recent Work of the U.S. Geological Survey in Alaska* (Washington, D.C.: Government Printing Office, 1902), pp. 7-8. John E. Sater, *The Arctic Basin* (Washington, D.C.: Arctic Institute of North America, 1968), pp. 2-10.

2. Richard E. Leopold, *The Growth of American Foreign Policy* (New York: Alfred A. Knopf, 1962), pp. 125-29.

3. *Current Literature* (June 1901): 684-86. In 1900, seven nations entered the race to the Pole: France, Canada, Germany, Norway, Italy, Russia, and the United States.

4. *New York Times*, December 11, 1900, p. 9; August 31, 1901, p. 6. *Current Literature* (June 1901): 684-86. Mary A. Fleming, "Russia and Siberia," *Bulletin of the American Bureau of Geography* 2, 1 (March

1901). The Russian icebreaking steamship *Ermak* was equipped with "Yankee inventions," including three screws (1 forward and 2 aft). In 1901, German shipbuilders at Wilhelmshaven built a submarine designed to descend 160 feet and remain submerged for 15 hours. Its speed of 3 knots would enable it to cover approximately 50 miles before it would need to surface.

5. *New York Times*, May 28, 1899, p. 19; September 7, 1900, p. 12. *American Geographical Society Bulletin* 33 (1901). *Scientific American* (February 28, 1903): 22712. Luigi Amedeo of Savoy, *On the Polar Star in the Arctic Sea* (New York: Dodd, Mead & Co., 1903), pp. vii, 30. The *Stella Polare* sailed under orders from the Italian King and Queen. While no new territory was discovered, the very absence of any islands indicated that previous reports describing Petermann Land, King Oscar Land, and a number of smaller islands were based either on mirage or, perhaps, were ice islands. American reporters noted that the expedition proved Italians were capable of enduring both high temperatures common to the Mediterranean and the extreme northern cold. The Duke and Cagni had suffered from frostbite but only because they had not been prudent in carrying out their duties. The officers and crew had actually gained weight during the expedition, contrary to reports from expeditions carrying crews from northern climates. The expedition's success was attributed to capable leadership and careful planning, including providing ample supplies. The ship was loaded with 350 tons of coal and 250 tons of provisions color-coded in case it became necessary to jettison supplies. Food included rice, 5 different qualities of macaroni, preserved chicken, tinned and dried beef, preserved vegetables, biscuits, flour, and 1,000 bottles of wine to be used on "festive occasions."

6. Evelyn B. Baldwin, "How I Hope to Reach the North Pole," *McClure* 17 (September 1901): 415-22.

7. *New York Times*, May 25, 1905, p. 9.

8. *Harpers Weekly* 45 (June 22, 1901): 638.

9. Leffingwell to Rudolph M. Anderson (n.d.), Rudolph M. Anderson Papers [hereafter cited as Anderson Papers], MG30 B40v14f13, Na-

tional Archives of Canada, Ottawa [hereafter cited as NAC]. *American Geographical Society Bulletin* 34 (1902): 56-60; 35 (1903): 192-93.

10. *New York Times*, February 4, 1901, p. 7.

11. *Bookman* 24 (January 1907): 480-82. *New York Times*, August 30, 1901, p. 7; April 29, 1902, p. 3; August 2, 1902, p. 3; August 6, 1902, p. 3. John E. Caswell, *Arctic Frontiers* (Norman: University of Oklahoma Press, 1956), pp. 173-83.

12. *McClure* (February 1900): 408. Andrew Croft, *Epics of Twentieth Century Polar Exploration* (London: Adam & Charles Black, 1939), pp. 129-30. In 1897, Andrée and two other Swedes attempted to reach the North Pole in a hot air balloon. The flight left from Danes Island off the northwest coast of Spitsbergen on July 11. Carrier pigeons delivered the message that the balloon had reached 88° north latitude but nothing else was ever heard from or about the expedition until 1930 when a Norwegian sealer at White Island found the remains of Andrée's camp. A diary found in the coat pocket of one of the men described the flight. When the balloon reached the colder atmosphere over the pack ice, the gas contracted and the balloon dropped. The party sledged toward Franz Josef Land but the ice drift carried them west to White Island. Provisions were sufficient and it was believed that the men died from fumes from their heater or from eating diseased bear meat. Per Olaf Sundman, *The Flight of the Eagle* (New York: Pantheon Books, 1970), pp. 1-88.

13. *The Times* (London), June 5, 1906, p. 5.

14. "Seeking the North Pole," *Journal of Geography* 4 (1905): 362. "Peary's Latest Work in the Arctic," *McClure* 14 (January 1900): 235-40. The following material on Peary appeared in *Fram: The Journal of Polar Studies* 2 (1985): 131-40; Nancy Fogelson, "Robert E. Peary and America's Exploration in the Arctic 1886-1910."

15. *American Geographical Society Bulletin* 34 (1902): 56-59. Brainard to Peary, May 12, 1902, letters received, Robert E. Peary Papers, Center for Polar and Scientific Archives, NA.

16. "Peary's Latest Work in the Arctic," pp. 235-40.

17. Cora to Peary, December 14, 1901; Brainard to Peary, May 12, 1902; George H. Stone, geologist, to Peary, February 6, 1901, letters received, Peary Papers, NA.

18. Peary to Bridgeman, December 22, 1902, letters sent, Peary Papers, NA.

19. Considering that Antarctica and the South Pole had yet to be explored, this is a curious statement.

20. *Harper's Weekly* 48 (July 9, 1904): 1053.

21. *American Geographical Society Bulletin* 35 (1903): 374-76.

22. Peary to Crandall, February 4, 1903, letters sent, Peary Papers, NA. September 18, 1903, letters received, Peary Papers, NA. American DeForest Wireless Telegraph Co. (New Jersey) expressed interest in installing a system and equipment used by the U.S. Army in 1902 maneuvers. The equipment, the company felt, "represents the originality and inventive genius of an American scientist." Wireless equipment was not used on American expeditions until the Donald B. MacMillan expeditions in the 1920s. Peary to Gilman, president of the Carnegie Institute, December 6, 1903, letters sent, Peary Papers, NA.

23. Whitelaw Reid, editor of the *New York Tribune*, was ambassador to England at this time.

24. Reid to Peary, January 7, 1904, letters received; Peary to Shepley, May 1903; Peary to Secretary of the Navy, July 7, 1903, letters sent, Peary Papers, NA.

25. *The Times* (London), November 5, 1906, p. 12.

26. E. O. Hovey letter, March 4, 1914, "Crocker Land." Expedition file 74, American Museum of Natural History, New York City.

27. R. J. McGrath, "For the Conquest of the Pole," *Review of Reviews* 32 (1905): 43-48.

28. Peary to the *St. Louis Dispatch*, October 10, 1903; Peary to Angelo Heilprin, February 24, 1904, letters sent, Peary Papers, NA.

29. Roosevelt to Peary, March 24, 1907, Theodore Roosevelt Papers, Microfilm Collection, Reel #345 S2v1 p408, University of Cincinnati Library.

30. Documents Box 25/1, Donald B. MacMillan Papers [hereafter cited as DBM Papers], Bowdoin College Library, Brunswick, Maine. See also Box 1, Correspondence 1908-9.

31. Peary to MacMillan, June 21, 1908, Correspondence 1908-9, Box 1, DBM Papers, Bowdoin College Library, Brunswick, Maine. Peary gave MacMillan minutely detailed instructions for securing supplies and storing them aboard the *Roosevelt*. Examples: oars should be "corded together in sets for each boat and . . . tied up between deck beams in the main hold . . . ." Notebook paper "should be light, thin, strong, with a surface that will take pencil easily" and measure "4 inches wide by 7 inches long and 1/2 inch thick."

32. Robert E. Peary, *The North Pole* (New York: Frederick A. Stokes, Co., 1910), pp. 5, 201-3.

33. Ibid., pp. 201-3.

34. Ibid., p. 19.

35. Peary Papers related to Arctic Exploration 1886-1909, NA.

36. Peary to Taft, September 8, 1909; Taft to Peary, February 9, 1910, William Howard Taft papers, Microfilm Collection, Reel #344, University of Cincinnati Library.

37. *Foreign Relations of the United States* (1910): xvii.

38. Cook had been the physician on Peary's previous expeditions. In the controversy over whether Peary reached the Pole, supporting evidence by Matthew Henson has been consistently overlooked. Matthew A. Henson, *A Negro Explorer at the North Pole* (New York: Frederick A. Stokes, 1912), Chap. 4. Bradley Robinson, *Dark Companion* (New York: Robert M. McBride & Co., 1947).

39. *New York Times*, 1909-10. *The Times* (London), 1909-10.

40. Biographical Materials, Testimonies, Awards 1886-1913, Peary Papers, NA.

41. Congressional papers, Retirement Bill 1910-11, Peary Papers, NA. Committee on Naval Affairs, *Congressional Hearings*, March 4, 1910, pp. 14-15. U.S. Congress, House Joint Resolution #247, August 2, 1916, 64th Cong., 1st sess. Peary to T. Roosevelt, December 26, 1911, Theodore Roosevelt Papers, Microfilm Reel #371, University of Cincinnati Library. Hon. Joseph Hampton Moore, *Peary's Discovery of the North Pole* (House of Representatives, March 22, 1910).

42. *National Geographical Magazine* 21 (1910): 63-82. At the annual banquet of the National Geographical Society, December 1910, representatives of those governments involved in arctic exploration congratulated Peary on his "conquest." Each man acknowledged Peary's accomplishment and noted that he had gone beyond their own explorers, all the while reminding each other, and the audience in general, of the heroic stature of each nation and its representative explorers. The Italian ambassador read a telegram from the "chivalrous" Duke of the Abruzzi, congratulating Peary as the "explorer whose courage and perseverance deserved rewards." French Ambassador Jussarand subtly reminded the group that France was a historic European exploring nation by referring to America as a place explorers came to, not from, a place itself relatively unexplored until the end of the nineteenth century. However, "that moment of great change" had come and the United States had begun producing geographic and scientific explorers. See also Thomas S. Gates, Jr., *The U.S. Navy and Its Influence Upon History* (New York: Newcomb Society in America, 1958).

43. July 1913, State Department Records (State Dept.), RG59 032.p31; April 1913, 093.516/5; January 1914, 093.546, NA.

44. Antarctic, 1910-13, Peary Papers, NA.

45. *New York Times*, June 7, 1913, p. 3.

46. September 1913, December 1916, Miscellaneous Subject File; October 12, 1917, Speeches; Peary to Boston Globe, September 14, 1916, letters sent; Aeronautics and Preparedness, 1918, Peary Papers, NA.

47. The crew of the "Crocker Land" expedition, educated and trained in the sciences and technology, is a good example of this emphasis on professionalism: W. Elmer Ekbalw (AB, University of Illinois, geologist and botanist, University of Illinois instructor 1910-13); Maurice Cole Tanquay (AB, AM, Ph.D., University of Illinois zoologist, Assistant in entomology Kansas State Agricultural College 1912-15); Harrison J. Hunt, MD; Ensign Fitzhugh Green (U.S. Navy wireless operator assigned to expedition by the government); Jonathan Cook Small, mechanic and cook. Donald B. MacMillan, *Four Years in the White North* (New York: Harper & Bros., 1918), pp. 4-5.

48. Everett S. Allen, *Arctic Odyssey: The Life of Rear Admiral Donald B. MacMillan* (New York: Dodd, Mead & Co., 1962).

49. Miriam MacMillan, *Green Seas and White Ice* (New York: 1948). Interview with Miriam MacMillan (wife of Donald MacMillan), July 1981.

50. State Dept. Records, RG59 031.11 Am3, "Crocker Land," NA, American Museum of Natural History to State Dept., January 29, 1912.

51. See *New York Times* 1912-14 and *Periodical Guide to Literature* for same period.

52. "Crocker Land Expedition," Box 25, DBM Papers. *Congressional Record*, 63rd Cong., 3rd sess., February 25, 1915, pp. 482-84. Maps

issued by the Navy Department were reviewed for corrections regarding areas reported by Peary, including "Crocker Land."

53. *New York Times*, May 14, 1911, p. 4; February 14, 1912, p. 6; January 21, 1913, p. 5. DBM Papers, Box 25.

54. *New York Times*, May 17, 1913. General Electric believed the use of wireless so important, it furnished all electrical equipment. Atlantic Communication Co., supplied a complete outfit of Telefunken wireless with a range of 2,000 miles.

55. Peter Freuchen, *Arctic Adventure* (New York: Farrar & Rhinehart, 1935), p. 278. *Bulletin of the American Geographic Society* 45 (1913): 753-56.

56. Correspondence, 1914, DBM Papers. The dogs also succumbed to illness, possibly from too much salt in their pemmican.

57. MacMillan, *Four Years in the White North*, p. 80.

58. Box 1, DBM Papers. Allen, *Arctic Odyssey*, pp. 179-82. Fitzhugh Green told MacMillan he shot the Eskimo when the two men were trying to find their way back to camp after nearly being buried in a snow storm. Peewahto refused to follow Green's orders and it is likely Green panicked.

59. Allen, *Arctic Odyssey*, pp. 316-17.

60. State Dept. Records, RG59 031.11, 22.

61. *New York Times*, June 10, 1923, Amusement sec., p. 3.

62. Ibid., p. 17. *The Literary Digest* (November 24, 1923): 25. *Scientific American* (December 1923): 388. *Outlook* (October 1, 1924): 151.

63. Ironically, military expeditions in the 1920s, especially those using aircraft, were publicized as seeking new land, a tactic to gain popular support and promote the sponsoring branch of service.

3

Canadian Arctic Expeditions, 1894-1921

What We Have We Hold

By the end of the nineteenth century, arctic explorers had produced accurate maps of many of the islands along the rim of the Arctic Ocean. From 1900 to 1921, these explorers and their successors returned from long-term expeditions with detailed descriptions of the remaining islands and charts of inter-island waterways. When the furor subsided over reaching the North Pole, explorers encouraged their governments to consider developing, and in some cases colonizing, arctic islands for strategic and economic purposes. Greenland, Ellesmere Island and surrounding smaller islands in the east, the Northwest Passage, and Wrangel Island in the west became the focus of competitive expeditions by Norway, Denmark, Canada, and the United States. American activity in the Canadian Arctic, in particular, caused Canada great concern over what it perceived as a violation of its territorial sovereignty. The American expeditions were so widely publicized Canadians feared the United States would annex the area, fear fueled by the Alaskan Boundary Dispute.[1] There was no real basis for this fear, but explorers, the press, and the American government exacerbated the tension by publicizing expansive schemes and exaggerated claims.[2] Canadian exploration during this period was both an attempt to open the Arctic for economic development and to protect the area from encroachment by foreign powers, especially the United States.

The need for establishing incontestable sovereignty over arctic islands became apparent at the end of the nineteenth century. Great Britain had funded most of the exploration in the Canadian Arctic, claiming all islands discovered for the British Crown. In 1880, it ceded its claims to

Canada which then confronted the need to protect the territory against counterclaims from countries whose explorers had established regular bases on certain islands.[3] As a way to broadcast its right to the islands in question, the Canadian government set out to occupy and administer the region. In 1884 and 1897 it authorized navigational surveys of inter-island waterways, and in 1893 established Royal Canadian Mounted Police (RCMP) posts at Herschel Island and in the District of Mackenzie.[4] These actions provided a Canadian presence at scattered spots, but neither the RCMP posts nor the surveying parties were sufficient protection against foreign expansion. The RCMP could not control exploration in those areas hard to reach, and island exploration by non-Canadians resulted in conflicting claims when sponsoring countries attempted to apply the criteria of discovery instead of occupation and administration as the basis for establishing sovereignty.

Confusion over control over arctic islands was only part of the problem. In 1903, Canada became aware that sovereignty over mainland territory was also in jeopardy when a conflict erupted between Canada and the United States over the boundary between Alaska and the Yukon Territory. The ensuing Alaskan Boundary Dispute seemed to prove to Canadians that the United States had not only decided to ignore Canada's right to settle matters pertaining to its territory by negotiating primarily with Great Britain, but had also begun to implement a program of northward expansion. The territory involved was small; the principle was not.

The controversy was rooted in an 1825 treaty between Russia and Great Britain that divided the Yukon Territory from its northern border at the Arctic Ocean south along the 141° longitude to Mt. Saint Elias. However, from that point to Prince of Wales Island at 54° 40' north latitude, the boundary was drawn across an unnamed crest of mountains that turned out to be a profusion of peaks with no clearly defined or mutually acceptable demarcation. A second point of the treaty stated that if the mountain summit was more than ten marine leagues (approximately thirty miles) from the ocean, the boundary line should be drawn parallel to the winding coast so that at no time would the boundary exceed the ten league designation.[5] The lack of precision in the treaty wording created opportunities and problems. Because the treaty did not stipulate whether the boundary should follow the heads or mouths of deep inlets, the real issue was control over port areas situated at these inlets. The United States claimed that the treaty granted to Russia exclusive rights to extensive ocean ports which, in turn, were transferred to the United States with the purchase of Alaska.[6] This strip of territory and its waterways became major points of contention during the 1896-1897 gold strikes when it became clear that the area was important as a point of entry to the gold fields and equally necessary for shipping ports.

By 1903, the contested boundary had become a serious problem. In his annual message to Congress, President Theodore Roosevelt noted that rapid and increasing development in the Arctic had made it necessary that the boundary issue be settled. The area in question included the entire mining district of the Porcupine River and Glacier Creek.[7] Rich veins of gold and silver had been located and had attracted the attention of the press and prospectors. The chance to get rich was irresistible, but Roosevelt believed that the wealth and well-being of the country were more dependent on new coal deposits, described as the best in the Pacific Ocean area. Government aid in opening these resources to development would encourage further exploration and development of other valuable resources such as petroleum, gypsum, and marble.[8] Roosevelt sent 800 cavalry men to the disputed area, allegedly because of the new gold discoveries, but probably to be in a better position to protect the area in case a satisfactory agreement was not reached.[9] The President vehemently opposed making any concessions to Canada and arranged for the dispute to be settled by an arbitration commission weighted so that the final convention would actually be between the United States and Great Britain rather than with Canada.[10]

The crisis ended with a settlement solidly in favor of the United States with a treaty that ceded to the United States the coastal strip of land and islands from north of Skagway to the Portland Canal. Canadians were as angry over the manipulation of the agreement as they were over the loss of territory and protested this example of "American imperialism" to the United States and to England. The English response was to stress the international advantage of a close cooperative relationship with the United States while reminding Canada of the tenuous legitimacy of its claim. This approach soothed the Canadians somewhat, but not enough to compensate for the churlish gloating by the American press, and Canada remained suspicious of American intentions regarding expansion northward through the 1920s.[11]

The Alaskan Boundary settlement coincided with the increase in exploration through the Canadian Arctic by Europeans and Americans. Canadians, angry over what they considered a national affront by the United States in the Alaska dispute, were equally distressed at the assumption by foreign powers that the Canadian archipelago was a *terra nullius* that could be explored at will. Canada insisted that the region between its eastern and western shores and the North Pole came under Canadian jurisdiction. Having lost the battle over one boundary, Canada was intent on protecting all others.[12] The issues were not just national pride, but were economic and political. Coal, fish, minerals (including petroleum), and ports were important reasons for claiming this inhospitable land, but Canadians also believed their national sovereignty was being undermined by open use of this area. If Canada were to be considered a great power, it would have to assert its authority as an independent nation and what more logical place to do so than in the Arctic.[13]

American and Norwegian expeditions were considered the most serious threats to Canadian sovereignty. Canada responded to this encroachment with a series of arctic expeditions. The first, in 1902, commanded by Captain Joseph E. Bernier, was a four-year expedition designed to reach the North Pole using Nansen's drift method.[14] Bernier planned to drift for three winters and two summers until he was within 100 to 150 miles of the Pole and then make a final dash over the ice using sledges and dogs. He set out from Vancouver in July in a steel-sheathed ship similar to the *Fram* but with "many modern appliances" such as electric and steam heat, distilling equipment, two electric stoves, and a telephone system for communication between the wheelhouse, engine room, crow's nest, and cabins.[15] Bernier hoped to use a telescopic pole to try to keep in contact with Dawson City (Yukon) and planned to telegraph communications to either Dawson or Hammerfest, Norway, 1,200 miles away.[16] It appears the contest was not only to reach the Pole, but to have Canada recognized as a "modern" and "progressive" nation.

Although not officially sponsored, Bernier's expedition had been organized to secure Canada's territorial rights and had the tacit approval of the government. The expedition planted the British flag on every island reached, claiming not only Ellesmere Island and the Axel Heiberg group (discovered in 1898 by the Norwegian Otto Sverdrup), but also 25,000 square miles of territory stretching beyond the route actually taken by Bernier. This grand, or grandiose, maneuver embarrassed as many Canadians as it pleased, and caused considerable consternation among Norwegians in general and with Sverdrup in particular.[17]

Otto Sverdrup had left Christiana, Norway, in June 1898, for a four-year expedition to find how far Greenland extended toward the North Pole and to determine the geomorphology of the island. He announced that he would consider trying to reach the Pole if circumstances were favorable, but the primary purpose of the endeavor was scientific. The *Fram* sailed with sixteen men, six of whom were trained in the sciences of geology, botany, and zoology. The expedition spent the spring and winter of 1898-99 on Ellesmere and Baffin islands, mapping and hunting, and remained in the Canadian archipelago until 1902. When the group returned that September, it claimed a number of new discoveries along the southern coast of Ellesmere, including a group of small islands named for Sverdrup and claimed for Norway.[18] A less publicized goal of the Bernier expedition was to reclaim these islands for Canada on the grounds that discovery alone did not entitle a country to claim sovereignty, that occupation and development, long recognized principles of international law, had to accompany the discovery.[19]

Canadians had problems with another Norwegian. In 1903, Roald Amundsen began his expedition to locate the magnetic North Pole, an investigation he insisted was "very different from Peary's or Nansen's." He did not plan to do any geographic mapping or any specimen collecting, but hoped to bring back important information for sailors navigating the northern seas and for mathematicians who prepared sea charts. Amundsen emphasized that his primary purpose was the study of the magnetic Pole, but that he would consider continuing his voyage to the Bering Straits. By promoting the scientific aspect of the expedition, Amundsen probably hoped to increase support for the voyage and counter a growing popular opinion that exploration should be backed by geographical societies, not governments.[20] This expedition, made famous as the first successful traverse of the Northwest Passage by ship, sailed through channels and along the coasts of southern arctic islands claimed by Canada.[21] Canadians expressed their concern that Norway might try to claim these islands and declare the Northwest Passage an international water route, open to ships from all nations, in an attempt to establish jurisdiction over the entire area, including the channels between the islands.[22]

Amundsen's successful transit of the Northwest Passage in 1906 made him an international hero. Called the "Norse King" by Adolphus Greely, Amundsen described the exploits of the tiny ship *Gjoa* in a cool, detached manner, which made good copy.[23] Unfortunately for him, the very copy that profited the newspapers nearly ruined Amundsen. Strapped for funds and owing shipbuilders and most of the tradesmen in Norway, he hoped to sell the story of this expedition to Norwegian newspapers, pay off his debts, and realize a profit. The story was reported in the American press first, and Amundsen's contracts with Norwegian papers were cancelled.[24] Amundsen's journey through the Northwest Passage did not bring him the riches he had hoped for, but it did result in broad publicity and helped establish his reputation as a calculating, fearless explorer.

Canadian reaction to Amundsen's feat was mixed. Unable to deny the success of the venture, officials still disapproved of Norwegian activity in Canadian territory, and attempts were made to discredit at least part of Amundsen's accomplishment. Captain Bernier reported that his expedition had discovered two boots belonging to the Franklin expedition. This claim, it was hoped, would establish Canadian title to the area by citing an expedition conducting official business (gathering the remains of the Franklin expedition) as proof of administrative activity. Amundsen refuted Bernier's claim and maintained that the remains had actually been found and brought "back to civilization" by him.[25] Bernier's irascible manner was no match for Amundsen's cool aloofness and the episode only resulted in more publicity for Amundsen, Norway's support for arctic exploration, and the idea that the Northwest Passage might be considered an international waterway and not an inland sea route.

Having lost out on publishing his story, Amundsen turned to the speaker's circuit. In February 1907, he spoke before the Royal Geographic Society, stressing the expedition's contribution to scientific inquiry. Nansen corroborated Amundsen's description of the voyage as one engaged in geographic investigation, removing it from the realm of pure adventure. Nansen, a respected scientist and the only trained expert engaged in arctic exploration at the time, insisted that scientific accomplishments far outweighed personal or national aggrandizement as reasons for many explorers in solving the problems of the North: Peary's mapping of the northeast extension of Greenland, Sverdrup's discovery of new northern islands in the "American" arctic archipelago, and his

Captain Bernier on the bridge of C.G.S. Arctic.
(National Archives Canada)

own and the Duke of Abruzzi's delineation of the north and west coasts of Franz Josef Land.[26]

The broad coverage given to Amundsen and Peary contributed to an increased interest in the Arctic and, as Americans wrote enthusiastically of the need to acquire more knowledge about arctic geography, Canadians became more vocal in their protest against what they had come to view as an invasion of their territory. In 1907, Sir Richard Cartwright, Minister of Trade and Commerce, addressed the Canadian Senate regarding the country's sovereign rights to all islands north of the dominion. He stated that he "thought Canada had a good reason for regarding Hudson's Bay a closed Sea," a decision he based on Canadian expeditions that had planted the flag and established ports, thereby adhering to principles of international law specifying occupation and administration as requisites for territorial claims.[27] The lands might not have been valuable at the time, but, Cartwright reminded Parliament, they could become so at any time hence. Because of the indefinite nature of economic possibilities, such as a Klondike gold strike, Cartwright further cautioned the Senate not to set a limit on the claims being made.[28]

When Amundsen turned his ship and his sights away from the Arctic and headed toward Antarctica and the South Pole, Canadians were free to concentrate on American exploration, especially the ramifications of Peary's expeditions. Persistent references to the "American North Pole" or to "Peary's American Pole" continued to annoy Canadians. In 1910, Joseph Bernier set out on a second expedition north. Unlike his first excursion, he made this trip with government ships under sealed orders. Bernier's purpose was to assert Canadian sovereignty over all islands in the North and to investigate rumors of deposits of coal, lignite, and other minerals.[29] In an attempt to counter Peary's claims, Bernier also hoped to find Bradley and "Crocker Lands," described by Peary, and claim them for Canada. Concerned over Peary's claiming the North Pole for the United States, he suggested dividing the Pole among the six nations interested, seven if the United States cared to participate.

Americans thought Bernier was somewhat of an upstart, a characteristic they attributed to Canadians in general because of claims that everything north of the Canadian-American border belonged to Canada. The deepening resentment between the two countries was expressed in the New York Times which noted that Americans believed it would have been more proper if "present proprietors of the Pole" had made the offer.

The Pole was considered "American" by the grace of Peary's discovery, and Americans were skeptical about accepting Canada as one of seven "nations" because Canadians insisted they were part of the British dominion and not a separate entity.[30]

The antagonism between the two countries increased with the proliferation of reports in newspapers and magazines describing Peary's accomplishments in terms of national attainments. In 1912, Bernier accused the United States of stealing Canadian polar regions, a charge applauded by his countrymen. The proof he offered was Peary's use of American names for Canadian soil, land which he insisted Peary "never touched with his foot." Bernier wanted the land renamed, citing proper occupation by the "Canadian Navy" as evidence of Canadian rights. A *New York Times* editorial wryly commented that Bernier could easily rename the territory in question, but it would be a "harder job to haul the American flag down from the peak of the continent, so tightly did Peary nail it to the Pole." Although this competition over the Pole appeared petty, something like a gold strike could make the question of sovereignty important and Americans wondered it Canadian preoccupation with sovereignty issues indicated they "knew something."[31]

There is no evidence that concern over jurisdiction was related to any knowledge of gold deposits; Canadian promotion of arctic exploration and development was stimulated by a need to protect political interests, by scientific curiosity, and by economic motivation. Bernier's campaign to convince Parliament to fund arctic expeditions was successful. When the young Canadian explorer Vilhjalmur Stefansson appeared before the House of Commons in February 1913 to request funds for a four-year expedition into the Canadian Arctic, his proposal was enthusiastically received.

Stefansson, Canada's counterpart to Peary, was educated in the new twentieth century professions, sociology, anthropology, and ethnology.[32] While Peary had merged his inherent nineteenth century individualism with the new twentieth century corporate form of organization, Stefansson did the opposite, applying the methodology and information from the new disciplines, but promoting and glorifying a traditional individualism.[33] He savored the contest between man and nature and worked best alone or in charge of a very few men, handpicked for their ability to demonstrate physical endurance. Stefansson, the twentieth century scientist, succeeded in his arctic explorations when he was able to function alone, the heroic individual.

Stefansson's first arctic expedition was in 1906 as an anthropologist on the Anglo-American Expedition sponsored by the American Museum of Natural History. The expedition explored the Beaufort Sea area hoping to determine the nature of the continental shelf between the American mainland and the Polar Ocean and investigating the possibility that land could have risen above the surface of the sea in the form of large islands. This curiosity about the possibility of land masses grew from a study of tides, and special attention was paid to those between Harrison Bay and Herschel Island, although the main area of investigation took place between Banks Land and Prince Patrick Island. Stefansson's role on this expedition was to complete ethnological studies.[34] His scholarly, detailed reports described an isolated group of Eskimos whose physical and cultural characteristics differed from previous anthropological studies. Unfortunately for Stefansson, the press was not content with these reports, and embellished them with stories about the "Blond" or "Copper" Eskimos who were the sole survivors of historical voyages from Scandinavia. Because of this sensational publicity, Stefansson's study was poorly received and his findings severely criticized.[35]

When he returned from the Anglo-American expedition, Stefansson immediately began preparations for a second arctic excursion, this time to explore the western Canadian archipelago. He contacted the American Geographical Society and the American Museum of Natural History for financial support, but found he was too late. These organizations were interested and offered Stefansson partial funding, but indicated that their primary interest was in MacMillan's search for "Crocker Land."[36] Stefansson then went to the Canadian government and suggested it would be to Canada's advantage to sponsor him. After all, he reminded Parliament, these expeditions were in Canadian territory and any land found and explored should be claimed by Canada.[37] Prime Minister Robert L. Borden agreed that Stefansson should be supported, noting that it would be "more suitable if the government that had the greater interest directed the expedition," and recommended Stefansson sail "under the flag of the country which is to be explored." Canada, he maintained, should be entirely responsible for the expedition so that any land discovered could be added to Canadian territory.[38]

Stefansson proposed equipping a whaling vessel and heading first to the Bering Strait and then to Herschel Island. From there, he planned to head north and east to explore land and waterways under Canadian jurisdiction and hoped to return with valuable reports on mineral, fish, and meteorological and tidal conditions. As an additional benefit and added inducement for support from the Canadian government, he suggested that he check on American whalers and enforce customs regulations.[39]

The expedition was organized under the direction of the Naval Service, which authorized Stefansson to assume full responsibility, and granted him $75,000 to $85,000 to spend at his discretion for men, ships, provisions, and supplies.[40] The expedition was divided into two parts, each with different assignments. Stefansson, in charge of a northern party, set out to explore the Beaufort Sea and annex any lands discovered for "His Majesty's dominion."[41] If no lands were found, the party would then engage in ocean studies. The southern party, under the leadership of Canadian naturalist Rudolph M. Anderson, engaged in areal mapping and investigated copper-bearing rocks on the mainland between Cape Perry and the Kent Peninsula.[42] The expedition was unusual, not only because it was fully supported by the Canadian government, but in the makeup of the staff. Half of the men had Ph.D.s and were chosen for their scientific abilities rather than for any knowledge or experience as arctic explorers.[43] Five out of the fifteen were Canadian, three were British, two American, one Australian (photographer George Hubert Wilkins who, later in 1928, flew from Point Barrow to Spitsbergen), one New Zealander, and one staff member each from Denmark, Norway, and France.[44]

The Canadian Arctic Expedition (CAE), scientifically and financially Canada's biggest operation, discovered Brock, Meighen, and Lougheed islands and claimed them for Canada. Hydrographic soundings were taken 100 miles northeast of Cape Isaches. The expedition explored approximately 65,000 square miles of the Arctic Ocean west of Prince Patrick Island and 3,000 square miles of land and sea northeast of the island.[45]

These accomplishments tell only part of the story. The expedition's ship, the *Karluk*, caught in the ice at the beginning of the voyage, was soon crushed and the survivors made their way to Wrangel and Herald islands.[46] Seven of the men died and the benefits of discovering new islands were weighed against the cost in lives. An investigation of the episode disclosed bitter controversy over Stefansson's ability to choose proper equipment and staff and to lead an expedition so large and complicated. The *Karluk* was described as unfit, although the evidence was more confusing than conclusive as experts testified on both sides.[47]

When the ship became iced in, Stefansson, always impatient, left to forage for food and explore. While he was gone, the ship drifted and Stefansson and his party were left behind to live off the land and improvise until they finally made their way to Anderson's camp. Stefansson was denounced for abandoning the *Karluk* and for trying to convince Anderson to part with some of the southern party's supplies so that Stefansson could continue his explorations in the north.[48] Here too, the evidence is not solid. It is doubtful Stefansson deserted as charged. His need for action and insistence on utilizing local food supplies were probably the reasons he decided to leave the ship. In his mind, he was performing correctly by searching for food and carrying out his orders to explore. However, Stefansson's persistent stand that men could live off the land without elaborate supplies, such as those carried by Peary, conflicts with his own purchase of enormous amounts of provisions and his attempts to convince Anderson to part with his supplies.[49]

Stefansson had been uncomfortable with the enterprise from the beginning. He had wanted to train the scientists in survival techniques and have them devote what he felt was necessary time and energy to hunting. The scientists had insisted they were employed to carry out complex experiments that would never get done if they used their time for hunting seals. As the conflict continued, it became clear Stefansson lacked executive ability. He had outfitted the expedition by relegating authority to numerous crew members, each of whom then acted independently. He had also ignored attempts by the Naval Service to coordinate the process and provide practical supervision. The result was that too many decisions were made independently by too many people and, consequently, Stefansson was reprimanded for being inefficient and the conclusion reached that he had been an unqualified leader.[50]

On receiving news of the iced-in *Karluk*, the Canadian government was then faced with two difficult rescues. Survivors of the ship had to be found and brought home safely.[51] Also, the southern party was poorly equipped and could run out of provisions by summer.[52] The nearest base to equip a relief expedition was Herschel Island and any rescue attempt could be dangerous as it had been for the *Karluk* because of ice, lack of harbors, and low-lying shore. To further complicate matters, Stefansson seemed to have disappeared. Determined to complete the exploration, when he left Anderson's camp he set off to the north. Stefansson accomplished the goal he set for himself and, when he returned, he wrote *The Friendly Arctic* in defense of his methods and decisions, pointing to his discoveries and the amount of territory explored as justification for the expedition. His evaluation of the escapade was not shared by the government after it examined a full account of the *Karluk* disaster and decided to take no more risks on sponsoring expeditions, especially those promoted by Stefansson who, it concluded, was "not worth it."[53]

When Stefansson returned in 1917, he was surprised and amused that he had been feared dead. When confronted with the *Karluk* episode, he maintained that the crew had been adequately supplied and had ample opportunity to live off seals and other land and marine life as he had. He insisted the cause of illness and deaths of the crew must have been because of a defect in the supplies, one he could not have foreseen. He decided the pemmican had been bad, that, at best, MacMillan had made an error in the formula he had given Stefansson and, he hinted, it was possible that MacMillan had attempted to sabotage the expedition by poisoning the dogs.[54] He had the remaining pemmican tested numerous times for defects but, alas for Stefansson, none were found. Not one to be easily diverted, Stefansson, although he finally accepted the reports, insisted the people doing the analysis were less than competent to judge the suitability of this foodstuff because they were not experienced in arctic life.[55] The controversy dragged on, and years later Anderson, referring to Stefansson's attempts to clear himself, described him as a "clever writer and talker . . . merely a clever opportunist." He argued that Stefansson had done nothing original, but instead had stolen or adapted ideas and methods used by numerous explorers from Schwatka to Peary.[56] Furthermore, Anderson maintained, even Stefansson's views on air exploration, then being published, were developed "while working as a sort of international spy in Washington, Ottawa, and London." Anderson probably was referring to Stefansson's attempts to get a government to sponsor his expeditions, but his bitterness toward Stefansson is clearly evident in this statement and an expression of the growing estrangement between the two men brought on by Anderson's jealousy of Stefansson and the latter's own arrogance.[57] Stefansson's continued efforts to promote his ideas and justify himself finally prompted Amundsen, himself no model of modesty, to note that "Mr. Steffansson [sic] is the greatest humbug alive."[58]

Stefansson attempted to counter the unfavorable publicity by charging that the southern party had been guilty of insubordination and even mutiny.[59] At the heart of the controversy was Stefansson's book which included an introduction by the former Canadian Prime Minister, thereby implying that the government supported his story. Stefansson's geographic contributions were never disputed. The conflict appears to have been primarily over his methods. He was a rugged individualist, more interested in forging character and living off the land than in specifically defined and organized work projects. Stefansson, the iconoclast who flouted authority, had demonstrated extraordinary ability in devising methods for survival that would aid explorers examining arctic regions over extended time periods. However, because he refused to follow standard bureaucratic practice, the bureaucracy he chose to ignore censured him.[60]

Stefansson's devotion to exploring and developing the Arctic lasted throughout his lifetime. Neither the sinking of the *Karluk* nor the personal criticism from Anderson and official criticism from the government deterred him. His next project, in 1921, was a colonizing expedition to Wrangel Island. His interest in the island went back to 1914 when the *Karluk* survivors had been marooned there, and he used that episode as evidence of Canadian rights to the island, citing the act of raising the Union Jack on July 1 "as part of a formal ceremony of reasserting British rights." Wrangel could be a profitable acquisition because of abundant fishing waters, Stefansson argued, but a more important long term goal was to establish an air base for future air routes.[61] He believed conditions for aerial navigation "on the whole" were better in the Arctic than anywhere else and that, although full use of aircraft was not immediately possible, it would be only "two or three decades in the future" before aviation were commonly employed.[62]

Stefansson urged the Canadian government to settle its claims to arctic islands, adding that new islands should also be claimed "against the time when they will be valuable both intrinsically and through their strategic position as supply stations along the airways." He had observed an increase in settlements along Siberian rivers and in northern Canada and noted that the polar ocean was the smallest and therefore "easiest" to cross, that this "polar Mediterranean [would] continually increase in importance through airways above it connecting to various lands."[63]

When Loring Christie, the legal advisor to the Canadian Department of External Affairs, received the colonization proposal, he objected, believing it unwise to consider occupying Wrangel because the "British Empire was already so large" and the cost of development would be a burden. Furthermore, he wrote, it was not worth the envy and suspicions of other countries.[64] Because international law had decreed that territorial ownership did not confer exclusive commercial advantage, other countries wishing to exploit Wrangel's economic potential could do so despite any Canadian claim. Similarly, Canadian traders could expect fair treatment if another country held the island. Therefore, Christie saw no advantage for Canada in claiming the island.[65]

While the government clearly had reservations about the project, the press carried enthusiastic reports and speculated on long-range benefits that might be gained. Wrangel was described as an island about the size of Jamaica whose location strategically dominated northeast Siberia, "one of the most important islands in the Arctic region." Stefansson fueled these exaggerated statements by suggesting that control of the island was necessary to thwart Japan's expansion northward into Siberia, a move that would antagonize the Russians as the two nations came into conflict over the Siberian fur trade.[66]

When word of Stefansson's plans reached Washington, the American government conducted an investigation regarding previous claims to Wrangel. The United States had been alerted to a possible controversy over Wrangel and surrounding islands as early as 1916 when the Russian government formally announced that it had incorporated into the empire all arctic islands north of the Russian coast to the North Pole. The State Department had acknowledged receipt of the announcement but carefully refrained from acknowledging the claim itself.[67] In 1921, the government was unwilling either to contest the Canadian expedition or acknowledge that Wrangel was open territory and chose instead to refer to the 1916 Russian claim, noting that the island was Russian property and should "be held in trust for the Russian people until such time as a stable government is established in Russia." Although the United States could claim rights to the island due to discovery in the nineteenth century, such rights were unclear.[68] Furthermore, various executive departments believed the island had, at the time, "little or no value."[69]

Stefansson's expedition and a plan to patrol the northern waters of the eastern Arctic were debated in the Canadian House of Commons. The question was raised as to government policy in these areas and answered succinctly with "What we have, we hold." Prime Minister Mackenzie King assured the members that Wrangel Island was definitely the property of Canada. At that moment, Ellesmere Island was of immediate importance because of questions concerning a Danish expedition led by Knud Rasmussen, but there was "no doubt that in the years to come it will be a matter of very great regret" if the extreme North, including Wrangel, were not secured to Canada.[70]

Reports of the expedition's progress were noted by the State Department which objected to "any nation obtaining undue economic advantage in any part of Russia." American interest in Wrangel was partially economic, but primarily because of its closeness to Siberia. The United States saw Wrangel as a possible step along a path that Japan could take if it attempted to establish a presence in Siberia. If the Japanese did attempt such a move, Wrangel would provide them with both a valuable trading spot and a "fine strategic airplane base."[71] What had begun as just another of Stefansson's impractical and extravagant plans was turning into an international contest. Americans who had shown no interest in Wrangel at the start of the proposed expedition rapidly found numerous reasons for opposing it, including the need to secure Wrangel from Japan which had at that time shown no interest at all in the island.

Despite all of the protests and publicity, Stefansson proceeded with his plan to send a colony of men to settle Wrangel. The Wrangel expedition, led by the Canadian Allen Crawford and staffed with young Americans, landed safely and established camp with no difficulty.[72] The great adventure quickly turned into a greater tragedy when the men found that they were unable to find food either by hunting wildlife or by fishing, and by the following year all but one expedition member had died. The press blamed Stefansson and hinted he had lured innocent youths for his own and Canada's gains.[73] The stories were greatly exaggerated, stressing that the young American men on the expedition had been sacrificed in order to further Canada's expansionist policy.[74] In all of this clamor over who had the right to colonize Wrangel and what the consequences of such an attempt might be, little attention was paid to Russia which promptly sent the ship *Red October* to Wrangel to confiscate any furs and, by planting the Soviet flag, make it known that Wrangel was indeed a Russian possession.[75] Stefansson was undeterred by either the tragedy or the press and continued to insist that the question of Canadian rights to Wrangel and all arctic islands was important to Canada's security. He maintained that if the 110 miles between Russia and Wrangel meant that the island was Russian, then the 10 miles separating Ellesmere from Denmark could mean Danish sovereignty over that island, and that certainly was not acceptable to him personally or to Canada. Stefansson, it appeared, would make any analogy to prove his point, even to posing a hypothetical situation that had no basis in evidence. Denmark simply had shown no interest in annexing Ellesmere Island. Stefansson continued to press his claim that Wrangel had an intrinsic value as a British wireless station and as a supply base for petroleum when a usable commercial transpolar air route had been developed.[76] His comments were forwarded to the Air Council which disagreed, stating that it was improbable that Wrangel would ever possess any value as an air base, especially for civil aviation.[77] Stefansson's belief that the Arctic would become a strategic line of defense became a reality after World War II. The problem was in the details such as Wrangel Island and in his need to justify the decision to develop these isolated, barren arctic islands.

The controversy over Wrangel Island continued long after the lone survivor had been rescued. As long as the press continued to print Stefansson's remarks about the potential value of Wrangel, the question continued to be raised about American and Canadian interests. The Canadian and American governments were kept busy reassessing the value of this little island because of comments admittedly improbable, that in fifty years Wrangel could become "one of the chief theaters of air commerce" because it was located straight across the polar ocean from Greenwich, England.[78]

The possibility of using Wrangel Island for any kind of base, naval or air, had always been slight but the deeper issue was the general importance of the Arctic for air routes and communication centers. Rapid advances in aviation and radio technology were cited as evidence that arctic regions were rapidly becoming more important for air and radio bases on air routes connecting Europe with Asia. Russian claim to Wrangel disturbed both Canada and the United States but appeared at the time to be a possible compromise that would keep either nation from expanding into the north Pacific. What had begun as a traditional quest to tame nature turned into an irritating international problem that kept the military and foreign service of both countries busy speculating about the intention of the other.

The knowledge that aviation was going to continue to be more important for commerce and defense affected arctic exploration. While explorers and scientists continued to probe the Arctic and exchange information, their governments became increasingly wary of each other. Altercation among Norway, Sweden, Denmark, Canada, and the United States continued to erupt through the 1920s. Although none was of major significance, the result was increased government surveillance and military involvement in arctic expeditions, and this in turn created even greater uneasiness among those nations involved, especially between the United States and Canada.

Notes to Chapter 3

1. Norman Penlington, *The Alaskan Boundary Dispute: A Critical Reappraisal* (New York: McGraw Hill, 1972), p. 33. Canadian suspicions could have been related to historic rhetoric concerning relations between the two countries, such as Grover Cleveland's hostile stance regarding Canada as part of the British empire and, in 1895-96, the Republican Party platform item calling for annexation of Canada.

2. *Review of Reviews* 32 (1905): 397; (1907): 484. An example of this is the charge that failure to acquire Canada along with Alaska was "the most colossal blunder of American statesmanship." A later article on the importance of Canada to the U.S. called for the establishment of a commercial union rather than annexation.

3. Gordon W. Smith, *Canada's Arctic Archipelago: 100 Years of Canadian Jurisdiction*, government pamphlet, Northern Affairs Program, Ottawa, 1980.

4. Noah Storey, *The Oxford Companion to Canadian History and Literature* (Toronto: Oxford University Press, 1967), p. 33. The 1884 expedition was led by Lt. Andrew Robertson Gordon and the 1897 one by Commander William Wakeham.

5. Robert Craig Brown, *Canada's National Policy 1883-1900: A Study in Canadian-American Relations* (Princeton, NJ: Princeton University Press, 1964), pp. 281-84.

6. Charles Thonger, *Canada's Alaskan Dismemberment* (Ontario: Charles Thonger, 1904), pp. vi, 10.

7. Theodore Roosevelt, "Annual Message of the President of the United States," *Foreign Relations of the United States 1903*, pp. xvi-xvii.

8. *Journal of Geography* (January 1906): 37-39.

9. Frederick W. Marks, III, *Velvet on Iron: The Diplomacy of Theodore Roosevelt,* (Lincoln: University of Toronto Press, 1979), pp. 105, 106.

10. *Foreign Relations of the United States 1903*, p. 488.

11. Penlington, *The Alaskan Boundary Dispute*, pp. 111-117.

12. R. H. C. Browne, *The Canadian Polar Expedition: Will Canada Claim Her Own*, pamphlet, (University of Toronto, 1901), Thomas Fisher Rare Books Library, Toronto. Canadians were as angry over the manipulation of the agreement process as they were over the loss of territory.

13. *Journal of Geography* (January 1906): 37-39. *The Times* (London), February 22, 1907, p. 5. Morris Zaslow, *The Opening of the Canadian North 1870-1914* (Toronto: McClelland & Stewart, 1971), pp. 262, 278.

14. Canadian arctic exploration by Norway refers to Nansen's drift across the Arctic Ocean 1893-96 and Sverdrup's 1898 exploration of islands north of the Canadian coast.

15. *Current Literature* 32 (April 1902): 397-98.

16. *Scientific American* 86 (February 15, 1902): 403.

17. R. A. J. Phillips, *Canada's North* (Toronto: MacMillan of Canada, 1967), pp. 98-113. In the excitement over Bernier's voyage, the Canadian Senate introduced a bill to claim formally all land north of its boundaries to the Pole. The reason given for such a claim was the necessity of notifying explorers and whalers that they were exploring, using, and claiming land illegally. This and future claims northward mark a decided change in direction for land claims. David Hunter Miller, "Political Rights in the Arctic," *Foreign Affairs* 4 (1925-26): 56-57. Previously, claims similar to those defined under the sector principle had been exercised from east to west, such as the original land grants in the United States. As seaboards were settled along latitudes, claims tended to extend inland. In these new proposals defining claims by longitudes extending northward, the north became the equivalent of inland or hinterland. The United States opposed the sector principle in the Arctic and, later, in the Antarctic, by simply not recognizing it. A reason for nonrecognition may have been the relatively small area encompassed by the east and west longitudes demarcating Alaska's boundaries. The government also opposed recognizing sovereign rights on the basis of discovery. Division of Western European Affairs, "Attitude in the Past of Nations Towards Polar Lands," pp. 14, 59-61, State Department Records, RG59, 1910-29, NA.

18. *American Geographical Society Bulletin* 34 (1902): 329. Sverdrup used Nansen's ship for this voyage.

19. Richard Finnie, "Farewell Voyages: Bernier and the Arctic," *Beaver* (Summer 1974): 44-54.

20. *Scientific American* (August 15, 1903): 23095. *The Times* (London), February 12, 1907, p. 12. Roland Huntford, *Scott and Amundsen* (New York: G. P. Putnam's Sons, 1980), p. 71.

21. Roald Amundsen, *My Life as an Explorer* (New York: Doubleday, Page & Co., 1927), Chap. 3.

22. *The Times* (London), February 12, 1907, p. 1.

23. Adolphus W. Greely, "Amundsen's Expedition and the Northwest Passage," *Century* 73 (February 1907): 625-33.

24. Messages between the Norwegian Dept. of Foreign Affairs and the State Dept., December 6, 7, 1905; April 7, 1906; May 16, 1906; January 17, 28, 1907; June 12, 1907, State Dept. Records, RG59, Microfilm M862, reel #189, NA. Amundsen sent a detailed account of the adventure to Nansen in a secret and personal telegram through the Norwegian consulate at Seattle. The telegram was intercepted and prematurely relased to the press by a U.S. Signal Corps officer in charge of the Alaskan telegraph. Nansen's brother, Norwegian Minister of Foreign Affairs, who had been handling Amundsen's legal and financial affairs, demanded retribution from the American government. The case went on for well over a year with calls for legal action by the Norwegian government against the Signal Corps and even the diplomatic service. The case was finally closed in June 1907, when Secretary of State Elihu Root refused payment or further consideration of the claim, citing affidavits by newsmen that the story was common knowledge and, therefore, public property. Norway dropped its case; no payment was made by the United States.

25. *The Times* (London), January 9, 1907.

26. *Geographical Journal* (July-December 1907): 470.

27. Dept. of Marine, RG42 v463 f84-1-1, PAC. A Hydrographic Survey conducted by the Naval Service sent expeditions to Hudson Bay in 1910-14 to gather information on the feasibility of navigation and to find a suitable terminal port. These studies were made on the advice of the government which, in 1904, had felt the waters of Hudson Strait, as well as the Bay, were Canadian territorial waters.

28. *The Times* (London), February 22, 1907, p. 5.

29. *New York Times*, July 26, 1910, p. 3.

30. Ibid., February 1, 1910, p. 2.

31. Ibid., February 8, 1912, p. 8.

32. Vilhjalmur Stefansson, *Discovery* (New York: McGraw Hill, 1964), pp. 33-76. Stefansson was born in Canada. Although he lived in the U.S. most of his life, he still regarded himself as Canadian. In order to gain a more balanced view of Stefansson see William H. Hunt's *Stef: A Biography of Viljalmur Stefansson* (Victoria: University of British Columbia Press, 1986).

33. Stefansson to Roosevelt, October 15, 1913, Theodore Roosevelt Papers, ser. 1, Microfilm Reel #181, University of Cincinnati Library.

34. *The Times* (London), January 19, 1906, p. 6; April 21, 1906, p. 13; September 5, 1907, p. 3.

35. Stefansson, *Discovery*, pp. 106-44. Richard J. Diubaldo, *Stefansson and the Canadian Arctic* (Montreal: McGill-Green's University Press, 1978), pp. 49-50.

36. Stefansson, *Discovery*, p. 146.

37. *New York Times*, February 5, 1913, p. 20.

38. Vilhjalmur Stefansson, *The Friendly Arctic: The Story of Five Years in Polar Regions* (New York: The MacMillan Co., 1922), p. xvi. *New York Times*, February 15, 1913, p. 1.

39. Rudolph M. Anderson Papers, MG30 B40, v12, NAC. *New York Times*, February 23, 1913, sec. IV, p. 5. Anderson Papers, MG30 B40, v12; Amundsen file, RG13 B6, v196 f2, NAC.

40. February 22, 1914, Anderson Papers, MG30 B40, v10 f3, NAC. *New York Times*, February 15, 1913, p. 1.

41. Anderson Papers, MG30 B40, v10 f3, NAC. The agreement Stefansson negotiated included the condition that he receive no pay, one he had insisted on in earlier enterprises. As compensation, he was to have all newspaper rights. No member of the expedition, including Anderson,

was to engage in any correspondence with newspapers during the trip unless Stefansson authorized material to be forwarded in order to fill his contract with the *London Chronicle* and, if published, Stefansson was to receive a percentage of the fee. John D. Craig Papers, MG30 B57, NAC. Report of the Canadian Arctic Expedition, 1913-18, vol. 12, Ottawa, 1923, p. 5. Correspondence between Stefansson and Anderson's wife indicates that he was actually counting on Anderson issuing press releases. See Hunt, *Stef*, pp. 111-112.

42. Canadian Arctic Expedition Papers, MG30 B57, NAC. Official instructions stated the goals in order of importance: first exploration, then studies in geography, oceanography, biology, geology, magnetism, anthropology, and photography. The southern party was to engage in the same activities minus exploration.

43. Diubaldo, *Stefansson*, p. 70.

44. Stefansson, *The Friendly Arctic*, p. xviii. This emphasis on scientific expertise was an important part of MacMillan's "Crocker Land" expedition at the same time. See previous chapter.

45. Diubaldo, *Stefansson*, p. 127. Leslie H. Neatby, *Conquest of the Last Frontier* (New York: H. Wolff, 1960), pp. 399-401.

46. Dept. of Marine, RG42 v463 f84-2-1, NAC.

47. Memo in O. E. LeRoy letter file, Anderson Papers, MG30 B40 f3, NAC.

48. Dept. of Marine, RG42 v463 f84-2-1, NAC. Memorandum on Investigation of Canadian Arctic Expedition, 1918-19, Anderson Papers, MG30 B40 f10, NAC.

49. Dept. of Marine, RG42 v463 f84-2-1, NAC.

50. Anderson Papers, MG30 B40 v10, NAC.

51. Dept. of Marine, RG42 v480 f84-2-35, NAC. Bartlett reached St. Michael, Alaska, and sent a relief ship to the survivors.

52. O. E. LeRoy (Geographical Survey), November 3, 1913, Anderson Papers, MG30 B40 v10 f3, NAC.

53. Anderson Papers, MG30 B40 v10 f3, NAC. Hunt, *Stef*, Chap. 7.

54. Conference report from Stefansson, Dept. of Marine, RG42 v490 f84-2-56, NAC. The issue was the amount of salt which may have been high enough to cause illness. MacMillan had commented on his concern about the salt content, but the laboratory reports did not find any abnormalities.

55. Debates from U.S. Dept. of Agriculture, November 30, 1920; January 5, 1921, Dept. of Marine, RG42 v480 f84-2-35, NAC.

56. Anderson to Amundsen, March 4, 1926, Anderson Papers, MG30 B40 v10 f3, NAC.

57. Hunt, *Stef*, Chap. 12.

58. Anderson Papers, MG30 B40 v11, NAC. Hunt, *Stef*, Chap. 9. The Canadian historian Richard Diubaldo's interpretation of Stefansson is far more critical than Hunt's, which is an attempt to provide a more balanced analysis of Stefansson and his accomplishments. This author still questions if Stefansson's decisions during the Canadian Arctic Exploration and the 1921 Wrangel episode were objective and sensible or if they were heavily influenced by Stefansson's determination to prove his theories correct.

59. Ibid.

60. In 1925, when Parliament was asked to appropriate $10,000 for the publication of the results of the Canadian Arctic Expedition, the whole episode was again raised in regard to benefits from arctic exploration. Members asked, "Of what practical value was it all?" "Is anybody going

to take a boat into these regions?" "Are we locating icebergs?" "Are we gaining territory of any value?" Canada, *House of Commons Debates*, 4th sess., 14th Parliament, vol. 13, May 8, 1925, pp. 3011-13. Anderson Papers, MG30 B40 f13, NAC.

61. March 3, 1921, Northern Affairs Program, RG85 v582 f565, NAC. Vilhjalmur Stefansson, *The Adventure of Wrangel Island* (New York: The MacMillan Co., 1925).

62. Handwritten memo by Stefansson, Loring Christie Papers, MG30 E44 v6 f19, NAC.

63. Ibid.

64. Secret memo, February 1921, Loring Christie Papers, MG30 #44 v6 f19, NAC. Christie was the legal advisor to the Canadian Department of External Affairs from 1913 to 1923.

65. The Spitsbergen Treaty (1920) was probably the precedent for this conclusion. The Treaty provided for equal opportunities for all nations involved. *U.S. Treaties*, vol. iv, 1923-27, pp. 4861-67. Nancy Fogelson, "The Tip of the Iceberg: The United States and International Rivalry for the Arctic 1900-25," *Diplomatic History* 9, 2 (Spring 1985): 131-48.

66. Dept. of Marine, RG42 v463, NAC.

67. Correspondence between Russian Ambassador and State Dept., November 13, 1916; January 4, 1917, State Dept. Records, RG59 861.014/2-3 M316, Reel #77, NA.

68. In 1867, Capt. Long, Commander of the American whaler *Nile*, approached within 15 miles of the island, naming it Wrangell [sic]. In 1881, American officers from the revenue cutter *Corwin* landed and raised the U.S. flag, claiming the territory for the U.S. *Foreign Relations of the United States* 1 (1923): 278-280.

69. Anderson Papers, MG30 B40 v11 f13, NAC.

70. Canada, *House of Commons Debates*, 1st sess., 14th Parliament, 1922, p. 1750.

71. Newsclippings, March 1922, State Dept. Records, RG59 861.0144/ 11, M316, Reel #77, NA.

72. *New York Times*, September 28, 1921, p. 21. The expedition included three young American men and an Eskimo woman, Ada Blackjack. Stefansson planned to go to Wrangel the following year with a larger expedition of volunteers drawn from the "25 daily applications" he had been receiving.

73. "The Tragic Crusoes of Wrangel Island," *Literary Digest* 79 (December 8, 1923): 36-47.

74. Richard J. Diubaldo, "Wrangling Over Wrangel Island," *The Canadian Historical Review* 48 (1967): 201-26.

75. Stefansson to Christie, June 9, 1922, Loring Christie Papers, MG30 E44, v3 f6-8, NAC.

76. Air Council memo, July 15, 1922, Air Board, MG30 B57, NAC.

77. Clipping, June to October 1923, State Dept. Records, RG59 861.0144/ 22-24, M316, reel #78, NA.

78. State Dept. Records, RG59 861.0144/52, NA.

4

Flying the Arctic, 1920-1921

If Anyone Can Do It, the Navy Can

Diplomatic and political questions concerning arctic territory became more complex in the 1920s with increased use of aircraft for transportation and exploration. As air routes were planned, Americans recognized that the shortest air lanes connecting Europe with Asia would cross the North American Arctic and the government began to use a polar perspective to measure geographic relationships with European and Asian nations. This polar view vividly illustrated the proximity of Russia, Japan, England, and Germany to the United States and Canada, and created a need in the minds of Americans for improved defense facilities along arctic borders. Improved aviation technology appears to have stimulated military interest in the Arctic and facilitated economic expansion. The combination of advances in aviation and the search for and development of mineral resources encouraged the American government to consider arctic territory, sea lanes, and air routes, essential aspects of strategic and economic interests.

Economic development in the North American Arctic depended on access to mineral deposits. In the 1920s, experimental flights opened previously inaccessible areas for mining operations, and successive flights demonstrated that the areas could also be valuable as supply bases along future air routes.[1] Widely publicized flights helped stimulate the American and Canadian aviation industries by promoting the feasibility of aviation for exploration, transportation, and defense.[2] Although most early flights were not economically or mechanically satisfactory, problems encountered were not insurmountable.[3] In the United States, companies engaged in aviation research and development were aided by government contracts for air mail service, and the industry showed steady growth.[4] Companies such as Loening, Ford, and DeHaviland tested their products by engaging in cross-country flights and air races, and by encouraging government-sponsored flights over arctic territory. Information gained from cold-weather flying, especially in the Arctic, was vital for the general development of aircraft because temperature conditions in the Arctic were more similar to than different from high flying at any latitude.[5]

An important element in the contest over arctic islands and unexplored territory was a need for aircraft bases along transpolar air routes around the arctic perimeter.[6] Because of the relatively short range of airplanes in the 1920s, it was necessary to position air bases at Franz Josef Land, Spitsbergen, Greenland, the islands comprising the Canadian archipelago, and Alaska. In 1920 as part of his effort to build a national air force, Army Air Force advocate William (Billy) Mitchell launched the most ambitious project at the time to test both the potential of airplanes and the idea that distances between major industrial powers should be measured across arctic and subarctic latitudes.[7] Mitchell's primary goal was the establishment of an independent air force, and he was willing to employ any method, no matter how flamboyant, to promote this goal. One such tactic was a round-trip flight from Minneola, Long Island, across Canada to Nome, Alaska.

Mitchell had established the Civil Affairs Division in the Training and Operations Group of the Air Service and, in 1919, supervised the development of a master airways plan that could be used for commercial air routes in peace time and by the military in case of war. In planning these routes, he included provisions for the defense of the Panama Canal and advantageous use of Alaska's strategic position in relation to Asia.[8] He considered Japan a major threat to the United States and believed the best defense against a possible Japanese attack would be to provide military protection and the means for a counterattack in Alaska.[9] The military importance of Alaska became apparent in the defense of the Aleutians in World War II, but in 1920, Mitchell's plans could not be implemented because meteorological knowledge of the Bering Strait was insufficient, and aircraft were unable to fly successfully in the notoriously poor weather conditions prevalent along the coast of Alaska.[10]

The new domestic aircraft industry had barely begun to develop the necessary technology for successful flights when it lost its contracts for military equipment at the end of the war. Faced with a surplus of planes and engines, companies sharply curtailed research and development. Technical improvements were costly, and the necessary funding for research was difficult to obtain without assurance of a market that would provide sufficient return for research investment.[11] Mitchell's vision of an aviation-supported American triangular defense system through Alaska, Canada, and the Panama Canal was, in 1920, theoretically correct but technologically not possible. Furthermore, unless there was active support to begin to build such a system, explorers and military men such as Mitchell feared it still might not be in place twenty years later.

Mitchell recognized that global and space geography required considerable changes in the traditional definition of national defense, which then concentrated on protecting national borders and strategic sea lanes. This new perspective also challenged aspects of foreign policy that defined relationships among the United States, Europe, and Asia in terms of the Monroe Doctrine.[12] Given the closeness of Asian nations above 60° north latitude, and what appeared to be increased efforts at economic and political expansion, Mitchell estimated that the mouth of the Yukon River could become increasingly vulnerable to attack by aircraft and should, therefore, be included in a comprehensive defense plan.[13]

As part of Mitchell's effort to establish an air force and extend defense perimeters into Alaska, he proposed government-sponsored air expeditions over areas of Alaska not yet explored, in order to search out commercial wealth and establish air routes and air support systems. He predicted that air space, in addition to land masses would, in the future, delineate sovereign boundaries and noted that strings of island bases developed for transportation and communication could and would be seized by hostile powers for use by aircraft unless properly secured and defended.[14] A flight from New York to Alaska could demonstrate the range of aircraft and prove the feasibility of establishing defense bases in the Arctic.

A major consideration in planning the Alaskan air route was securing the consent of the Canadian government to United States military airplanes crossing over Canadian territory and establishing depots in Canada. An additional complication involved communications. The shortest air route should coincide with communication lines in order to track planes and supply them with information regarding weather conditions and descriptions of the terrain, should emergency landing become necessary.

1920 flight from New York to Nome.

The flight, commanded by Captain St. Clair Streett, was scheduled to take forty-five days and cover 9,000 miles round trip, crossing areas that were mountainous and sparsely populated.[15] The expedition was designed to establish an aerial route to the northwest corner of the American continent so that if "military considerations required it, it would be possible to move air service units to Asia by direct flight." A secondary, but perhaps equally important, aspect of the flight provided for extensive photographing of inaccessible parts of Alaska. The plan, authorized by the Secretary of War, was submitted to the Canadian government which granted permission, providing there was no unnecessary risk to those taking part.[16] Allowances were also made for supplies to be brought into Canada free of customs duty as long as they were the property of the American government.[17]

The flight, called the "most difficult feat in the history of aeronautics," was set to begin July 15, 1920. From May 1, the date of final approval, until takeoff time, vast amounts of equipment, supplies, gasoline, oil, and personnel were shipped to remote areas which were to serve as depots. Commander Streett acknowledged the flight's military significance and added it would also prove the commercial importance of air power. The *New York Times* questioned Streett's conclusion, calling the

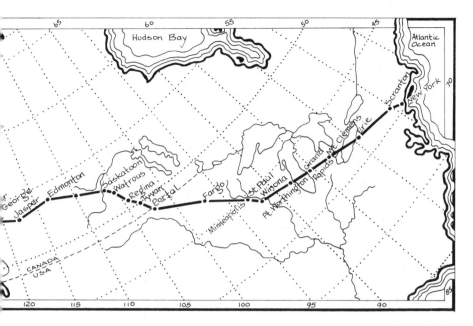

expedition a "waste of time and material," an opinion not shared by businesses, including Boeing Airplane Company of Seattle and a number of Chambers of Commerce.[18] Mitchell noted the expedition would be the first American overland flight of any magnitude to cross another country's territory. The extent of the effort can best be appreciated by examining the flight organization which included complete auxiliary services such as storage and distribution of fuel, maps, and spare parts. By providing extensive services, Mitchell believed that each part of the Army Air Service would then be ready to function in a manner similar to that necessary for "preparation for war."[19]

Commander Streett had been instructed to photograph the previously inaccessible area south of the Tanana River between McCarty and Hot Spring. Although the expedition was limited to establishing an air route to the northwest corner of Alaska and exploring by air regions that were difficult to reach, the temptation to continue the flight was hard to resist. The fifty-six hour flight had been routine, if continual replacement of airplane parts and difficult landings on makeshift fields could be called routine, and the men were eager to make Nome just another makeshift stop rather than the final destination.

The landing at Nome was uneventful, but had almost been a disaster. Final preparation of the landing field was completed only shortly before the flight was due, and the crew was cautioned about field conditions which were described as "sandy" except for a hole one foot wide and fifty yards long, discovered when the grass had been cut. The planes landed safely alongside and not in the hole, and the flyers, even more confident of their ability, insisted they could easily continue the flight by crossing to Siberia, circling the Siberian coast, and returning to Alaska.[20] Commander Streett suggested the proposed flight extension was important for proving the feasibility of air mail routes, but considering the small demand for mail to Siberia, the reason for continuing with the flight could easily have been the challenge, and because the men were infected with that heady excitement that comes from winning an arduous and dangerous goal. Streett and his flyers did not get a chance to demonstrate their prowess. The War Department canceled the Siberian plans, claiming political disturbances in northern Siberia.[21]

Even without this additional adventure, the expedition was a great success.[22] The flight returned with entirely new map information and proved the reliability of the engines which never failed despite regular repairs on all other parts of the planes.[23] The flight crossed over 300 miles of glaciers, flying at an average height of 6,000 feet, sometimes climbing as high as 12,000 and descending to a low of 200. The Liberty engines never missed a cylinder and maintained an average speed of 80 mph. The flight proved an airway to Nome could be permanently established if it included relay stations. Furthermore, such an airway was considered a necessary part of the general growth of aviation, important because the "nation with the best aviation development will be the best in transportation and preparedness for war."[24]

William Mitchell's success with the New York to Nome flight and his unrelenting campaign for a unified air force provided serious competition for the navy in its contest with the army for research and development funds. A number of flyers in the Navy's Bureau of Navigation feared that simply opposing Mitchell's campaign for a unified air force would produce no tangible benefits to the navy and warned that if the Bureau of Navigation did not begin developing its own aviation program, the department could become an adjunct to a new air force. However, if the navy were able to offer adequate competition by proposing its own program, it might be able to reverse the advantage the army had and succeed in establishing hegemony over an air force.[25] The army's Alaskan flight had included those elements with which the navy had been associated in the nineteenth century: discovery, exploration, and the Arctic. If the navy began its own exploration program, it could promote its peacetime role as a stimulus for scientific and industrial achievement. By engaging in arctic exploration and opening new frontiers, the department would also be participating in the development of aviation technology useful to its Bureau of Aeronautics.[26]

Over the next eighteen months, numerous articles and editorials describing the economic and strategic importance of the Arctic appeared regularly, making it difficult to ignore the possibility of utilizing arctic regions for air routes and air bases.[27] Reports of new expeditions by explorers such as Amundsen, and articles written by Stefansson promoting arctic air routes as the key to economic success and national prestige, laid the foundation for seriously considering development of arctic air routes that could be critically important in safeguarding national borders against foreign attack.[28] In 1923, the navy began work on a flight over the Beaufort Sea north of Alaska.[29] The well-publicized plans for extensive exploration over the Arctic Ocean with a naval airship provided the navy with an opportunity to reinforce its reputation as a military unit with definite peacetime functions, including testing modern equipment, acquiring scientific information, mapping, discovering new land, and, as a matter of national defense, providing "for the maximum possible development of aviation."[30]

Arctic air routes planned and developed by the U.S. Navy could serve two functions: to expand commerce and to function as a defense perimeter. American shipping to Japan and Norway amounted to approximately one billion dollars. Arctic air routes between Christiana, Norway, and Nagasaki, Japan, could eliminate 5,000 miles of rail and shipping distance and significantly reduce the cost of transporting freight. If those routes bypassed the United States, the country could lose a substantial amount of trade.[31] Furthermore, the projected value of arctic shipping would increase with the future development of natural resources in Canada and Siberia and concomitant need for machinery, supplies, food, and manufactured goods. If the United States were to remain a dominant nation in international trade, it would be advantageous to become a leader in the development of such air routes and any necessary bases.

Polar air routes could also be of military value. World War I had demonstrated the effectiveness of naval blockades and, in case of a second war with Asian or European powers, that tactic would assuredly be used again. However, the introduction of aviation had changed the nature of warfare and, in any subsequent battles, air power would be equally as important as sea power. The Arctic, a "northern Mediterranean" between Eurasia and North America, would then assume a strategic significance similar to that of the Panama Canal.[32]

Debate over exploring the Arctic by air continued while government committees met to discuss the merits of an expedition. Secretary of the Navy Edwin Denby announced the decision to proceed after he consulted with President Coolidge who commended the navy's heroic participation in exploration, particularly Peary's achievement in reaching the "final goal" (the discovery of the North Pole).[33] The primary purpose of the expedition was to locate land and chart the one million square mile area between Alaska and the North Pole. In addition, it was hoped the United States would be the first to establish an usable air route between Europe and Japan.[34]

The dirigible *Shenandoah*, whose size and range of operation were unexcelled at that time, was chosen as the lead aircraft.[35] The airship, an example of "American skill, ingenuity, and engineering ability," was designed by the Navy Department, fabricated at the naval aircraft factory in Philadelphia, assembled at the Lakehurst naval air station, and manned by naval officers and personnel.[36] In addition to the *Shenandoah*, plans called for airplanes to transport equipment and supplies. A preliminary report indicated there were six seaplanes under construction capable of cruising the required range of approximately 2,200 miles, but unable to carry more than a few basic scientific instruments because of space needed for fuel. Improvements in cruising speed and alterations in flight plans could be completed, but the greater problem was in allocating these six planes to the arctic project. Initially, they had been scheduled for duty in the Pacific, and, if diverted to the Arctic, maneuvers in the Pacific and Caribbean would be delayed a year or more. If, however, the planes were assigned to the expedition and the arctic experiment succeeded, a three-pronged defense perimeter through the Pacific, Caribbean, and Alaskan Arctic could be developed which would protect the three strategic and commercial sea approaches to the United States while future air routes were developed.[37]

There was some serious disagreement amid the general enthusiasm for the project. Dirigible accidents were among the most tragic, especially that of the *Dixmude*, a French airship that had burned, and the press advised caution in regard to supporting dirigible flights because of the belief that they were dangerous except under the most favorable conditions. Considering the cost of the expedition, $180,000, and the size of the crew, a *New York Times* editorial questioned whether the "lives of officers and men should be hazarded for vain glory."[38]

Charges that the expedition would surely result in "virtual suicide" were dismissed by naval authorities who stressed the scientific value of the voyage and the importance to the country of the possibility of annexing new land.[39] Discussions about the destiny of the Arctic to become the "Mediterranean of the future" reflected Stefansson's theory about the strategic importance of the North Polar regions. The navy used this idea to show that it had an obligation to contribute to the exploration and development of this area in order to protect American interests as well as to further international communication.[40] Secretary of the Navy Edwin Denby warned that another power "would and could win" the race to find new land if the United States did not undertake an expedition before the year was out. He added that he believed the area was "certain to be of high strategic value if we look forward to warfare and commerce in the future." He realized that the possibility of finding new land was slim, but supported the search because "whether there is land out there or not it should be the property of the United States." On hearing of the proposed expedition, Captain Bob Bartlett gave his hearty approval, commenting, "What are we going to do with the *Shenandoah* if we don't fly to the Pole? I want to see the Stars and Stripes carried to the North. Don't read American history! Make it!"[41]

Congressional committee hearings on the proposed expedition began in December 1923. Denby, testifying before the House of Representatives, referred to scientific studies indicating that a continent or land mass could be present in the area directly north of Alaska.[42] The secretary believed it was highly desirable that the United States discover any such land because of its "contiguity to the United States and its strategic value if we are to look forward to the advance in the material warfare and of commerce." He alluded to glories of past explorations, particularly in Alaska, as the historic precedent for searching for new territory. Denby acknowledged that material benefits might not be realized immediately but stressed the importance of the area north of Alaska as a future base for planes flying between Europe and Asia. Therefore, he could not "view with equanimity any territory of that kind being in the hands of another power," and reminded the committee that "beyond the Pole there is territory in the hands of another power, the more reason why something in that Arctic Circle, if there is anything there, should be in the hands of the United States."[43]

Expedition plans provided for systematic aerial photography, extensive reconnaissance, mapping, and the establishment of bases capable of servicing airplanes and dirigibles. Because the proposed scientific studies would provide information important for the establishment of commercial trade routes, the expedition's results could speed up commercial aviation design. Arctic exploration was considered a valuable stimulus to technology, which, in turn, enhances national defense. The consensus in the Navy Department was that "short of actual war there has been nothing that has acted as more of a prod to designers and operators than the order of the Secretary of the Navy to do this work by aircraft."[44]

The actual exploration was to be carried out by the *Shenandoah*. Airplanes assigned to accompany the dirigible were to gather aerological data during short flights and test weather conditions which then would be broadcast to the *Shenandoah*. The aircraft were to use Nome as the primary base of operation because existing landing fields and early ice breakup would aid in delivery of supplies.[45] Regular navy personnel, selected for both officers and crew, included competent navigators who consulted with those who were to receive their data to confirm what proofs would be required.[46] Gilbert Grosvenor, director of the National Geographic Society and member of the committee, offered to contribute $40,000 of the society's funds to help defray costs, adding that the contribution "would not affect the status of the project being entirely under the Navy." He recommended launching a careful publicity campaign stressing the expedition's scientific value in order to avert adverse public opinion that might arise if the project were considered some kind of stunt. He also offered the assistance of the society's scientists in preparing a statement concerning the value of exploring polar regions by air, an offer that was readily accepted. Although the committee debated every aspect of the plan from the route it would take to the type of gas the *Shenandoah* would use, all members did agree the dirigible would be capable of returning with valuable economic, military, and scientific information.[47] Captain Bob Bartlett described the importance of the mission:

"The flying route across the Pole is the aerial Panama Canal of the future. It is absolutely essential that, for trade and military purposes, the United States should control the area on the American side of the Pole— just as essential as that the United States should control the Panama Canal.

"To have some other nation find this land would cause endless trouble for future generations when flying from the American to the European side of the Pole is going to be so valuable commercially that military control of the area between the American flag already planted by Peary at the Pole and the American territory of Alaska will be essential."[48]

Speculation over national benefits that could materialize from the *Shenandoah* flight reflected a growing public acceptance of political and economic expansion. The *Literary Digest* justified the possibility of annexing the Arctic by claiming that sovereign rights could be established based on discovery of territory while exploring by air. Economic advantages were described in terms of coal deposits such as those in Spitsbergen, and military advantages were associated with air routes traversing the general arctic area. The *New York World* echoed Secretary Denby's enthusiasm over possible land claims, adding, "We need the North Pole to strengthen our defenses," and warning that, after annexation, the Pole and adjacent ice fields would have to be covered with long-range guns to protect the area and secure it for bases for a flying fleet, ice cruisers, and destroyers.[49]

Lt. Commander Fitzhugh Green described the *Shenandoah* flight as a practical experiment in transportation, less dangerous than the press had feared.[50] He agreed with Stefansson's conclusion that the cold had been overemphasized, adding that similar or worse temperatures were present in Winnipeg (Manitoba, Canada) or Michigan. Forced landings were always a concern, but would be no more disastrous than if they occurred in an isolated area. Provisions carried aboard the dirigible and fresh meat available from sea and land animals would be sufficient to keep the stranded crew safe until a rescue team arrived. Rescue could even be quicker if the landing location were radioed and a rescue team dispatched by air.

Green emphasized possible economic advantages of claiming arctic land by describing geological formations he and MacMillan had discovered on previous expeditions. Coal and oil fields, he explained, could be worked by establishing preliminary bases in Alaska, whose own coal and oil fields were just beginning to be developed. He also stressed the potential strategic importance of the Arctic, describing Europe and Asia as "two great reservoirs of trade . . . connected by long thin pipes of traffic via Panama and Suez." Transpolar traffic could greatly increase the commercial traffic between the two continents and would need to be defended, the traditional role of the navy.[51] American bases in Alaska were necessary, but not sufficient to defend the general area. "From a military point of view" the United States should establish a "terrestrial oasis somewhere between Alaska and the Pole. That there is such an oasis we have excellent reasons to believe. But it will not be ours unless we get there first." Green concluded that the precedent for arctic exploration had been set by Wilkes, Kane, and Peary, and that Alaska had provided national profit. Therefore, this new venture was a logical continuation of naval procedure that had already proven advantageous to the country.[52]

Despite the many disclaimers, arctic flying in 1924 was hazardous.[53] Winter flights were not practical because of the lack of equipment necessary for night flying, and summer flights, while able to take advantage of the long daylight, had to contend with dangerous fog.[54] Economic advantages described by the press and explorers were real, but the ability to exploit natural resources was still many years away. Not only was transportation unreliable, but the machinery and technology necessary for cold weather mineral extraction were insufficiently developed. The potential was there; the tools were missing.

Arguments advanced by Secretary Denby and those who testified at the hearings had not convinced Congress to allocate sufficient funds for the operation. The expense was too great and the hearings continued for too long, leaving too little time to complete preparations for the expedition that year. The operation was cancelled and the *Shenandoah* was assigned to regular naval duties.[55]

Cancellation of the *Shenandoah* flight did not deter the navy from continuing with plans to explore the Arctic with aircraft. On learning that Donald MacMillan was planning to return to the Arctic in 1925 with the *Bowdoin* on an expedition sponsored by the National Geographic Society, the new Secretary of the Navy, Curtis Wilbur, suggested the two organizations cosponsor the operation. Wilbur had been notified of

MacMillan's expedition by E. F. McDonald, a lawyer who was concerned about ongoing Canadian claims to arctic territory and an increasing number of arctic expeditions sponsored by European governments. He reminded Wilbur that MacMillan had been a Lt. Commander in the U.S. Naval Reserves and suggested this link to the navy be used to combine resources to explore the interior of Baffin Island, Axel Heiberg, Ellesmere, and the North Greenland ice cap, and to search for undiscovered land which, he believed, "should be under the United States flag" because it was "too quickly accessible from Europe and Asia for hostile operations against us from the air." McDonald's views were reinforced by Rear Admiral William A. Moffett, chief of the Bureau of Aeronautics, who considered it extremely desirable for the navy to participate as much as possible in scientific expeditions. Moffett offered to supply aircraft and equipment from the Bureau of Aeronautics and recommended that MacMillan be temporarily detailed to the bureau. By participating in this arctic expedition, the navy would be able to "keep its present lead in the exploring field."[56]

Interested in expanding navy functions and promoting his own career, Richard E. Byrd also was convinced that aircraft could open the Arctic. He had attempted to secure a post on the *Shenandoah* flight and, when it was cancelled, contacted members of the committee about a flight over the North Pole using an airplane rather than a dirigible.[57] Admiral Edward W. Eberle, chief of Naval Operations, and Secretary of the Navy Wilbur expressed interest and suggested incorporating Byrd's proposal with the MacMillan expedition if President Coolidge approved the plan.[58]

Coolidge conferred with MacMillan about the proposed voyage, and the two men agreed that the United States should make a major effort to claim additional territory near the North Pole. MacMillan reminded the President that Denmark already had a "foothold" in the Arctic with Greenland, a situation that could prove embarrassing to the United States if landing fields for airships and airplanes were needed in the North.[59] When the plans were completed, MacMillan was chosen to command the expedition on the basis of his arctic experience and Byrd, who had hoped for a prominent spot, settled for second in command, in charge of naval personnel and aircraft.[60] The joint venture appeared to be a good solution to the problem of funding and congressional approval and also allowed the navy to concentrate on developing those aspects of aviation technology it considered most important.

The expedition sailed from Wiscasset, Maine, on June 17, 1925, with MacMillan's *Bowdoin* leading the way and the *Peary*, a converted French trawler, carrying the navy's planes. After setting up headquarters at Etah, Greenland, the men planned to investigate over approximately one million square miles of previously unexplored territory northwest of the Canadian archipelago. They also hoped to explore Ellesmere Island, the northern part of the Greenland ice cap, northern Labrador, and the interior of Baffin Island. The first task was to relay gas and supplies to Cape Thomas Hubbard on Axel Heiberg and then, from there, the men would proceed to the center of the unknown area.[61] Byrd, in charge of leading the aerial excursions, planned to land planes and supplies on the east side of Smith Sound near Cape Sabine and then fly two Loening amphibian planes to set up the next depot at Cape Columbia, 300 miles north, making two or three trips with each plane. When a sufficient supply of fuel was established, one plane would fly north as far as possible over the Polar Sea and, on returning, would then fly to Axel Heiberg.[62]

The expedition was well planned and should have been a success.[63] It did result in a considerable accumulation of scientific data and the reconnaissance of over 30,000 square miles of territory, but it was plagued by bad weather, poor working relations between Byrd and MacMillan, and even poorer relations between the United States and Canada. When reports of the proposed expedition reached the Canadian government, it again expressed concern over sovereignty. The Department of National Defence insisted MacMillan comply with Canadian regulations prior to sailing because of the possible threat to Canada due to the inclusion of military personnel in the expedition and the possibility of claiming land for the United States.[64]

Canadians were particularly worried about plans to fly across Ellesmere to Axel Heiberg and establish a base. These two areas were the only ones where questions of Canadian sovereignty could be raised because of Sverdrup's discoveries and American explorations in the nineteenth century. Both areas had probably been chosen because MacMillan was familiar with them from previous expeditions. However, Canadians worried that the choice was not accidental or just convenient but a test of Canadian sovereignty. The fear was not groundless. MacMillan, in a note to Wilbur, affirmed that "all lands discovered in the great unexplored area by the United States with planes will be claimed in spite of Canada's protest." He included not just the unknown area north of Alaska, but also the "northern end of Ellesmere Land . . . and Axel Heiberg Island," both of which had been explored by Americans between 1854 and 1917. MacMillan claimed these areas were valuable as future air bases and as areas in which to conduct scientific studies, and he hoped that the government would agree to support his plans for annexation.[65]

The Canadian government responded to the perceived threat of MacMillan's expedition by passing the Northwest Territories Act in June 1925, regulating foreign expeditions bringing aircraft into Canada. The Act required that scientists as well as explorers file an application for permission to enter the country and submit information on the nature of their expeditions. Applicants were also to submit evidence of aircraft registration and names and qualifications of pilots. The new regulations were not unknown to the American government. Wilbur notified Secretary of State Frank Kellogg about the details of MacMillan's expedition and requested clarification regarding American acceptance of Canadian regulations. The Canadian Deputy Minister of the Interior had notified Wilbur and the Chief of the Bureau of Aeronautics that Canadian permission should be obtained before the flight proceeded.[66] Wilbur advised the government to acknowledge the communication, notify the Canadian government of the proposed flights, and apply for a permit.[67] After considering the points in the Canadian Northwest Territories Act, the State Department decided it would make no final statement until MacMillan's reports were received. The department questioned the validity of the Canadian position regarding arctic territory, citing Canada's status as part of Great Britain, and considered invoking the Monroe Doctrine to curb Canadian expansion. This ploy appeared quite attractive until it was realized that repercussions could be disadvantageous if applying the Doctrine caused "strained relations for years to come." The matter was further complicated by communications from the Canadian government offering assistance to the expedition and noting that the RCMP had been alerted and were ready if assistance were necessary.[68]

As the expedition sailed in June, the CGS *Arctic* was informed of the voyage and Commander George P. MacKenzie was instructed to look for MacMillan's ships while on annual patrol.[69] The diplomatic process had been acted out in detail. Notes had been exchanged between proper dignitaries, personal visits had been made, letters to the United States explaining Canadian rules had been sent, received, and acknowledged, and the United States had been alerted that the RCMP and patrol ship *Arctic* were on the lookout for MacMillan and would check to see if he had complied with Canadian regulations.[70] The United States had responded to each of these steps in a noncommittal fashion, leaving Canadians with a choice of two conclusions: that it was unimportant to the United States to comply with Canadian regulations or that this expedition was a test to see if the Canadian position was valid.[71]

The *Bowdoin* and *Peary* arrived at Etah on August 1 in the middle of a snowstorm. MacMillan had planned to remain in the North only until August 25, but the departure date could be extended to September 1 if necessary. He made it clear that there could be no more than a week's leeway because the expedition carried only enough provisions for the thirty-nine man crew for a maximum of three months. MacMillan's close planning was done in recognition of the dangerous and unreliable arctic weather. Should any mishap occur, wintering over by one or both ships would be a "very serious matter." To avoid even the possibility of putting the men in danger, departure dates had to be rigidly set to make sure the expedition could leave soon enough to avoid an early freezing of the waterways. Because of concern over weather, the entire project, including landing and assembling planes, establishing food and fuel depots on Ellesmere, and flying at least 2,000 miles, had to be accomplished in an orderly and efficient manner. By August 3, the preliminary work was finished and the first flight was able to survey part of Greenland.[72] Returning from that flight, MacMillan found radioed instructions stating that a reporter aboard the approaching *Arctic* had rights to exclusive news articles but that MacMillan was to give no interviews or let any of the personnel on the *Arctic* use American radio facilities. Furthermore, the crew was cautioned to avoid talking to any outside news agency.[73] Although this secrecy was considered necessary in order to fulfill a contract between MacMillan and the National Geographic Society (NGS) for the exclusive story of the expedition, it also effectively barred the exchange of information between the American and Canadian ships.

All planes were operational and engaged in flights by August 5, but none was running satisfactorily. Minor engine trouble and unusually heavy rain, fog, and low-lying clouds kept the flights short and hindered attempts to set up supply depots. On August 8, a successful flight was made over Smith Sound which was covered with ice pans. Flying over Ellesmere, the planes reached altitudes of 5,500 and 7,000 feet but the flights were abruptly shortened when heavy storm clouds appeared, and all attempts at landing to cache supplies were abandoned.[74] By August 18, the planes had covered 6,000 miles despite technical problems and constant poor weather.[75] MacMillan, aware that all spare parts were then in use and that the weather appeared to be getting even worse, recommended no further attempts be made to establish aircraft bases and that the expedition abandon original flight plans to explore Baffin, Greenland, and Labrador.[76] Byrd protested the decision and expressed his disappointment to the Navy Department, but made no attempt to do other than follow orders.

As the *Arctic* approached Etah, Byrd received orders from the Navy Department to be forwarded to MacMillan. The expedition apparently had caused sufficient discomfort for the government that the State Department had decided to comply with Canadian rules by ordering MacMillan to obtain the necessary licenses from Canadian Commander George Mackenzie in order to "avoid an embarrassing diplomatic situation." The request was to have been made personally in an informal manner. The State Department described the situation as "most delicate" and cautioned the explorers to handle the license matter diplomatically. If the matter could not be resolved and the men were unable to obtain the license, it would be impossible to secure it from Washington.[77]

The *Arctic* reached Etah on August 19. The next afternoon, Commander Mackenzie met Byrd who described the various flights he and his men had made. Mackenzie knew that when he departed from Quebec no permit had been granted for the MacMillan expedition, and he sent his secretary to Byrd to inform him that a permit would be issued. Byrd, in full uniform, returned to the *Arctic* and stated that he had conferred with MacMillan who said a permit had already been granted before departure, and that the incident had been reported in the press. Mackenzie insisted he knew of no such permit but added that if the Canadian government had tried to radio him, the message may not have gotten through because the ship's radio was not working properly.[78] With inadequate radio facilities of its own and unable to use the *Peary's* radio, the Canadian patrol was unable to verify Byrd's claim and the ship left Etah to continue its patrol.

It appears the permission Byrd referred to was ambiguous at best and probably a fabrication. The State Department reviewed the episode when the expedition returned, and MacMillan testified that he had neither a license from Canada nor had he received any instructions to obtain one. Before sailing, the matter had been discussed with the NGS and naval authorities who decided that no license should be applied for since "it was not admitted that Canada had any claim" to the areas to be explored. MacMillan added that Byrd "knew perfectly well" that no permit had been issued but probably made the statement to ease out of a difficult situation.[79]

Although the 1925 expedition was cut short, flights made during the few days when weather was favorable surveyed 30,000 square miles of territory in just a few hours, compared to months of backbreaking effort.[80] MacMillan, on his return, described the Arctic as a "strange and wonderful place" that had aroused the curiosity of men continually from the time of Norse voyages to the present and would continue to attract explorers until "every square foot of this little world of ours will be explored." He believed polar studies, aside from measurable benefits for commercial interests, added to the "sum total of human knowledge," and he attempted to answer the question of why exploration should continue by describing the need for information about the two million square miles north of Alaska. Scientists had speculated that large land masses might exist in the area but observations had been inadequate. The Arctic Ocean had been described as the "birth place of the iceberg," and scientists and explorers had developed theories on the nature of the Polar Sea, its depth, configuration, currents, tides, water temperature, and its unique characteristic, ice. MacMillan argued that information should be collected to test these theories regardless of commercial benefits.[81]

MacMillan hoped aviation would provide the means to accomplish a full investigation of the arctic area in question, but was skeptical about the degree of success that could be expected. He felt planes had been given a fair trial, especially in 1925, but was "convinced that far northern work [would] never be done at least with a single engine airplane" because of difficulty in landing and taking off. He thought three-engine planes might be useful but preferred dirigibles at that time. He reasoned that although dirigibles also needed better design and construction to withstand low temperatures and gale winds, the improvements could be made within the next few years.[82] MacMillan's forecast of usable improvements in aviation in the immediate future was quite accurate. In 1925, Byrd's flights had been cancelled because the planes could not be flown in bad weather, but the next year dirigibles and planes would both be used to cross the Arctic without incident. In 1926, Roald Amundsen completed the first successful transpolar dirigible flight, and Byrd made the first successful flight from Spitsbergen to the North Pole in a tri-motor airplane.

Byrd began planning his flight over the North Pole immediately after returning from the MacMillan expedition in 1925. He believed the flight was important for testing the ability of airplanes to fly at high altitudes and that, if successful, the flights would increase chances of finding unexplored land because planes had a wider viewing range than diri-gibles. He also thought a successful flight across the Pole might stimu-late public interest in aviation and that such a flight could encourage support similar to that generated by flights across the Atlantic. He hoped the navy would provide four Wright air-cooled motors and the necessary spare parts, meteorological and camping equipment, and two aviation machinist mates. In return, he offered to submit a report on engine and equipment performance.[83] Rear Admiral William A. Moffett endorsed the plan in the "interest of science" and sent it on to Secretary Wilbur, but the navy was hesitant to sponsor so expensive and large an expedition.[84] Failure to complete the flights planned for the MacMillan expedition could have been an important factor in rejecting Byrd's proposal.

Although there was no financial support from the navy, Byrd and his machinist mate, Floyd Bennett, were granted leave for the expedition which was scheduled to depart from New York early in April 1926.[85] Byrd then went to the NGS and a number of wealthy friends for funding, all in the tradition of earlier explorers. The NGS made a substantial contribution and Edsel Ford, Vincent Astor, and John D. Rockefeller, all wealthy American entrepreneurs, each contributed $20,000. The Federal War Shipping Board loaned Byrd a 4,000 ton steamer, the *Chantier*, for which Byrd paid a token leasing fee of one dollar a year.[86]

Byrd stressed that the venture was an all-American expedition, staffed with 46 adventure-seeking volunteers.[87] Using a Fokker tri-motor plane equipped with air-cooled 200 hp Wright motors, Byrd planned to fly from King's Bay, Spitsbergen, in May. The route crossed 375 miles to Cape Bridgeman, Greenland, where bases would be established while he explored the area. If the region proved impractical for landing, he would still be able to explore 40,000 square miles of unknown territory during the flight. In addition to the flight, he planned to sail to Etah in September and freeze the ship in for the winter.[88] Byrd emphasized that his object was not to find the North Pole; Peary had already done that. He hoped to prove the airplane safe for arctic travel and demonstrate the commercial value of arctic aviation.[89] Byrd believed the area was becoming crowded, that there was a need to act quickly and not wait "while foreigners locate and take over land that probably is in the Polar Sea and that may within twenty-five years be of value to the United States as a landing base for transpolar flights of a commercial or a military nature."[90]

Publicity for Byrd's flight elicited the expected reaction from the Canadian government which promptly reminded him that the RCMP regularly patrolled arctic islands. Byrd was also informed that caches of food and gas had been set up which he was welcome to use if necessary. If Byrd desired to obtain a permit to fly over and land on Canadian territory, he was to contact the Department of the Interior. Byrd replied that he did not think he would be "likely to fly over Canadian territory until late in the spring," and if he did land, it would be in Greenland.[91] Although Byrd's plan to base his expedition at Spitsbergen and Cape Jessup, Greenland, reduced the "danger of his planting the American flag on territory claimed by the Dominion Government," Canada wanted further clarification from the United States as to its attitude regarding Canadian sovereignty.[92]

When he found that a dirigible flight by Amundsen was to leave from Spitsbergen at the same time, Byrd cancelled all aspects of his flight except the dash to the Pole. The flight left May 9, 1926, with Bennett as aviator and Byrd as navigator. The completed flight followed a straight line to the area of the North Pole, circled, and returned to Spitsbergen. It was a triumph for Byrd, an example of his able preparation and audacity, and a triumph for Americans who were then able to claim that the first conquests of the Pole were by American naval officers.[93] Despite great acclaim, the actual value was minimal because the flight had been too brief to test the plane's ability to withstand prolonged flight in the Arctic. Flying over the polar area required skilled navigation, but the information brought back was too little to be of much scientific or technical use. As it had been with Peary's assault, Byrd's flight was both praised and severely criticized.[94] The importance of Byrd's adventure was questionable. Although he returned with little new information, he had accomplished a spectacular feat in completing the first flight over the Pole with no mishaps. He also proved MacMillan wrong in his assertion that airplanes could not yet be used in the Arctic. Peary may have been the first to use twentieth century technology. Byrd's flight brought exploration fully into the twentieth century.[95]

The press described Byrd's flight as characteristic of the United States, a country that had achieved major feats in the Arctic. The flight had added a "golden page to the history of aviation and exploration" and was acclaimed a "first" for the United States, a country that accomplished things first and better. The flight was more than a heroic gesture. It was an "example of technology defeating nature." Commander Byrd may have added no new territory to the country's possessions and he may not have made a great contribution to science, but he was regarded as a hero because he had "written a brilliant chapter into the history of Anglo-Saxon pioneering."[96]

In January 1927, Richard E. Byrd was awarded the Congressional Medal of Honor for "distinguishing himself conspicuously by courage and intrepidity at the risk of his life in demonstrating that it is possible for aircraft to travel in continuous flight from a now inhabited portion of the earth over the North Pole and return." The next month, Floyd Bennett also received this award as a member of the Byrd arctic expedition for "distinguishing himself conspicuously by courage and intrepidity at the risk of his life . . . thus contributing largely to the success of the first heavier than aircraft flight to the North Pole and return." Byrd and Bennett were congratulated for promoting "peaceful relations between the nations of the world" through the use of aviation. Byrd, Bennett, and Lindbergh had significantly contributed to the view of airplanes as peace advocates rather than as instruments of destruction.[97] Byrd had not been able to secure the information nations had been so eager for, evidence of the existence of land in the region north of Alaska, but his flight over the North Pole, coupled with MacMillan's annual sea excursions, established an American presence in the eastern arctic. Aircraft had not, in 1926, developed enough for regular use in arctic regions, but American expeditions in 1925 and 1926 had demonstrated that American economic and strategic interests could and would expand into the Arctic with improvement in aviation technology and development of air routes.

From 1920 to 1926, exaggerated claims for future air routes led reporters to speculate that new empires in the North would likely shift the North Pole to the center of the world as developments in aeronautics produced a geographical revolution. Some credited the United States with leading the way in both development and revolution, further intensifying the opinion many Canadians had of the United States as an expansionist nation. Canadian distrust of American interest in the Arctic was fueled by American newspapers and the government personnel they quoted. In 1926, a Navy Department representative explained that control of lands in the north polar region was a valuable asset to the United States or to any country from a "commercial and expansion standpoint." He felt that the land above Point Barrow could become the "junction point of commercial aviation," as airlines from Russia and the East passed near the Pole and those flying from the opposite direction did the same.[98] Until new land north of Alaska were found, Canadians could only wonder if the land referred to by the United States Navy included islands within the Canadian archipelago, a speculation that prompted Canada to sponsor its own program of exploration by aircraft.

Notes to Chapter 4

1. "Northern Aerial Minerals Exploration," p. 1, Northern Affairs Program, RG85 v783 f594, National Archives of Canada [hereafter cited as NAC].

2. Margaret S. Mattson, "The Growth of Canadian Civil Commercial Aviation 1918-1930," unpub. Ph.D. diss., University of Western Ontario, 1979, p. 294.

3. Canadian Air Board Report, #10, October 1921-March 1922, Department of National Defense, RG24 v3897 f8-2-1, NAC. Faculty at Canadian universities experimented with operating aero engines at low temperatures and reducing the required starting time. Suitable antifreeze mixtures were tested and studies made of lubrication problems that occurred under winter conditions. Experiments were also conducted testing the strength of streamline wires, tapered aerofoils, and different shapes of wing tips.

4. Philip S. Dickey, III, "The Liberty Engine 1918-1942," *Smithsonian Annals of Flight* 3 (1968).

5. Grover Loening, *Our Wings Grow Faster* (New York: Doubleday, Doran & Co., 1935).

6. Memo, Commandant 12th Naval Dept. to Sec. of Navy, April 19, 1924, General Correspondence, Navy Dept., RG80 29455, NA.

7. Alfred F. Hurley, *Billy Mitchell: Crusader for Air Power* (Bloomington: Indiana University Press, 1975), p. 53.

8. "The Opening of Alaska," p. 3A, unpub. ms., William Mitchell Papers, Box 20, Library of Congress, Washington, D.C. [hereafter cited as LC].

9. Hurley, *Billy Mitchell*, pp. 52-87.

10. Lt. Col. C. V. Glines, USAF, *Polar Aviation* (New York: Franklin Watts, Inc., 1964), pp. 163-65. Richard Finnie, *Canada Moves North* (New York: The Macmillan Co., 1944), Chap. 6.

11. Hurley, *Billy Mitchell*, p. 41.

12. "The Opening of Alaska," Chap. 2, p. 15, Mitchell Papers, LC.

13. William Mitchell, *Winged Defense* (New York: G. P. Putnam's Sons, 1925), pp. viii-xvii.

14. Ibid., p. 12. Commander G. C. Westervelt and H. B. Sanford, "Possibilities of Transpolar Flight," *U.S. Naval Institute Proceedings* (May 1920): 675-712. Elmer Plischke, "Trans-Polar Aviation and Jurisdiction Over Arctic Airspace," *The American Political Science Review* 37 (December 1943): 995-1013.

15. Army Air Force, RG18 f373B, NA. Plans specified use of four bi-motor remodeled DeHaviland planes with Liberty engine.

16. War Dept. memo to chief of staff, April 8, 1920, Army Air Force, RG18 f373B, NA. Condition applied to bases and route in Canada.

17. British Embassy to State Department, March 16, 1920, Army Air Force, RG18 f373B, NA.

18. *New York Times*, July 16, 1920, p. 5; July 9, 1920, p. 12; May 23, 1920, sec. 2, p. 1.

19. Ibid., July 16, 1920, p. 5.

20. Correspondence, July 1920, Army Air Force, RG18 f373B, NA.

21. Ibid.

22. Praise for the expedition was repeated by Gen. H. H. Arnold in *Global Mission* (New York: Harper & Bros., 1949), pp. 94-98.

23. Army Air Force, RG18 f373B, NA. This file contains copies of purchase orders for airplane parts. Propellers, wings, tail parts, and items for repair of the fuselage were replaced often. There are no requisition orders for replacement parts for the engines. *Literary Digest* 66 (September 11, 1920): 92-96. Members of the Manufacturers' Aircraft Association described the flight as "the most significant aviation event of the western hemisphere this year."

24. *New York Times*, July 16, 1920, p. 5; August 26, 1920, p. 17; August 29, 1920, p. 15; October 21, 1920, p. 10; October 24, 1920, sec. 2, p. 2. "Alaskan Expedition, 1920-21," Mitchell Papers, LC.

25. Charles J. V. Murphy, *Struggle: The Life of Commander Byrd* (New York: Frederick A. Stokes Co., 1928), pp. 99-120.

26. Office of U.S. Naval Intelligence, *The U.S. Navy in Peace Time* (Washington, D.C.: Government Printing Office, 1931), pp. iv, 48.

27. *Annual Report of the Navy Department, 1921*, p. 3.

28. *New York Times*, March 7, 1923, p. 1; March 8, 1923, p. 16.

29. The first dirigible designed and manufactured entirely in the U.S. was chosen for the flight. Facilities were constructed at Lakehurst, N.J., consisting of the largest hangar in the world with sufficient room for 2 airships. *Annual Report of the Navy Department, 1920*, p. 45.

30. *Annual Report of the Navy Department, 1921*, p. 3.

31. Commander Fitzhugh Green, USN, "Across the Pole by Plane," *U.S. Naval Institute Proceedings* (June 1923): 943.

32. Ibid., pp. 945-81.

33. Edwin Denby to Calvin Coolidge, November 16, 1923; November 20, 1923. Calvin Coolidge to Edwin Denby, February 15, 1924. Calvin Coolidge Papers, Microfilm reel 21, series 18, University of Cincinnati Library.

34. W. R. Furlong, "Arctic Exploration by Air," p. 4, Navy Department Records, RG80 111-99, NA.

35. "Star Trip of the Stars' Daughter," *Literary Digest* (December 29, 1923): 12-13. The *Shenandoah* was as large as an ocean liner (680' long, 78' wide), powered by six engines, and had a cruise radius of 4,000 miles.

36. *Annual Report of the Navy Department, 1923*, p. 47. Gas capacity was 2,150,000 cubic feet. Helium was to be used because it was non-flammable and nonpoisonous.

37. W. R. Furlong, "Memorandum," November 25, 1923, Navy Department Records, RG80 111-99, NA.

38. *Literary Digest* (January 12, 1924): 15. *New York Times*, January 4, 1924, p. 12.

39. *New York Times*, January 17, 1924, p. 2.

40. D. M. LeBourdais, "The Aerial Attack on the Arctic," *The Nation* 118 (1924): 60.

41. *New York Times*, January 17, 1924, p. 2. Denby's and Bartlett's comments elicited an irritated response from the Canadian press which described the *Shenandoah* flight as an example of Mr. Denby's "spread-eagling" and concluded that because land in the area to be explored

would be hard to locate from an airship, the chances of finding unclaimed land were slim and it would be "difficult for the *Shenandoah* to find unexplored territory upon which the American eagle can find a place to perch." State Dept. Records, RG59 842.014, NA. Memo from American Consul General Albert Halstead, including press clippings. Stefansson's enthusiastic support of the flight further annoyed Canadians, especially his claim that "thriving American cities on the shores of the Arctic Ocean in direct touch with the rest of the world" would be a possible result of the *Shenandoah* expedition. His use of hyperbole was well known, but this new item was answered by the Canadian government with the acerbic comment that the "Patriotic Vilhjalmur was trying to give it [the Arctic] to Canada last year. What country is he working for anyway?" Northern Affairs Program, RG85 v582 f565, NAC. The British were as concerned as Canadians over possible American encroachment and requested an official statement from the State Dept. regarding plans to use Canadian territory as a base of operations. What appeared to be the beginning of a heated exchange dissolved when the State Department answered that Canadian territory would not be used. Memo, State Department to Navy, February 6, 1924, General Correspondence, Navy Dept., RG80, 1916-26, 29455, NA.

42. "Arctic Exploration by Aircraft," p. 21, General Correspondence, Navy Dept., RG80 111-99, NA.

43. U.S. Congress, House Resolutions #149, #78-198, Hearings before the Committee on Naval Affairs of the House of Representatives, 68th Cong., 1st sess., 1923-24.

44. Navy Dept. Hearings, First Day, December 5, 1923, Navy Dept., RG80 111-99: 1-105, NA.

45. "Plan for the Exploration of the North Polar Region," Navy Dept., RG80 111-99: 1-105, NA. Point Barrow, although closer to the Pole, was less accessible because of severe ice conditions. A second base was planned for Spitsbergen as an emergency facility in case return to Nome was not possible.

46. These details may be related to the controversy over data and proofs offered by Peary in 1909.

47. Navy Dept. Hearings, First Day, December 5, 1923, p. 3; Third Day, December 7, 1923, Navy Dept., RG80 111-99: 1-15, NA.

48. Ibid., Sixth Day, December 11, 1923, p. 61, Navy Dept., RG80 111-99, NA.

49. "To Annex the Arctic by Air," *Literary Digest* (February 23, 1924): 18.

50. Green had been a member of the MacMillan "Crocker Land" expedition.

51. Commander Fitzhugh Green, USN, "The Navy and the North Pole," *U.S. Naval Institute Proceedings* (March 1924): 373-85.

52. Fitzhugh Green, "Over the Top of the World," *Literary Digest* 135 (December 1923): 681-83.

53. "Polar Perils Await the *Shenandoah*," *Current Opinion* (March 31, 1924): 344-46.

54. Vilhjalmur Stefansson, "Arctic Air Routes to the Orient," *Forum* (December 1924): 721-32.

55. *Annual Report of the Navy Department, 1924*, pp. 31, 616, 617. Dismay over canceling the flight was expressed by many, usually in terms of fear of competition from other countries. President Coolidge received a letter protesting the cancellation that included a clipping describing German plans for an arctic air expedition. The writer hoped to convince the President to reactivate the American expedition, urging that "no one will dispute the logic that the land should not fall into the hands of a foreign power." William A. Hechard (New York) to Calvin Coolidge, February 11, 1925, General Correspondence, Navy Dept., RG80, 1916-26, 29455, NA.

56. Memo to Curtis Wilbur, February 28, 1925; Memo from Moffett, March 10, 1925, General Correspondence, Navy Dept., RG80 1916-26 29455, NA.

57. Murphy, *Struggle*, pp. 123-28. Richard E. Byrd, *Skyward* (New York: G. P. Putnam's Sons, 1928), pp. 140-41.

58. Byrd to Bartlett, February 24, 1925; March 30, 1925, Robert A. Bartlett Papers, Bowdoin College Library, Brunswick, Maine. Byrd, never one to submit easily to routine protocol, was irked and regretted "extremely that the Secretary finds it necessary to take such a small matter up with the President." Rear Admiral William Adgar Moffett was the Chief of the Bureau of Aeronautics 1921-1930. Admiral Edward Walter Eberle was Chief of Naval Operations 1923. *Who Was Who In American History—The Military* (Chicago: Marquis' Who's Who, 1975), pp. 388, 150.

59. *New York Times*, March 31, 1925, p. 1. Clipping from *Washington Star*, March 30, 1925, Dept. of Marine, RG42 v463 f84-1-1, PAC. MacMillan's concern was correct as evidenced by the development of an American Air Force base at Thule, Greenland.

60. Secretary of the Navy to Byrd, June 15, 1925, State Dept. Records, RG59 842.014, NA.

61. "To Seek the Unknown in the Arctic," *National Geographic Magazine* (June 1925): 673-75.

62. Byrd to J. A. Wilson, May 1925, Northern Affairs Program, RG85 v759 f831, PAC.

63. One aspect was successful. Byrd was the first to fly over the Greenland ice cap. John Grierson, *Challenge to the Poles: Highlights of Arctic and Antarctic Aviation* (London: G. T. Foulis & Co., 1964), p. 198.

64. Confidential report: Northern Advisory Committee, Dept. of External Affairs, RG25 D1 v717 f18, NAC. Although Canada's concern over

exploration in the Canadian archipelago began early in the century, the intense hostility to American explorers in 1925 appears to have been founded less on actual American goals and more in response to reports in the press which continually stressed the historic mission of the U.S. to be the first to find and claim territory, establish air bases, and participate in whatever else may have had economic or prestige value. Canadian antagonism was directed more at MacMillan, with whom they had had to deal for many years, than with Byrd whom they regarded as a gentleman, charming, correct in his manner, and ingenuous. The expedition was judged against the publicity that had accompanied the proposed *Shenandoah* flight, proclaiming that the U.S. had been looking for prestige by adding territory and possibly air bases in the North. Secret dispatch #104, June 4, 1925, Dept. of Marine, RG42 v463 f84-1-1, NAC. While much of the problem could be attributed to press sensationalism, the U.S. had persistently ignored Canadian authority. Moffett to Chief of Naval Operations, Navy Dept., RG80 1916-26, 29455-88: 8, NA. By publicly announcing a route that encompassed Canadian territory without first consulting the host country, the expedition became a test of Canada's influence and role as a rising power.

65. MacMillan to Wilbur, June 5, 1925, Navy Dept., RG80, 1916-25, 29455-83: 10, NA.

66. *Foreign Relations of the United States, 1925*, pp. 570-73.

67. Wilbur to Secretary of State, June 10, 1925, Navy Dept., RG80, 1916-26, 29455-83: 3, NA.

68. "Canada's Claim in the Arctic Ocean," July 13, 1925, State Dept. Records, RG59 800.014, NA. Note from British Embassy, June 15, 1925.

69. Northern Affairs Program, RG85 v759 f482, pt. 1, NAC.

70. U.S. Naval Message, July 31, 1925, Navy Dept., RG80 111-99: 3, NA. As the ships were approaching Etah, MacMillan and Byrd received a radio message that the Canadian government had requested that the *Peary* establish communications with the *Arctic*, then on its way to Etah.

71. General Board #438, ser. #1284, July 14, 1925, Naval Historical Center Archives, Washington, D.C.

72. Everett S. Allen, *Arctic Odyssey: The Life of Rear Admiral Donald B. MacMillan* (New York: Dodd, Mead & Co., 1962), p. 258. "1925 MacMillan Arctic Expedition With Airplanes," unpub. ms., Donald B. MacMillan Papers, Box 20, Bowdoin College Library, Brunswick, Maine [hereafter cited as DBM Papers].

73. August 1925, Navy Dept., RG80 111-99: 3, NA.

74. "1925 MacMillan Arctic Expedition With Airplanes."

75. D. H. Dinwoodie, "Arctic Controversy: The 1925 Byrd-MacMillan Expedition Example," *The Canadian Historical Review* (March 1972): 51-61.

76. August 18, 1925, Navy Dept., RG80 111-99: 3, NA.

77. August 20, 1925, Navy Dept., RG80 111-99: 3, NA.

78. Documents and letter from British Embassy to Secretary of State Kellogg, December 21, 1925, State Dept. Records, RG59 031.11 m221, NA.

79. Memo of conversation between Under Secretary of State Green and Commander MacMillan, March 1926, State Dept. Records, RG59 031.11 m221, NA.

80. Grierson, *Challenge to the Poles*, pp. 93-98.

81. "Arctic Exploration from the Air," n.d., DBM Papers, Box 17/1, Bowdoin College Library, Brunswick, Maine.

82. Ibid.

83. Byrd, *Skyward,* p. 166. Edwin P. Hoyt, *The Last Explorer: The Adventures of Admiral Byrd* (New York: The John Day Co., 1968), p. 100.

84. The expedition was estimated to cost $140,000. Northern Affairs Program, RG85 v764 f5052, NAC.

85. *Annual Report of the Navy Department, 1926*, p. 37.

86. Hoyt, *The Last Explorer*, pp. 97-100. Edsel Ford, Henry Ford's son, was president of the Ford Motor Company from 1919 to 1943. John D. Rockefeller was founder of Standard Oil Company. Vincent Astor was the son of John Jacob Astor, financier. *The Columbia Encyclopedia*, William Bridgewater, and Seymour Kurtz, eds. (New York: Columbia University Press, 1963), pp. 741, 1816, 121.

87. *New York Times*, April 2, 1926, p. 8.

88. Hoyt, *The Last Explorer*, pp. 97-100. Byrd's Fokker had been built in Holland and shipped to the U.S. Bernt Balchen, dictated notes entry 1, RG401-99, NA.

89. *New York Times*, April 3, 1926, p. 7.

90. Quoted in Hoyt, *The Last Explorer*, p. 100.

91. W. W. Cory to Byrd, February 13, 1926; Byrd to Cory, February 24, 1926, Northern Affairs Program, RG85 v764 f5052, NAC.

92. Confidential Report, "Claims of Dominion Government to Sovereignty Over Certain Arctic Territory," March 8, 1926, Northern Affairs Program, RG85 v764 f5052, NAC.

93. "The Byrd Flight to the North Pole," *Aviation* (May 24, 1926): 780-83. The flight, described as a technical triumph particularly for the Wright engines, took approximately 9 hours 3 minutes round trip and covered 1,200 miles.

94. A critical appraisal of Byrd's flight appears in Capt. Finn Ronne, *Antarctica My Destiny* (New York: Hasting House, 1979), pp. 182-89.

95. "Over the Top by Air," *The Independent* (June 5, 1926): 649-53.

96. "Crowding the North Pole," *Literary Digest* (May 22, 1926): 8-11.

97. Calvin Coolidge Papers, Microfilm reel #179 #3580, University of Cincinnati.

98. R. M. Anderson to O. S. Finnie, Director, NWT Branch of Dept. of Interior, March 16, 1925, Northern Affairs Program, RG85 v582 f565, NAC. See *Asia* (April 1925): 290-95. See also *Washington Post*, May 1926, clippings, Northern Affairs Program, RG85 v584 f571-6, NAC.

5

Canadian Response to Foreign Expansion through the Eastern Arctic, 1920-1927

William Mitchell's 1920 U.S. Air Service flight from New York through Canada to Alaska aroused little concern in Canada. The air route, dependent on intermediate bases in Canada, had been negotiated through standard diplomatic channels with full regard for Canada sovereignty and in full compliance with Canadian law.[1] The Canadian government was much more concerned about foreign expeditions establishing bases on eastern arctic islands. Traditional scientific expeditions sponsored by Denmark and new air expeditions from the United States used these islands, claimed by Canada, as bases of operations. The data collected and returned to both countries could be valuable to businesses, and Canada feared that governments might be tempted to establish some kind of official presence on the islands in order to facilitate commercial development. Through the 1920s, Canada patrolled this area to protect it against foreign claims, especially by the United States and Denmark, as businesses sought access to natural resources, such as coal and oil, and governments expressed an interest in establishing air routes though the Arctic. Canada believed that its claims could be overridden if countries sponsoring exploration for commercial or scientific purposes tried to claim territory by using expedition bases and staffs as evidence of occupation and administration.[2] Questions regarding legal jurisdiction over eastern arctic islands became more complex as international expeditions sponsored jointly by governments, scientific societies, and businesses carried out long-term projects. If these expeditions, which sometimes lasted for four or more years, were accepted as evidence of effective occupation and administration, an area could be claimed by one or more of the participating countries.[3] Canada objected to foreign interests in eastern arctic islands because the government was aware that earlier Canadian claims could be jeopardized if an unregulated foreign presence were permitted.[4] As early as 1907, Canadian Senator Pascal Poirer had proposed that Canada protect these islands against foreign claims by applying the principle of contiguity and extending Canadian jurisdiction to all land between its northern coast and the North Pole.[5] The area claimed fell within a sector defined by longitudes extending to the North Pole from Canada's eastern and western boundaries.[6] Neither contiguity nor the idea of a recognized national sector was accepted internationally, but Canada continued to promote both principles.[7] Serious controversies arose over the sector principle in the 1920s when the United States and European countries began to plan international air routes that crossed the Arctic. If the sector principle were accepted, areas previously open to international use would be subject to national jurisdiction, and countries expanding shipping lanes would then have less freedom in planning air and water routes. The United States, in particular, rejected any consideration of dividing the Arctic into international sectors or spheres of influence, a decision consistent with its history of preferring an "open door" commercial policy.[8] With the sector principle rejected, Canada could be sure of its sovereignty over eastern arctic islands only by proving it occupied the land and had established an administrative system, conditions difficult to accomplish if a foreign power also occupied a designated territory.[9]

A dispute erupted over the status of Ellesmere Island between 1916 and 1924 when Denmark sent Knud Rasmussen on a series of expeditions into the Ellesmere area. The Canadian government concluded that the Rasmussen expeditions were part of an attempt by Denmark to expand into territory where Canada's claim was tenuous.[10] In 1919, in response to a request from England for an evaluation of Denmark's control over arctic territory, the Canadian Department of External Affairs suggested Great Britain recognize Danish sovereignty over Greenland only on the condition the British empire be given priority regarding purchase should Denmark decide to dispose of the island.[11] The suggestion was accepted, the proposal made, and other nations informed. The United States objected to the proposal, replying that it was "not disposed to recognize the existence in a third government of a right of pre-empting."[12]

The controversy continued and the RCMP were sent to protect Canada's claims. The Deputy Minister for External Affairs requested RCMP patrols be stationed on Banks and Victoria islands to provide evidence of permanent administration. The Department of the Interior supported the recommendation which emphasized the importance of these posts and advised setting up additional police posts on Bylot, North Devon, and Ellesmere as a means of establishing an administrative process that would protect Canada's claims to all islands in the Arctic north of the American continent.[13] According to international law, Canada held these islands only by inchoate title.[14] Any other power could attempt to establish possession by presenting similar evidence of compliance with the criteria of occupation and administration.

A desire to promote national prestige was only one reason for interest in eastern arctic islands. There were also practical motives. Scientific observations taken during years of exploration had proven valuable in understanding ocean tides and weather patterns. Data brought back from previous expeditions had shown that weather conditions in the temperate zone of the northern hemisphere were influenced by meteorological conditions in different areas of the Arctic. Arctic bases equipped to study and transmit information on weather conditions and to investigate tidal characteristics, ocean depths, and ice formation became important information centers for businesses engaged in transocean commerce. Well-established shipping lanes, as well as the new air routes being planned to connect North America, Europe, Japan, and China, depended on accurate, regular weather reports and bases equipped for refueling and repair. Considering the expanded involvement of governments and businesses in plans to develop weather stations, air routes, and bases across the Arctic, it was logical that certain arctic islands emerged as key posts in this network.[15]

Foreign businesses also hoped to secure rights to natural resources and were serious competition to Canadian companies.[16] In 1923, Hudson's Bay Company directors protested against foreign companies' efforts to develop mineral deposits, specifically oil fields, in the Mackenzie district. A desire to protect its economic advantage was definitely a company priority but the government, in considering the protest, recognized that foreign control of natural resources in the far North also might be accepted as legal precedent for establishing commercial operations on arctic islands where Canadian title was not secure. After full consideration of potential danger from foreign encroachment, the government responded to the protest by adopting a resolution limiting foreign holdings to no more than 25% ownership in any one commercial enterprise.[17]

If the resolution could be applied to exploitation of the immense deposits of coal on Ellesmere, Axel Heiberg, and Banks islands, foreign development could be severely curtailed. The Canadian Geological Survey had determined that the four principal geological formations on Ellesmere Island contained all the important minerals necessary for industrial development, minerals that had been previously discovered in the United States and Canada. Canadians, wary of Danish development in Greenland and Danish expeditions through Ellesmere, wondered if Denmark contemplated occupying Ellesmere with the intent of seeking these minerals. The Canadian government also considered the possibility that the United States, realizing Canadian claims were tenuous, might also try to stake a claim to the island because "the most important economic problem of the United States . . . concerns her future oil supply."[18]

The situation regarding Canadian sovereignty became acute when Canadians received an official communication from the Danish government defining the arctic archipelago as a *terra nullius* or "no-man's land," thereby officially denying the legality of Canadian jurisdiction over Ellesmere. Although Canadians feared that Rasmussen's expeditions had been sent to test the *terra nullius* designation and as such were evidence of Danish expansion, there was no evidence of political motivation by Rasmussen as an individual or as an agent for the Danish government. In addition to suspecting Rasmussen's motives, the Canadian government wondered if Donald MacMillan's expeditions to Baffin Island in 1921 and 1922 were official American enterprises designed to establish American bases.[19] Although no evidence of political motives surfaced, the Canadian Department of the Interior insisted the situation was critical despite the absence of any evidence that either Denmark or the United States was encroaching on territory identified by Canada as under its jurisdiction.[20] However, to protect its claims, in 1921 a Canadian expedition was sent out to establish RCMP posts on Baffin and Ellesmere islands in order to conform to the legal requirements of occupation and administration.[21] The situation was believed to be so serious that consideration was given to using a dirigible or hydroplane to carry men and supplies to Ellesmere in case a ship were stopped by ice.[22] The expedition was canceled at the last moment but reorganized and sent out in 1922 as the first in a series of excursions authorized to patrol the Arctic annually through 1926.[23]

The 1922 Canadian Arctic Patrol differed from previous patrols in that it was a cooperative venture between the Northwest Territories Branch of the Department of the Interior and the Canadian Air Board.[24] The patrol surveyed and photographed Craig Harbor on Ellesmere Island and conducted wireless radio experiments that yielded results exceeding all expectations. Broadcasts from radio posts on Ellesmere were clearly heard by power stations in the United States, England, France, Germany, Italy, and Canada.[25]

Robert A. Logan, formerly a pilot in the Royal Flying Corps, was assigned to the expedition and directed to investigate the possibility of using arctic islands for air bases, RCMP posts, supply depots for commercial flights, and radio bases that would be part of a unified communications system.[26] Logan conducted a thorough survey of land areas reached by the patrol and submitted a detailed report including directions for building an air route and radio system in the North. Logan's directive was not implemented, and its importance has been overlooked. He was one of a small group of men who recognized the need for long range development in the Arctic and who had the foresight to suggest methods for that development.

In his preliminary report, Logan noted that establishing air operations in the Arctic would require several years of work before a reliable network was completed. He suggested beginning the process with a practical communications system immediately valuable for transmitting daily weather reports. Aircraft, he maintained, could be used to travel among the numerous arctic islands to assist exploration, investigate the extent of natural resources, locate mineral deposits, and transport personnel and supplies in case of an oil strike. The more area fully explored, the greater the possibility of discovering natural resources and, consequently, the greater the commercial opportunities. Logan recommended that plans to establish an airways system include provisions for the RCMP, geological survey, and military air bases as well as for commercial interests.[27]

Logan's study produced valuable information on weather conditions that could be used in planning air routes across Canada and establishing

F. D. Henserson, D.L.S., making survey of group lot no. 2134. This survey on Rice Strait is the most northerly in Canada being in latitude 78°47'N, Ellesmere Island, N.W.T., ca. 1924. (National Archives Canada)

Unloading supplies at Craig Harbour, Ellesmere Island, N.W.T., August 1925. (National Archives Canada)

international air bases in Canadian territory, a move he advocated because he felt it could contribute to Canadian economic development.[28] Logan strongly urged building a research and development program for equipment and air bases and suggested sending a small detachment of the Air Force to the northern end of Baffin Island in the summers of 1923 and 1924 to gather necessary data.[29] The project might not yield immediate profits, but "even if it were twenty years before an urgent demand arose for extensive operations in the Arctic archipelago, the information gained on such an experimental station as suggested would be of the highest value in determining the proper organization and equipment to be used."[30] Logan's proposal was passed from department to department. Because there appeared to be no immediate benefits except for the establishment of a wireless station in the Mackenzie area, the government, especially the air force, was reluctant to appropriate the necessary funds. The proposal was ultimately tabled and the government applied its resources to developing aviation across Canada south of arctic territory.[31]

Logan was dismayed at the government's shortsightedness. In 1925, he applied for leases and air harbor licenses in the Canadian archipelago to demonstrate the validity of Canadian claims. The lease terms, approved in June 1925, included prohibitions against subleasing to non-nationals and required the lessee permit use of bases by government aircraft at all times. The designated area included the northern end of Axel Heiberg, Craig Harbor on the southern coast of Ellesmere, and an area at 141° west longitude, 83° 20' north latitude named Beaufort Air Harbor. The application was accepted, but the leases were never issued.[32] Logan urged the government to establish an official procedure for regulating foreign use of Canadian arctic territory so that countries would know where "Canada stands astride." He stressed he had no personal interest but only wanted to keep the United States, especially Donald MacMillan who was at that time engaged in exploring the Canadian Arctic with Richard E. Byrd, in its "place, which was not the Canadian Arctic."[33]

Logan's continued efforts to promote the establishment of air routes and radio and aircraft bases in the Canadian Arctic paralleled Stefansson's insistence that future commercial growth depended not just on aviation development, but also on northern development in general. Stefansson stressed the importance of moving from relying on sea lanes for trade and transportation to considering the space "above the partly ice-filled water" as an "unhampered ocean of the air, free to be navigated in any direction by ships of the air." In reviewing the controversy over arctic flying conditions, especially fog, winter darkness, and storms, he emphasized that differing opinions regarding the reliability of aircraft to operate in these conditions arose in part because authorities were considering the state of aircraft development at the time and neglecting to consider future developments. Stefansson believed that progress would accelerate rapidly and that difficulties experienced in 1924 would be overcome by 1930.[34]

Stefansson's insistence that it was necessary to develop an aviation industry that utilized arctic and subarctic areas did not result in any great following by Parliament. Despite concern over the possibility of foreign countries encroaching on Canadian claims, Parliament was hesitant to appropriate funds necessary for the establishment of government agencies in the Northwest Territories, even though these agencies would have been the best protection at the time against foreign expansion.[35]

When Parliament reviewed the record of appropriations for exploration and development of arctic territory between 1912 and 1924, members questioned whether there had been any definable value from continued support for such ventures. Throughout the debate, Parliament acknowledged that reliable reports of mineral deposits compiled by earlier patrols were important enough to warrant protecting the area against any "chances of anybody else going into that territory and laying claim to any land that belongs to us."[36]

The question of an enforceable policy that would require only moderate appropriations but would protect Canadian interests was argued doggedly until June 1925, when the Canadian House of Commons passed an amendment to the Northwest Territories Act of 1906 requiring scientists and explorers who wished to enter the territories to obtain permits or licenses. The regulation was considered necessary because exploration of northern islands in the Northwest Territories was no longer an occasional event, but rather had become annual occurrences. The purpose of the new regulation was to protect Canadian claims and would also protect the natural wildlife which was being threatened by the increase in expeditions killing game to feed crew members.[37] The application of provisions of this act to the MacMillan-Byrd expedition had mixed results.[38] The expedition had not complied with the provisions, nor had it been turned back.[39] However, it was the last American expedition to enter Canadian territory without a Canadian permit. Furthermore, after 1925, expeditions originating in Europe and planning to explore the Canadian Arctic all complied with the Canadian regulations.

Following the adoption of legislation limiting access to arctic islands, the question of Canada's right to act unilaterally on foreign policy matters was discussed at the British Institute of International Affairs. The participants were concerned over the possibility that Canada could apply the new arctic regulations to England, a move that would allow Canada rather than England to make decisions pertaining to rights of access. The primary issue was not use of the islands but the position taken by the Canadian government that it was an independent unit, rightfully capable of negotiating with other countries and pursuing its own national interests, especially in regard to relations with the United States. The conference ended on a tense note with the assertion by Loring Christie, the legal advisor for the Department of External Affairs, that the dominion government was devoted to defining Canada's self-image and identity as a national and even world power.[40]

Questions of sovereign rights to arctic islands involved more than establishing the authority to control a given territory. An equally important issue was the right to control access to the territory and to use and develop all resources within the area. In the early 1920s, interest in locating and developing areas rich in coal, oil, and other minerals increased with technological changes in transportation and communications and in corporate organization. Expansion of commercial interests required protection for investments in mining operations. Rich deposits of coal, oil, and other minerals had been located all along the arctic rim from Spitsbergen, Greenland, Alaska, Baffin Island, Ellesmere Island, and on some of the smaller islands in the Canadian archipelago, to the area of the Bering Strait. Mining operations were well developed in some of these areas and had not progressed beyond the planning stage in others. Tied to the economic development of these arctic regions was the problem of accessibility. Shipping routes traversed by icebreakers could be used to transport supplies to and/or from mines close to the coast, but inland deposits could not be developed without a reliable connecting form of transportation. Aircraft could provide that link, but neither Canadian nor American aviation technology was sufficiently developed in the 1920s to provide airplanes or dirigibles that could operate with consistent success.[41] Despite this lag in technological development, aviation would be the key to exploitation of arctic resources and the Arctic, in turn, would become of greater importance as improvements in aviation produced aircraft capable of transarctic flights. Through the 1920s, contests over sovereign rights to arctic islands involved the immediate problem of establishing jurisdiction over land for the purpose of mineral exploitation and the long-range goal of securing both air bases and rights to air space.

Technology did improve as predicted, and from the middle of the 1920s through the early 1930s the race to fly over the North Pole paralleled the race to reach the Pole at the beginning of the century. Canadian vigilance in protecting its claims to arctic islands continued, although land expeditions decreased and were replaced by flights over Canadian territory by expeditions from the United States, Norway, Italy, and Germany. Rapid improvements in dirigibles and airplanes made it possible to fly greater distances without landing, and the islands targeted as valuable air bases in the early 1920s were no longer necessary by 1927. A series of arctic flights between 1926 and 1932 demonstrated that aircraft could travel the Great Circle and North Pole routes without intermediate stops. Canada continued to patrol the eastern Arctic, but the adversarial relationship with those countries sponsoring air expeditions, in particular the United States and Norway, eased when observations taken during these transarctic flights proved that no new land existed.

Notes to Chapter 5

1. "Application of Air Regulations 1920," p. 5, Air Board, RG24 v3897 f1034-82 v1, National Archives of Canada, Ottawa, Canada, [hereafter cited as NAC].

2. Lawrence P. Kirwan, *A History of Polar Exploration* (New York: W. W. Norton & Co., 1960), p. 319. The International Metallurgical and Chemical Society of Billings, Montana, was organizing an expedition to investigate land north of 70° latitude. Although the purpose of the survey was limited to a study of natural sciences, it could have been used as evidence of occupation and administration for future claims. Loring Christie Papers, MG30 E44 v6 p5848, NAC.

3. *New York Times*, April 2, 1926, p. 8.

4. Kenneth V. Johnson, "Canada's Title to the Arctic Islands," *Canadian Historical Review* 14 (1933): 25-41.

5. Gustav Smedal, *Acquisition of Sovereignty* (Oslo: I Kommisjon Has Jacob Dybwad, 1931), pp. 7-9, 60, 63. This principle allowed a country to claim territory adjacent to that previously recognized as under its jurisdiction. In the case of northern islands, Canada claimed not only contiguity but jurisdiction based on connection to its mainland by the continental shelf.

6. Canada, *Senate Debates*, 1906-09, 3rd. sess., 19th Parliament, pp. 266-74.

7. Russia, which supported and encouraged Canada to apply these measures, had also been eager to apply the same principles because of the great expanse of territory between its eastern and western borders. Promotion of the sector principle came from both the Czarist and Communist governments. W. Lakhtine, "Rights Over the Arctic," *American Journal of International Law* (1930): 703-17.

8. David Hunter Miller, "Political Rights in the Arctic," *Foreign Affairs* 4 (1925): 47-60.

9. Correspondence, April, 1921, John D. Craig Papers, MG30 B57, NAC.

10. Therkel Mathiasen, *Report of the Fifth Thule Expedition* (Copenhagen, 1945), vol. 1. *U.S. Treaties, Conventions, International Acts, Protocols and Agreements 1910-1923*, p. 2564. The 1916 convention for ceding the Danish West Indies to the U.S. refers to North Greenland as an area Peary claimed for the U.S. because of his multiple explorations. Loring Christie Papers, MG30 E44 v6 f19, p. 5839, NAC. Canadian claim was not clear because Ellesmere was equally contiguous to Greenland and Canada. Lawrence Preuss, "The Dispute Between Denmark and Norway Over the Sovereignty of East Greenland," *American Journal of International Law* 26 (1932): 469-87.

11. Northwest Territories Council Minutes, M-11, p. 26, October 1920, NAC.

12. Loring Christie Papers, MG30 E44 v6 f13, NAC. Marie Peary Stafford, "Peary's Ideas About U.S. Rights in Greenland," *Arctic Encyclopedia*, Reel #27. Peary protested surrendering U.S. rights to northern Greenland. He felt Greenland belonged to North America and therefore came under the aegis of the Monroe Doctrine. Greenland could be economically valuable because of its coal deposits and glacial streams which could be turned into electrical energy, but the most important reason was its strategic value as a naval and aeronautical base. This second consideration became a reality with the establishment of an American military installation at Thule. See also Gordon W. Smith, "Historical and Legal Background of Canada's Arctic Claims," unpub. Ph.D. dissertation, Columbia University, 1952, p. 260.

13. Deputy Minister to Colonel Perry, Commissioner, RCMP, December 22, 1920, Northern Affairs Program, RG85 v582 f567, NAC.

14. Inchoate: not fully formed or secured. "National Status of Heiberg, Ringes, Ellesmere and Other Islands in the Canadian Arctic Archipelago," p. 8, RG85 v584 f571 v6, NAC.

15. Smedal, *Acquisition of Sovereignty*, pp. 7-9. Charles Rabot, "New Annexation of Polar Lands," pp. 1-2, RG85 v584 f561 v6, NAC. Vilhjalmur Stefansson, "The Arctic as an Air Route of the Future," *National Geographic Magazine* (August 1922): 205-18. In 1922, the sea and land route from England to Japan through Canada was 11,000 miles. An air route crossing North Cape, Norway, and Novayla Zemlya would involve less than 5,000 miles. A similar route could be developed crossing northern Canada. See also, "Shall We Have an Aerial Route by Way of the North Pole," *Literary Digest* (March 3, 1923): 70-74.

16. D. M. LeBourdais, "When America Looks North," *Outlook* 135 (November 1923): 451-52.

17. *New York Times*, July 5, 1923, p. 23; July 24, 1923, p. 37.

18. Correspondence, April, 1921, John D. Craig Papers, MG30 B57, NAC. *New York Times*, July 5, 1923, p. 23; July 24, 1923, p. 37. "The Economic Importance of the Northern Fields," RG85 v576 f378, NAC. Finnie to Craig, February 26, 1924, RG85 v582 f565, NAC.

19. Memo from Christie, October 1920, John D. Craig Papers, MG30 B57, NAC.

20. All reports of Rasmussen's expedition indicate its goal was to study the origins of the Eskimo people. See especially Knud Rasmussen, *Across Arctic America: Narrative of the Fifth Thule Expedition* (New York: G. P. Putnam's Sons, 1927).

21. Canada, *House of Commons Debates*, 5th sess., 14th Parliament, July 24, 1921, p. 37.

22. Confidential memo, February 16, 1922, John D. Craig Papers, MG30 B57, NAC.

23. Canada, *House of Commons Debates*, 3rd sess., 14th Parliament, 1923, p. 3944.

24. Craig to Corry, May 19, 1922, Northern Affairs Program, RG85 v582 f567; February 1923, v610 f2713, NAC.

25. Ibid., September 1922, v610 f2713, NAC.

26. Excerpt from Report of Air Board of Canada, 1922, p. 19. Copy sent by Robert A. Logan to author.

27. "Aviation and Northern Canada," Robert A. Logan Papers, MG30 B68, NAC.

28. Logan noted several peculiar wind patterns such as strong winds at sea level, similar to those described by explorers, that were absent at very high altitudes. Also, winds seemed to be confined to narrow corridors. He described winds of 30-40 mph at the entrance to Pond's Inlet, but 15 miles inland the air was dead calm.

29. Canada, *House of Commons Debates*, 3rd sess., 14th Parliament, 1924, vol. 2, pp. 1109-10.

30. Logan to Craig, October 16, 1922, Northern Affairs Program, RG85 v610 f2718, NAC. Letter from Robert A. Logan to author, November 1981.

31. Desbarats to Finnie and Craig, January 24, 1923, Northern Affairs Program, RG85 v610 f2718, NAC. Margaret Mattson, "The Growth of Canadian Civil Commercial Aviation 1918-1930," unpub. Ph.D. dissertation, University of Western Ontario, 1979, Chap. 7.

32. June 5, 1926, Robert A. Logan Papers, MG30 B68, NAC.

33. Ibid., June 19, 1925.

34. Vilhjalmur Stefansson, "Arctic Air Routes to the Orient," *The Forum* (December 1924): 721-29.

35. Canada, *House of Commons Debates*, 3rd sess., 14th Parliament, 1924, vol. 2, pp. 1109-10.

36. Ibid., 4th sess., 14th Parliament, 1925, pp. 4083-95. Auditory General's Report of expenses for patrol of northern waters of Canada, 1912-14, RG85 v582 f565, NAC.

1912-13	$ 15,688.97	1919	$ 65,000.00
1913-14	174,388.69	1920	60,027.72
1914-15	95,172.16	1921	15,000.00
1915-16	75,616.44	1921-22	8,198.42
1917	20,333.75	1922-23	9,001.14
1917-18	25,863.67	1924	7,987.94

37. Canada, *House of Commons Debates,* Bill 151, "An Act to Amend the Northwest Territories Act, June, 1925."

38. "Canada's Arctic Claims," *Literary Digest* 85 (June 20, 1925): 14.

39. The expedition had been shortened due to adverse weather.

40. February 24, 1926, Loring Christie Papers, MG30 E44 v26, NAC. See also file 106, NAC. The debate continued through 1928. Canada, *House of Commons Debates,* 2nd sess., 16th Parliament, 1928, p. 3691. W. L. Morton, *The Canadian Identity* (Madison: University of Wisconsin Press, 1972), p. 71. Fred Alexander, *Canadians and Foreign Policy* (Toronto: University of Toronto Press, 1960), pp. 33, 89.

41. "Northern Aerial Mineral Exploration," RG85 v783 f5941 pt. 1, NAC. *New York Times,* May 27, 1923, p. 17. Archibald Williams, *Conquering the Air* (New York: Thomas Nelson & Sons, 1930), pp. 193-211.

6

International Transarctic Flights, 1922-1928

Canada's resolve to protect its political rights to islands in the Arctic meant complying with the traditional criteria of occupation and administration which it did by establishing a series of RCMP bases, a regular patrol of arctic waterways, and a Canadian Arctic Administration. This policy of administration and development helped ease international tensions by eliminating much of the uncertainty regarding territorial sovereignty in the region. Furthermore, long standing conflicts among Denmark, Norway, and Canada were resolved. By the late 1920s, Denmark had settled the controversy with Norway over Greenland and had turned its efforts toward developing that territory. Norway, under the leadership of Roald Amundsen, then began a program of air expeditions and, when Canada made a cash settlement for the Sverdrup Islands, tension between these two countries significantly decreased. Also, relations between Canada and the United States improved after Byrd's flight over the North Pole in 1926 when American exploration began in the Antarctic.

Although these issues influenced each country's relations with Canada, a more important factor was the change in the direction and method of exploration characterized by transarctic flights. These flights were designed to survey large areas within the Arctic, test the ability of aircraft to fly long distances in Arctic weather, and lay out air routes connecting Europe, North America, and Asia. These air expeditions did not endanger Canada's arctic claims because they either chose to establish bases in Greenland and Spitsbergen or bypassed Canadian islands on long-distance flights.

Relations with Canada may have improved, but a new set of tensions developed among the participating nations, particularly the United States, Norway, and Italy.[1] The antagonism, rooted in competition and nationalism, became a barrier to successful international cooperation on transarctic flights staffed with commanders and crews from not only those nations with arctic borders but also countries geographically distant from arctic regions. International crews were one source of irritation. Funding and provisioning by different governments and individuals also led to disagreements, bickering, and confusion. Norway funded Roald Amundsen's air expedition, but substantial backing also came from Lincoln Ellsworth, a wealthy American explorer and adventurer. Italy promoted the Amundsen dirigible flight, hoping to establish an international reputation as a leader in the field of aviation engineering.

The American aviation and engine industries also saw the advantages of sponsoring arctic flights to test aircraft and did not hesitate to use non-national flyers as well as Americans with proven reputations. Pan American Airways contracted with Charles Lindbergh to fly a northern air route to Asia. The flight was successful but the route was temporarily abandoned in favor of one on a southern course. Intrigued with both the Arctic and flying, the Australian Hubert Wilkins convinced a group of Detroit businessmen to sponsor his flights along the rim of Alaska and Canada. Wilkins' eventual success in flying nonstop between Alaska and Spitsbergen was heralded as a great "American" triumph. The "American" part of the feat was not accepted everywhere and Wilkins was knighted by England for his accomplishment and the honor it brought to the British Empire. Other experimental flights, such as the University of Michigan Greenland research expedition and the British arctic air expedition, also made important contributions to the development of arctic air routes, but the Amundsen, Nobile, and Wilkins flights represented the end of the period of arctic exploration. These men commanded the last of the expeditions that combined exploration, adventure, and scientific inquiry. The Arctic was becoming too important to be left to explorers. It was time to establish national policy and engage in development.

After Roald Amundson's success in navigating the Northwest Passage and reaching the South Pole, he continued to dominate the field of arctic exploration with a series of daring polar flights. Obsessed with the need to be "first," he persisted in his search for new horizons and new passages to conquer. He had studied the use of aircraft before and during World War I and recognized that aviation could provide the means to accomplish long-distance exploration. Amundsen purchased his first airplane in 1914, but the expedition he planned was cancelled with the outbreak of World War I. He was unable to organize another attempt until the war was over, a circumstance that fortunately allowed him to utilize advances in aviation technology that had taken place because of the war. In 1922, Amundsen organized a combination sea and air expedition leaving from Seattle, heading for the Polar Sea north of Alaska. He planned to sail the *Maud* as far north as possible and then make short reconnaissance flights using two planes carried aboard the ship. The planes chosen were a Curtis, lent by the American Curtis Aeroplane Factory, and a Junker which he purchased after the plane completed a successful twenty-seven hour flight.[2] Plans for this expedition had grown out of a conference with Peary and Bartlett in 1916 when Peary had discussed the possibility of a transpolar flight using Etah as a base.[3] By relocating the base at Seattle, Amundsen hoped to accomplish two goals with one expedition: an easy navigation of the Northeast Passage and a successful polar flight.

The press viewed the expedition with considerable skepticism. The *New York Times* questioned whether any gain would accrue from the flight, suggesting that only arctic explorers would appreciate the effort and even they would be puzzled. Peary had already confirmed that the Pole was surrounded by a frozen sea and "to see that again is not very profitable." Because of Amundsen's demonstrated competence in the Arctic and Antarctic, he was expected to succeed, but as perilous as the flight was, it was expected to add little to his reputation because it did not entail the personal hardships of previous expeditions.[4] The *Maud* left in May 1923. First attempts to use the planes ended in forced landings before any significant amount of territory had been viewed and, because the flights were too short, no real benefit was derived in terms of testing equipment. The expedition was canceled and Amundsen brought the *Maud* and damaged planes back to Seattle in June, his first failure. The previous *Gjoa* and South Pole expeditions had been efficient and well-planned exercises that succeeded because of Amundsen's ability as a sailor and explorer. This attempt at using aircraft was different. Amundsen was not an aviator and had to rely on equipment and personnel unfamiliar to him. If he were to continue to use aircraft and succeed with future expeditions, he would need to acquire greater expertise himself or a crew experienced with airplanes. Amundsen realized the importance of this decision. If the latter option were chosen, exploration could become the province of engineers, pilots, and technicians, and the "hero" would be the machine.[5]

The aborted experiment only whetted Amundsen's determination to use aircraft to explore the Arctic. With the help of Haken H. Hammer, who had been hired to promote these expeditions, Amundsen located two Dornier Dolphin flying boats equipped with radio and capable of taking off and landing on ice, snow, or water.[6] He was now ready to launch a second expedition which he hoped would be ready by the summer of 1924. He began his search for a crew experienced with aircraft by asking the U.S. Navy Bureau of Aeronautics to provide him with a pilot qualified in handling seaplanes. The Bureau declined but did allow men to volunteer for the expedition.[7]

Amundsen had approached the Aero Club of Norway first for funding, but the donations were not enough and he continued his promotion by canvassing in the United States. In January 1924, the *Rochester Herald* published a story on the upcoming expedition, noting that Amundsen had promised to claim any land discovered during a polar flight for the United States because Norway had not been able to provide sufficient funds for the expedition. Amundsen vehemently denied he had made any such offer and insisted he would claim all land discovered for Norway. The incident created some tension between the Norwegian Foreign Minister and the U.S. State Department but was resolved when it was found that the basis of the story was a publicity move instigated by Hammer. Hammer had stated that "although Amundsen was Norwegian, he would not lay claim to any new lands discovered on behalf of his government and an American officer could, if so desired, claim it for his government."[8]

The State Department responded to Amundsen's assertion that he would claim any new land for Norway with a statement that sovereign claims by him would not be recognized because the United States did not accept traditional acts of discovery of unknown land as a basis for sovereign claims unless steps were taken to settle the land.[9] The United States would acknowledge data regarding any discovery Amundsen might make, but acceptance of the information should not be taken as an assent by the American government to any Norwegian claims or those of any other country. Any new territory would be considered *terra nullius*. The Norwegian Legation notified the State Department that Norway did not intend to press for jurisdiction over new land on the basis of discovery but did reserve the right to first priority in establishing sovereignty through settlement.[10] Any attempt by Norway to press its case for sovereign rights would probably have aroused major objections from Canada, which continued to safeguard its own national interests in the area.[11]

Amundsen's promotional campaign in the United States was not successful, and he was unable to raise the money necessary for his expedition. In September 1924, while Amundsen was in New York City between lectures, Lincoln Ellsworth, the son of a wealthy New York merchant, contacted him. Ellsworth, smitten with a desire for adventure, convinced Amundsen to take him on as a partner. The arrangement fulfilled Ellsworth's ambition and his family connections gave Amundsen access to new sources of support.

After his meeting with Amundsen, Ellsworth immediately contacted people he thought might cooperate in backing the expedition, particularly General "Billy" Mitchell, who he hoped would convince the government to donate parachutes, instruments, and equipment. Mitchell was interested, but reminded Ellsworth that release of materials required an act of Congress, which might or might not come about after months of debate. Ellsworth and Amundsen then approached the Aero Club of Norway which promised partial funding on the condition the men fly only to the North Pole and back.[12]

In order to secure the rest of the money necessary to complete the project, Ellsworth decided to introduce his father to Amundsen, hoping the elderly Ellsworth would contribute to the expedition. In September 1924, Ellsworth wrote his father asking him to fund arctic exploration not just for himself, but because he wanted to accomplish "something noteworthy." He had chosen exploration in the North in response to a "primitive" urge and because it was a "great field . . . for scientific work." In a subsequent letter, he begged for the chance to "make good" where his "individual conscience would be satisfied with the result." Ellsworth argued that the expedition was important because it would contribute benefits to "science for its own sake." He continued chipping away at his father's reluctance to finance an adventure that might end in his son's death until the elder Ellsworth agreed, with much misgiving, to contribute $85,000 for the purchase of the two Dornier flying boats.[13]

The expedition left from Spitsbergen May 21, 1925, with Amundsen as navigator in one plane and Ellsworth as navigator in the other. The planes flew for 8 hours at 75 mph and covered approximately 600 miles. Because of a heavy northeast wind, they traveled in a decidedly westward arc placing them short of the Pole at latitude 87° 44'. In a few hours, the planes had covered territory it had taken Peary years to travel. The terrain was obscured by fog much of the time, but during clear periods the men could see for 60-70 miles in every direction. Even with intermittent patches of heavy fog, the flight confirmed the absence of anything but an "immense void," an area of nothing but snow, ice, and ever-changing cracks in the ice indicating the movement of the polar pack.[14]

Amundsen's plane circled, looking for a place to land so he could take soundings and make observations. No satisfactory landing place appeared, but before Amundsen could change his mind, the plane's engine failed and he was forced to land rapidly. Fortunately, the men sighted an open lead between two icebergs. The plane landed safely, incurring only minor daramge, and, as prearranged, Ellsworth's plane prepared to land. He was not as lucky as Amundsen had been and was unable to find a similar open stretch of water. His plan crashed on the ice and, although the crew were unhurt, the plane was badly damaged.

When the flight did not return in the expected time, radio stations broadcasted news of the assumed crash. The U.S. Navy suggested a rescue mission using the *Shenandoah* and *Patoka*, then under consideration for an American arctic expedition. The possibility of using the dirigible and ship was enhanced when individuals made financial offers to Secretary of the Navy Curtis Wilbur and personnel from the private sector and the navy volunteered their service. The Detroit Flying Club urged the government to use the *Shenandoah*, arguing that if the airship were ready for its own expedition, it should be used to rescue Amundsen. The Navy Department answered that it had reconsidered initiating a relief expedition because Norway was handling the emergency and no official request for aid had been received from Norway or from Amundsen. If relief were requested, the naval expedition sent to Etah for the MacMillan expedition would be available.[15] No action was taken on any of the rescue proposals.

Damaged Dornier Flying Boat: Amundsen-Ellsworth Expedition, 1925.
(National Archives,Washington, D.C.)

Meanwhile Amundsen and his crew spent three weeks repairing the least damaged plane by using salvaged parts from the other and then carved a runway out of the ice with only the small tools and knives stored with their supplies. The six men then boarded the plane, designed to hold three, and with just enough fuel to reach Spitsbergen, returned in the expected eight hours—twenty-five days late. Although the expedition was a failure, it had proven the worth of a new sun compass which had been valuable in determining their location after the crash and was responsible for their success in navigating a safe return.[16]

Based on this experience, Amundsen questioned the practicality of using airplanes for exploration, citing a lack of appropriate landing areas. Because the Polar Sea was not smooth ice as it appeared from the air but solid walls of ice with areas between filled with hard masses of snow, the only place to land planes would be on open water and, even if such leads were found, there was considerable danger of being frozen in. During the flight, no land had been sighted between the coasts of known islands and 88° north latitude, confirming Peary's observations.[17] Airplanes, with their still limited cruising radius, might not be practical for arctic flying, but Amundsen was undaunted and immediately set out to put together another expedition, this time with a dirigible which he planned to fly across the North Pole from Spitsbergen to Alaska.

Fridtjof Nansen wrote that the expedition was more than an exercise in furthering national interests or demonstrating personal heroism. The venture was an opportunity to understand the rules of physics that governed the whole globe, principles that could become more clear with better information about the poles and influences they exerted on the rest of the world. He agreed it was certainly important to discover and survey any land encountered, but believed it was more important to determine the northern extension of the continental land masses which were fixed not by coastal lines above sea level, but by the edge of the continental shelf which extends beyond coasts at a moderate depth and must be considered part of a continent. As continental shelf delineations were made, the relationship of the continent to islands, particularly those off the coast of Siberia and the northern coast of Canada, would become clearer and questions of sovereign rights might be better settled.[18]

Writing about his escapades, Amundsen extolled the virtues of science and scientists, suggesting that the men who led arctic expeditions were both explorers and scientists. Amundsen was indeed an extraordinary explorer and his expeditions all returned with valuable scientific information. However, Amundsen was not a scientist, and voyages of exploration were rapidly becoming less important than expeditions designed to test scientific theories and developments in technology. The real heroes of air exploration were turning out to be technicians, engineers, pilots, and scientists, many of whom had had no personal experience in the Arctic but were experts in aviation and different branches of science and technology.

The conflict between explorer and technician is best exemplified by the conflicts between Amundsen and Umberto Nobile, the Italian engineer who designed the airship purchased by Amundsen for a flight from Spitsbergen to Alaska. Each man insisted he should be the commander of the expedition, Amundsen because of his expertise as explorer, and Nobile because of his knowledge of and experience with airships. Nobile thought Amundsen would only become important if the expedition failed and Amundsen's skill became necessary for survival on land, a situation that was Nobile's responsibility to avoid. The success of the expedition required that the airship complete the flight with no mishap, a condition that made use of few if any of Amundsen's abilities during the flight.

Amundsen was the visionary who had conceived of the flight and, with Ellsworth, had made it possible, but Nobile felt Amundsen was no longer an important part of it. The Scandinavian Viking had encountered a new antagonist, the Mediterranean mathematician.

Amundsen and Ellsworth arranged with Nobile for the sale of a semirigid airship renamed *Norge* (Norway). The transfer of the airship included provisions for an Italian crew and the services of Nobile who was to be in charge of the airship and navigation.[19] Problems of organization became evident during early contract negotiations when Nobile insisted he be designated expedition commander because of his knowledge of and experience with airships. Because the *Norge* was commanded by men from various countries which all hoped to benefit from the expedition, the question of command became a matter of international importance in determining the rights of countries represented on the expedition to claim territory sighted from the airship.[20]

The flight left Spitsbergen May 11, 1925, at 9:55 a.m., and reached the North Pole in eight hours. Although there had been fog during the early hours of the flight, above 83° north latitude the skies cleared, exposing a vast panorama of ice. As the airship crossed the Pole, Amundsen dropped the Norwegian flag, Ellsworth the American, and Nobile the Italian. After they crossed over the Pole, the weather worsened and as they approached the "Ice Pole" or "Pole of Inaccessibility," the *Norge* entered first heavy fog and then a strong wind and sleet storm that lasted for thirty-one hours.[21] Ice accumulated on the rubber envelope, and the propeller blades shot ice particles into the dirigible causing a series of holes that had to be patched. The men were unable to maintain radio communication for much of the time after the storm, and the sun compass was of little use because of fog and storms. Nonetheless, Nobile accurately navigated the *Norge* over Point Barrow and the airship was able to land at Teller on May 14, at 3:30 p.m., after a short detour over the Bering Strait. The trip covered 3,393 miles and had taken 72 hours.[22]

The difficulties experienced during the storms were serious evidence that aviation technology needed further refinements before flights through the Arctic could become commonplace. However, this transpolar dirigible flight and the airplane flight the year before proved that arctic weather was no barrier to aviation. The problems were technical and mechanical and could be corrected. The area surrounding the Pole might be a desolate wasteland, but the air above could be utilized as a natural

Mussolini honoring the officers of the 1925 Norge Expedition. Left to right, beginning front row center: *Nobile* (wearing hat) *Amundsen, and Ellsworth.* (National Archives, Washington, D.C.)

thoroughfare. The world of the 1920s was, indeed, characterized by "achievement, hope and vigor, of new beginnings."[23] Unfortunately, along with the excitement of advances in arctic exploration and aviation, one aspect of the "new beginnings" was an increase in nationalistic rhetoric.

Commenting on the expedition in an article for the *National Geographic Magazine*, Nobile stated he and his men were "proud that it was Premier Benito Mussolini who fostered the undertaking and gave for it the ship and the men to command her." For him, the flight symbolized the dream of Italian navigators to reach the Pacific by sailing north. Nobile was proud that during the "8,500 mile journey [from Italy to Leningrad, Spitsbergen, Alaska, and back to Italy], the cabin of the aircraft had on its front the fascist littorio . . . symbol of the old eternal Rome and of the new Italy."[24] Given the contributions for the purchase of the *Norge* from Norway and an American, Ellsworth, this statement was exaggerated and inaccurate, bound to raise the ire of both Amundsen and Ellsworth. Ellsworth attempted to counter Nobile's nationalistic posturing by describing the flight as an important example of changes in exploration, an issue of far greater significance than nationalism. He noted that aircraft had supplanted traditional heroic expedition leaders, that explorers were being replaced with scientists, engineers, and mechanics, and that exploration was becoming less dependent on personal strength and endurance and was more a matter of skill in mathematics and technology.[25] Exploration had once been a test of brawn. With the introduction of flying, it became a test of both brawn and brains. The crossing of the Polar Sea in the *Norge* was an experience he felt would be remembered as one of "life's great adventures for in all human experience never before had man traveled so fast and so far into the realms of the unknown. There [was] an indefinable something about such as experience where illusion and reality [were] hauntingly intermingled that well may color one's whole existence ever after."[26]

Amundsen's transarctic flight in the *Norge* was just one example of the internationalization of arctic aviation. From 1925 to 1928, the Australian George Hubert Wilkins made a series of short airplane flights exploring the northern coast of Alaska.[27] These flights, made in conjunction with American corporations, culminated in the first nonstop airplane flight from Alaska to Spitsbergen in 1928. The route was almost the reverse of that followed by the *Norge* and was a dramatic rebuttal to arguments that airplanes were not suitable for long-distance arctic flying.

Wilkins originally planned to fly across the Arctic in one airplane staffed with a skeleton crew consisting of a pilot, a mechanic, and himself as navigator. He began to raise the necessary funds in 1925 by contacting newspapers that might be interested in making a substantial contribution in exchange for exclusive publication rights to the story, a procedure previously used by Peary, Amundsen, Stefansson, and Macmillan.[28] Stefansson heartily endorsed Wilkins' plan, helped publicize the expedition, and introduced him to Isaiah Bowman, head of the American Geographical Society.[29] Stefansson's assistance was beneficial, and Wilkins successfully negotiated an arrangement with the North American Newspaper Alliance (NANA) which contributed $25,000 for the news rights to the story of the flight. Bowman also endorsed the expedition and his support helped convince a number of Detroit millionaires to finance Wilkins' project. The men formed a corporation to handle the details of the expedition and notified Wilkins that funding would be provided only if he consented to use not one but two or three planes. Personnel hired for the expedition rapidly grew to include mechanics, superintendents, photographers, wireless operators, assistants in charge of supplies, and spare pilots. A board of control was appointed as well as a committee of aeronautical engineers, a finance committee, and a staff of managers and assistants. The result was that the Detroit Arctic Expedition resembled a modern corporate bureaucracy and, it terms of leadership, became a "hopeless muddle."[30]

While the committee debated over which planes should be used, insisting that only American-made craft were acceptable, Wilkins went ahead and ordered two Fokker monoplanes, one with three Wright Whirlwind engines and one with a special Liberty engine, using $15,000 of his own money and obtaining credit toward the $80,000-$100,000 promised by the Detroit Aviation Society.[31] Wilkins wanted to explore the broad area of polar pack ice but the Society wanted a spectacular dash to the Pole. Wilkins won, not because of his persuasive powers, but because Byrd had beat him by completing his flight over the North Pole.[32]

The expedition suffered from a committee mentality in its planning stage and continued to function poorly as it became evident the expedition personnel were making decisions according to what they believed were the goals of the committee in Detroit, decisions that were not always proper for the conditions or activities of the expedition itself. There was no evidence of special loyalty to the commander, Wilkins; instead, any loyalty expressed was to the company. This was the first such expedition in which personnel felt a primary responsibility to a bureaucracy removed from the site of the expedition. Peary had used a complex system of command, but always retained complete control. As large as Stefansson's Canadian expedition was and regardless of the internecine fighting, it was still under his command. Wilkins was primarily a hired flyer, not a commander, and difficulties arose continuously in developing and executing plans.

In the initial planning stage, publicity men were hired for the express purpose of promoting the expedition as an adventure of heroic proportions. They arranged for three weeks of public appearances by Wilkins and at each of these appearances, he was introduced as a national hero about to go off on an expedition for the glory of the United States. Angered and embarrassed by the whole procedure, Wilkins protested that he was not a national hero. In fact, he was neither an American nor

Amundsen (with white beard, center) *and Ellsworth* (to Amundsen's right). (National Archives, Washington, D.C.)

a hero in any sense of the term. His purpose, he insisted, was to complete a series of flights to demonstrate the possibilities of using airplanes for transportation and research. The very mundane characteristics of the plans exempted the expedition from consideration as a heroic venture. Wilkins' protests were to no avail. He was persuaded to cooperate with the showmanship arranged by the publicity men, who reminded him that funds to complete the expedition would be more readily available if the public were convinced the expedition was in the national interest.[33] The hyperbole used by the press was successful and the necessary funds were raised. In the process, the flight was called "the greatest venture into the unknown since Columbus set out from the shores of Spain." With this image before the public, Detroit hoped to identify itself as the aviation center of the world. Readers were reminded that all great nations were aware of commercial possibilities of arctic air routes, that Norway and France were backing expeditions to find land usable for air bases, and that Japan, Russia, and Germany were planning similar expeditions. There was indeed a "struggle among several nations not only for honor

Detroit Arctic Expedition Fokker used by G. H. Wilkins, June 1926.
(R. M. Anderson collection, National Archives Canada)

and glory, but for the possession of the only important spot on earth not covered by a flag."[34]

The Detroit Arctic Expedition sailed from Seattle, Washington, to Seward, Alaska, in February 1926, and proceeded to Fairbanks by rail. When the planes were assembled and ready to fly, the newspaper representative assigned to the expedition, seeking some human interest material for a press release, decided to have the planes christened by a Catholic priest, a Presbyterian minister, and an Episcopal parson. The news was more exciting than the man had anticipated, for it included the notice of his own death. Wilkins had readied the three-motor *Alaskan* for testing, and when the crowd cleared the field, he called in the newsman to get a scoop of this first flight. The plane taxied to the runway, but stopped when its wheels became stuck in a soft snowbank. In order to release it, the men had to stamp down the snow into a hardened surface, a dangerous operation because the motors were positioned immediately in front of the wheels. Eager to be part of the excitement, the newsman hurried to help release the plane, but when it started to move, he accidentally walked back into the propeller, instead of maneuvering sideways away from it, and was killed instantly.[35]

With that ominous beginning, the *Alaskan* took off piloted by Carl Ben Eielson, a flyer who had initiated an Alaskan airmail route in 1923.[36] The plane handled well, but on the approach for landing Eielson misjudged wind currents and the plane crashed. Neither Wilkins nor Eielson were hurt but the plane was badly damaged and instructions were wired from Detroit to choose another pilot for the next trial flight. Against his better judgment, because he was convinced Eielson would not make the same mistake twice, Wilkins notified the reserve pilot, Major Thomas G. Lamphier, a former Air Service flyer, that he was to test the three-engine *Detroiter.*[37] It proved clumsy in the air, difficult to maneuver, and, on landing, the pilot made the same error as Eielson and it too crashed.

The crash of the *Detroiter* was the more serious mishap because the plane needed extensive repairs requiring sending for major parts. The repairs for the smaller *Alaskan* were completed in three weeks and Wilkins, realizing that too much time had passed to accomplish much in the way of exploration, decided to fly the *Alaskan* to the Point Barrow supply base without a preliminary test flight. Using U.S. Geological Survey maps, Wilkins, as navigator, and Eielson, as pilot, took off on March 31. Their route took them over the Endicott Mountain range, shown on their maps as reaching a height of 6,000 feet. As they approached the peaks, it became evident the maps were in error. The plane climbed to 9,000 feet, the maximum altitude possible with a heavy load, and was barely able to maneuver between the peaks. Flying at an unusually fast speed of 140 mph (ground speed), they reached the Arctic Ocean and were flying out over it before they realized it. Catching the error, Wilkins signaled Eielson to continue, excited that some exploration would actually take place. The flight covered 100 miles before Wilkins signaled to turn back and, using compass and dead reckoning, they flew into Barrow in a heavy blizzard after having flown through extensive cloud cover, a major navigational feat.[38]

This initial flight was all the expedition accomplished in 1926. The propeller of the *Alaskan* was damaged in a fire that had been set to keep the engine from freezing, and Lamphier insisted the *Detroiter* was incapable of making the flight from Fairbanks to Barrow. Wilkins and Eielson flew the *Alaskan* back to Fairbanks after making emergency repairs on the propeller. Wilkins, convinced that the *Detroiter* with its more powerful engine could make the trip, decided to try to fly it to Barrow with Lamphier as pilot, a copilot, and himself as navigator. They climbed to 11,000 feet over the Endicott Mountains and Wilkins gave Lamphier the compass course to Barrow. The copilot decided to go below the clouds and steer by land markings because he distrusted Wilkins' instructions. Dropping too fast, the plane fell rapidly in a dive that was almost not corrected in time. Wilkins again instructed the pilot to fly above the clouds. They climbed to 5,000 feet, but the course continued as erratic as before while pilot and copilot fought for control of the plane. Lamphier won, followed Wilkins' instructions, and the plane reached Barrow with no further incident, proving Wilkins' contention that the *Detroiter* was capable of the strenuous flight. Still, no exploratory flight could take place. It was too late in the season and the heavy May fogs had settled in. Wilkins dismissed the crew and all members of the expedition and returned to Detroit.

Without funds and having lost the support of the Detroit Aviation Society and the *Detroit News*, Wilkins went looking for new funds and new backers. He did not believe the flights had been without merit. Amundsen proved there was no new land in the Arctic Ocean, and that emergency landings could be made on sea ice. Additional flights in search of new land or over the North Pole would "add little to our knowledge of geography," but Amundsen's experience could be used in planning a series of short flights which included landings on sea ice to make observations. In early 1927, Wilkins arranged with William B. Scripps, a member of the Detroit Aviation Society, and George Miller (president of the North American Newspaper Alliance) to give free lectures at schools in Detroit and its suburbs in exchange for $5,000 backing. After reconsideration, the *Detroit News* offered to pay all expenses. Wilkins was then able to proceed with his plans to secure a Detroit-made Stinson biplane. This decision was instrumental in convincing the Detroit Aviation Society to support this expedition by supplying a second Stinson that could be used for spare parts.

The two crated Stinsons arrived at Point Barrow. Wilkins expected assembly would be easy because the parts were supposed to be interchangeable. Because of imprecise tooling, only one plane could be assembled using the parts that had been sent. The other plane could only be put together after the remaining parts had been refitted.[39]

On March 29, 1927, Wilkins and Eielson took off in the Stinson for the area west of Barrow. The weather was clear, visibility good, and the men sighted a number of areas of ice suitable for landings. As the plane crossed over an area of older ridged ice, the motor malfunctioned and they turned back toward the safe new ice just passed in order to make an emergency landing. Once down, Wilkins took a series of soundings and when the engine was repaired, the men took off easily.[40] The emergency repair, however, had not been enough to correct the problem and the engine stalled again, making a second landing necessary. Once again they corrected the malfunction and were able to take off. This time the men got to within 100 miles of Barrow when poor visibility forced them to climb to 5,000 feet. At that point the engine stopped again. Eielson held the plane in a steady glide and landed in a snowdrift about 65 miles northwest of Barrow on an ice floe that was drifting north at about 5-6 mph. Wilkins decided to abandon the plane and, drawing on the experience he had gained from exploring with Stefansson, he and Eielson walked out the 80 miles to Barrow.[41]

The crash and long walk back to Barrow had taken too much time. Summer fog settled in and there was little time left for exploratory flights. Wilkins sold the Stinson and the two Fokkers from the first expedition to pay his debts and, with the remaining money, arranged to buy one Lockheed Vega after observing the plane on a test flight.[42] He was determined to complete the series of experiments with planes in arctic regions and decided to fly from Barrow to Spitsbergen. The flight route would pass over 700 miles of unexplored territory north of Canada but would not cross over the North Pole, a maneuver Wilkins thought unnecessary, good only for publicity. He organized this flight with himself in full charge, believing the expedition could only be successful if he could avoid the bureaucratic complications that had accompanied the previous two flights. With minimal provisions and little publicity, Wilkins and Eielson took off from Barrow on April 15, 1928, for Spitsbergen, 2,200 miles away.

In the first five hours they covered about 700 miles with excellent visibility, but dense fog rapidly set it. It lasted only an hour and, as it lifted, the men could see for a hundred miles in each direction. There was no land and the ice below them was too rough for landing, a consideration they constantly kept in mind after the experiences north of Barrow. After 13 hours, they passed over Grant Land and, checking compass readings, found the instruments behaving erratically. Wilkins' navigation had been exact, nonetheless.[43] Passing over Greenland, they encountered heavy clouds and climbed to 8,000 feet. With only 30 gallons of gas left, they descended through a hole in the clouds only to find that they were in a bad storm and could not continue to King's Bay, Spitsbergen, in the driving snow. As they flew over the west coast of Spitsbergen, they circled and decided to land on an island just off the shore. After waiting five days for the storm to clear, they flew on to Green Harbor, Spitsbergen.

The flight was a personal victory for Wilkins, proving his assertion that airplanes were well suited for arctic flying, and also a victory for the air-cooled engine made famous by Lindbergh on his transatlantic flight.[44] The flight had not only demonstrated Wilkins' extraordinary ability to navigate, but had also produced meteorological data important for weather forecasting.[45] Wilkins had finally accomplished his original goal, to fly nonstop from Alaska to the eastern Arctic. There was no question about his ability as a navigator or his promotion of airplanes for long-distance flights over arctic territory, and the American aviation industry used the flight to promote advances in aviation technology.

National and international publicity surrounding transarctic flights in the 1920s contributed to general advances in aviation in each country engaged in arctic exploration. These air expeditions were also an important part of each country's decision to include the Arctic as an area important for the development and protection of national economic and political interests. Concerned about this increasing nationalism in arctic exploration, international societies of scientists and explorers, notably Aeroarctic, attempted to discourage national exploration by substituting a number of air and land expeditions composed of international crews and designed exclusively to gather data. (See Appendix 2.) The attempt was admirable, but the momentum of nationalistic expansion was already too strong and, despite years of work, the experiment failed.

Arctic development rapidly began to replace exploration. By 1930, the race to claim arctic territory was over. Competition for leadership in aviation intensified, but in this matter the Arctic was no more than a testing area. Businessmen vied with governments as initiators of arctic development, and expeditions focused more on establishing observation stations and gathering weather data than on traditional discovery and exploration. The Arctic had become a laboratory, a route between countries instead of a destination. The three decades of extensive arctic exploration accompanied by international rivalry ended in 1930 with one last major event, the Second International Polar Year.

Notes to Chapter 6

1. *Foreign Relations of the United States*, 1920-30. See also periodicals and newspapers published during the decade.

2. Roald Amundsen and Lincoln Ellsworth, *Our Polar Flight* (New York: Dodd, Mead & Co., 1925), pp. 6-8. Preliminary route: Norway to Siberia via the Northeast Passage.

3. *New York Times*, September 7, 1922, p. 8; August 6, 1922, p. 6.

4. Ibid., April 16, 1923, p. 16.

5. Ibid., June 3, 1923, sec. 1, p. 5; June 10, 1923, sec. 2, p. 1; June 14, 1923, p. 18; June 21, 1923, p. 7.

6. Ibid., November 9, 1923, p. 1; November 13, 1923, p. 5. Haken H. Hammer, Norwegian Consul and President of the Universal Trading and Shipping Company of Seattle, promoted Amundsen's expeditions.

7. Chief, Bureau of Aeronautics to commanding officers, October, 1923, Navy Dept., RG80 29455, NA. More than 30 men volunteered.

8. *Foreign Relations of the United States*, 1924, p. 518.

9. Division of Political Information, March 21, 1927, State Dept. Records, RG59 857.014, NA.

10. *Foreign Relations of the United States*, 1924, p. 518.

11. State Dept. Records, RG59 800.014, NA, April 6, 1925.

12. Lincoln Ellsworth, *Search* (New York: Brewer, Warren & Putnam, 1932), pp. 75-85.

13. Lincoln Ellsworth Papers [hereafter cited as LE], RG401 (36), Box 4, Center for Polar and Scientific Archives, NA. Ellsworth's father made the donation with great fear that his son would die in the expedition. When the planes were forced down and no word came from the men, his father suffered a heart attack and died believing his son was dead. See also, *New York Times*, February 2, 1925, p. 6. Each plane was 55' long with a wing span of 75' and powered with two Rolls Royce engines.

14. Amundsen and Ellsworth, *Our Polar Flight*, pp. 11, 36, 107. One plane was piloted by Norwegian Navy Lt. H. Riiser-Larsen with Adolph Feucht, the mechanic from the Dornier Wal factory, in charge of repairs and maintenance. The second plane was piloted by Lt. Lief Dietrichson with Lt. Oskar Omdal as mechanic. Also see Ellsworth, *Search*, pp. 42-57. Ellsworth had studied astrometry with the U.S. Coast and Geodetic Survey, taken engineering at Yale School of Mines, and spent a winter in London studying surveying and practical astronomy at the Royal Geographic Society.

15. May 1925, Navy Dept., RG80 29455, NA.

16. *Literary Digest* (July 14, 1925): 47-50; (August 8, 1925): 34-36.

17. *Review of Reviews* (August 25, 1925): 204-205.

18. *Forum* 75 (1926): 538-47.

19. One-third of the expedition's cost was contributed by the Italian government, one-sixth by Ellsworth, and the rest by the Aero Club of Norway. LE Papers, RG401 (36), NA. *National Geographic Magazine* (August 27, 1926): 177-215. The dirigible, a rubberized triple-ply fabric balloon filled with hydrogen, was powered by three 250 hp engines. Because of the unique characteristics of dirigibles compared with airplanes, there was a safety margin in being able to make repairs or take observations without having to land.

20. U.S. Navy War College report, "Jurisdiction Over Polar Areas," (Newport, RI: October 29, 1937), p. 13.

21. Nobile claimed he also dropped the flags of Rome, the Royal Geographic Society, Aero Club, and one given him by Fascists from the town of Grotte di Castro, although photographs taken showed only the three flags on the ground. *National Geographic Magazine* (August 27, 1926): 177-215.

22. Roald Amundsen, *Ellsworth, Across the Pole*. Roald Amundsen, *My Life as an Explorer* (New York: Doubleday, Page & Co., 1927).

23. *Yale Review* (July 1927): 739-49. *Living Age* (June 20, 1926): 670-73.

24. *National Geographic Magazine* (August 27, 1926): 177-215.

25. Ellsworth, *Search*, pp. 132-45.

26. *Annual Report, Smithsonian Institution*, 1927, pp. 321-39.

27. For implication of Wilkins' flights, see *Literary Digest* 93 (May 28, 1927): 42-46.

28. Lowell Thomas, *Sir Hubert Wilkins* (New York: McGraw-Hill, 1961), pp. 169-216.

29. December 23, 1925, Northern Affairs Program, RG85 v582 f565, NAC; R. M. Anderson Papers, NAC.

30. George Hubert Wilkins, *Flying the Arctic* (New York: G. P. Putnam's Sons, 1928), pp. 10-19. Detroit Aviation Society members: Edwin Denby, Hon. Pres.; William B. Mayo, Pres.; Col. Jess G. Vincent, First Vice Pres.; Howard Coffin, Second Vice Pres.; Charles T. Bursh, Treas.; Carl B. Fritsche, Sec.; Directors: Herbert W. Alden, Alex Dow, Harold H. Emmons, Edsel B. Ford, George W. Holly, W. H. H. Hutton Jr., William E. Metzger, Dr. Angus McLeen, E. LeRoy Pelletier, Macon P. Rummy, William B. Scripps, William B. Stout, Paul Strasburg, Ralph H. Apson, Sidney D. Waldon.

31. *The World* (January 31, 1926). Clipping in RG85 v764 f5052, NAC.

32. Wilkins, *Flying the Arctic*, pp. 13-18. The rest of the funds needed by Wilkins were raised by the Finance Committee which made a public appeal resulting in subscriptions from 80,000 people including many school children who each sent in as little as five cents.

33. In this report, there is a similarity to the treatment of the first astronauts. See Tom Wolfe, *The Right Stuff* (New York: Farrar, Straus & Giroux, 1979).

34. *The Independent* (February 27, 1926): 292-93.

35. Wilkins, *Flying the Arctic*, pp. 31-32.

36. Carl Ben Eielson Papers, Historical Society, Bismark, North Dakota. (A copy of the papers is with the author in Cincinnati, Ohio.) Jean Potter, *Arctic Encyclopedia*, reel 18. Before joining Wilkins, Eielson had proposed that the Army develop an air service route between the U.S. and China. He had also discussed with Mitchell the usefulness of an air base in Alaska that could be used for mapping and photography.

37. *New York Times*, April 2, 1926, p. 8.

38. Wilkins, *Flying the Arctic*, pp. 45-63. George Hubert Wilkins, "Flights North of Point Barrow," *Geographical Journal* (February 1928): 160-66.

39. Wilkins, *Flying the Arctic*, pp. 107-14.

40. Wilkins, "Flights North of Point Barrow," pp. 160-66.

41. Ibid.

42. *Literary Digest* 93 (May 28, 1927): 42-46. George Hubert Wilkins, "The Flight from Alaska to Spitsbergen 1928," *Geographical Review* (October 1928): 527-55. Richfield Oil Company and Penzoil paid to

have advertising on the sides of the plane. The Lockheed Vega cost $12,500 and instruments, parts, and transportation brought the total cost to $20,000.

43. *Geographical Review* (July 1928): 184-94.

44. "The First Hop Over the Earth's Roof," *Literary Digest* 97 (May 5, 1928): 1041.

45. Wilkins, "The Flight from Alaska to Spitsbergen 1928," pp. 527-55.

7

Aeroarctic

Conclusions drawn from flights by Byrd, Amundsen, and Wilkins were contradictory and inconclusive and only fueled the controversy over whether to use planes or dirigibles in the Arctic. Commercial interests as well as governments attempted to minimize the problems encountered on these flights and concentrated on publicizing only the details they thought might promote or contribute to business investments. New airline companies, such as Juan Trippe's Pan American Air Lines, hoped to use the results of these early flights to establish profitable air routes.[1] National and international mining operations hoped for faster development of equipment capable of being used in cold areas and for more rapid developments in transportation such as ice breakers and aircraft in order to hasten the discovery and development of fuel and mineral resources. By 1928, there was no question about the potential value of the Arctic. Still, information on weather, ocean, and ice conditions was incomplete. The challenge of accomplishing the research that would provide that information appealed to scientists and explorers and their governments. Germany, France, and England organized air expeditions in the Spitsbergen area, and Russia began an extensive program of arctic exploration that lasted through the 1930s and culminated in the establishment of permanent scientific stations operated from ice floes in the Arctic Ocean.

The possibility that aircraft could provide the means to conduct research without the arduous and dangerous years of labor associated with sledge expeditions stimulated scientific organizations to cooperate in an international study of the circumpolar Arctic. With great enthusiasm, a congress of explorers and scientists met in Berlin in 1928, fifty years after the first such gathering. The consensus of this second meeting was that an organized international effort to thoroughly probe arctic regions could be accomplished over an extended period and that it was appropriate to repeat the theme of 1882, the first International Polar Year. The second IPY was to begin in 1932 with dirigible flights and scientific stations established by a number of countries along the routes the dirigibles would follow.

Plans for Aeroarctic had been discussed throughout a series of international conferences held between 1900 and the outbreak of World War I. At these early meetings, a commission was formed to:

1. promote closer relationships among polar explorers;
2. develop uniform methods of observation;
3. share results of scientific studies;
4. support studies of polar regions.[2]

The meetings resumed after World War I in conjunction with an increase in polar exploration, especially in the Arctic. In Berlin in 1924, the German airship pilot Walther Bruns initiated a conference of German scholars that became the International Society for the Exploration of the Arctic by Means of the Airship.[3] The society was formally organized on an international basis in 1926 in Berlin with Fridtjof Nansen as general chairman. The group had great hopes of countering the growing nationalistic quality in polar exploration, a goal expressed in 1927 at the Hungarian Academy of Sciences at Budapest by Dr. Hugo Andreas Kruss:

"So we observe how the national leads to the international and that is based on the structure of science itself, even if scientific cooperation does not halt at the national borders. International cooperation may not lead to a leveling internationalization of scientific work. It may not even become organized. The primary factor and most valuable thing are the living powers of the individual persons, and in the cooperative work of nations, the work and values which each nation has to put into the common work in its own manner. Any piece of cooperative international effort can only become fruitful, therefore, if it permits free action and free development to the forces resulting from it."[4]

When the society met in Leningrad in 1928 for the first research and organizational meeting, 260 individual and 13 corporative members represented 19 countries. A statement of purpose noted that understanding polar conditions was important to the study of physics and a matter of great practical importance to weather forecasting.[5] Norwegian scientists, leading the research in meteorology, had described the impact of cold polar air on storm frequency and severity as the polar front moves through the North Atlantic. Improved weather forecasting, especially in the area of the North Atlantic, would benefit shipping, trade, and air traffic. The current system of weather stations operating in the Arctic had a definite impact on improved weather forecasting in Europe, but gaps existed because of the great area of arctic territory that was so difficult, if not almost impossible, to reach by traditional ship and sledge.[6] The society proposed using aircraft, particularly airships, as a means of transportation to inaccessible areas in order to establish permanent stations. Airships could carry in the necessary personnel and equipment and provide a steady supply of material and relief. They also could be outfitted with new echo sounding apparatus for determining sea depths and with photographic equipment for mapping and surveying. Airplanes might also be used for short flights from one post to another or for general reconnaissance, similar to the flights conducted by Wilkins. The project resembled the 1882 International Polar Year in the placement and utilization of scientific posts. This new enterprise, however, went beyond the scope of the first. Acknowledging national interests as a reality, the society hoped to balance the international quality of the expeditions by granting national enterprises their share of scientific control of the expedition.[7]

Nansen was a persuasive promoter for the society. In 1928, when President Calvin Coolidge received Nansen's request for American participation, he recommended that the U.S. cooperate with the society, a position enthusiastically supported by the Secretary of the Navy, Acting Secretary of Agriculture, and the Secretaries of the Smithsonian, National Research Council, and Carnegie Institute. Secretary of State Frank Kellogg asked Congress to appropriate the required annual contribution of $300, describing the project as deserving "serious consideration as a scientific enterprise of great potential practical value in several important fields. . . ."[8]

Canadians, having learned of the society's plans in the press rather than from a direct communication from Nansen, wondered if the oversight was meant as an insult and as one more threat to their claim to the arctic islands. Because they had not been invited to the initial planning sessions, they were worried that final plans would be made without their participation, a situation they felt was completely unacceptable. The government made it clear that Canada believed it had a greater stake in the Arctic than any other country did and should not be left behind in this new round of exploration.[9] Canadian sensibilities were soothed by a communication from Nansen, followed by a personal visit from Bruns, after which Parliament voted to contribute fully to the project.[10]

The expedition, scheduled for 1929 or 1930, was planned around a series of flights to be made by a Zeppelin airship contributed by the German government. In order for the flights to proceed successfully, crossing and landing at predetermined locations around the arctic perimeter, it was necessary that all countries bordering on the Arctic participate and that the host country assure access to designated posts. In this regard, Russia agreed to construct mooring masts at Leningrad and Murmansk, and the United States agreed to improve a mooring mast previously erected at Nome.[11]

Provisions for transportation of personnel and supplies using dirigibles was only the beginning. Orderly acquisition of scientific data could only take place if a set of stations were erected in every area of the Arctic, including Canadian territory. When Canada agreed to provide assistance from the RCMP and to contribute a sum ($10,000) equal to the cost of contributions from Germany, the United States, and Russia, the society had sufficient provisions and working capital at its disposal to begin the first dirigible flight.[12]

Although news of the impending expedition was generally received with considerable excitement and generated widespread support, there were some dissenting voices. H. K. E. Kruger, a German national and a prominent Greenland explorer, objected to the use of aircraft for either transportation or exploration in the Arctic. He warned that demonstrating the feasibility of arctic flying by pointing to successful flights was most dangerous. Unless all evidence regarding aircraft were examined, conclusions would be erroneous and could result in decisions that might be responsible for further deaths. He discounted the two flights across arctic territory by Amundsen and Wilkins, and maintained that the *Norge* flight had produced insufficient information of scientific value to warrant another attempt at long-distance dirigible flying. Wilkins' flight from Point Barrow to Spitsbergen, although successful, was only one example of an airplane completing long-distance maneuvers in the Arctic and did not assure that other flights would be equally successful.

Wilkins had, furthermore, abandoned aircraft as a means of travel and was currently experimenting with a submarine. Kruger summarily rejected the society's plans on two counts: first, aircraft could, he believed, produce no further scientific information of value concerning oceanography or topography and second, the dangers of using aircraft far exceeded any value they might have. The whole operation was planned around the assumption that nations other than Germany would cooperate in supplying the necessary aircraft and landing facilities. Kruger disputed this, insisting that the society would "knock at the doors of England or America in vain for such purposes, for only we Germans do not know evidently that this undertaking, which calls itself international, is in reality German-Russian."[13]

The British were also skeptical of the operation. They acknowledged the importance of long-range plans for studying arctic conditions, but the government was hesitant to make a commitment to full participation. The British were hopeful that a national air expedition would establish British priority in developing air routes and air bases, and felt that cooperation with the society could only occur if British national aims were more adequately recognized and their representative accorded greater responsibility for making decisions regarding the basic nature of the expedition.

Difficulties in gaining the necessary support from major countries continued, and the society turned to private sources for funds. The most promising were newspaper syndicates, and the society signed agreements for monopoly rights to all news of the expedition with the Hearst syndicate in the United States and England and the Wolff Telegraph Bureau in Europe. Although this arrangement funneled funds directly to Aeroarctic without going through the increasingly complicated process of obtaining approval from various governments, it also limited the society's purpose, that of making the results of the expedition immediately available to all interested nations.[14]

Additional complications arose over landing facilities in Alaska and Russia. Nome, the original choice, was rejected because of transportation difficulties and replaced by Fairbanks. Reasons cited for the change were the available assistance from U.S. Army personnel stationed in Fairbanks and the ability to utilize the faculty and student body of the Alaska Agricultural College and School of Mines in that city, along with weather conditions that allowed the expedition more flexibility. Russia reported that it preferred not to allocate the vast amount of money necessary for building an aerodome at Murmansk and recommended changing the site to Vadso, Norway. Without the responsibility for the aerodome, the Russians could apply their resources to developing bases along their Euro-Asian border. These decisions and the onset of the depression worked to delay the start of the expedition until 1931.[15]

Despite these complications, the Hoover administration recommended that the U.S. continue to participate on the basis of a report by the Senate Foreign Relations Committee, but approval of funding for the construction of a base in Alaska was difficult to obtain from the House of Representatives. Secretary of State Henry Stimson appealed to the House, reiterating the position of previous heads of the State Department that the wireless data resulting from the expedition would be of "inestimable scientific and economic value in the complex development of present day human activities."[16] President Herbert Hoover appealed for $30,000 in appropriations, submitting as evidence of the project's worthiness reports from the Departments of State, Commerce, Navy, Interior, and Agriculture indicating that information regarding radio transmission, weather, air routes, and coastal mapping would all contribute to American economic and diplomatic interests. J. A. Fleming, Director of Terrestrial Magnetism at the Carnegie Institute and also American delegate to the society, testified before the House Committee on Foreign Affairs that the information on radio transmission from the expedition would greatly aid in the development of American radio, telephone, and telegraph communications. He notified the members that American Telephone and Telegraph, recognizing this importance, was providing use of telephone lines in Arizona, Alaska, Maine, and New York.[17]

The first *Graf Zeppelin* flight left Friedrichshafen, Germany, on July 24, 1931, commanded by Dr. Hugo Eckener who had been elected to lead the expedition when Nansen died in 1930. The flight continued on to Leningrad and then to Franz Josef Land where it landed using air-filled rubber pontoons. The Russian ship *Malygin* met the airship and transferred its mail.[18] The expedition made some important geographic corrections, particularly in redefining some small land areas, previously identified as islands, as peninsulas. It also completed observations using the latest equipment, including German mapping cameras, to construct a more accurate set of isobaric maps.[19] Furthermore, new procedures were used to take soundings with sonic depth finders in the Arctic Sea and make atmospheric observations by using automatic radios equipped with balloons.[20]

The success of this first part of the IPY marked the end of the period of traditional land exploration. Scientists had replaced explorers, and geographic discovery had given way to studies of electricity and radiowaves. Through international expeditions of this kind, men would "cease to be Frenchmen, Englishmen, or Dutchmen and become Earthmen." The men who planned the second IPY thought it would be "worth all the money appropriated merely because it [proved] that nations [were] able to sink their differences and work together." They believed these new expeditions could signal the end of an era of adventurers seeking personal and national glory. The new breed of explorer-scientists would need "not only courage and hardihood but scientific training and knowledge." New marvels would be found in studies of the earth's crust and atmosphere, "marvels which [were] fully as exciting as any that greeted men who went down to the sea in ships."[21]

In 1932, there were high expectations for a new era of exploration and scientific cooperation. Faith in science and technology to solve human problems was equally strong. The hopes lasted a scant year. In September 1933, Congress canceled appropriations for participation in further society activities, and the State Department instructed the American ambassador in Berlin to cancel American membership in the society.[22] Nationalistic fervor had quashed this peaceful attempt at international cooperation. The Arctic, in 1933, had become an outpost for national interests. The North Polar era was closing and the drama was about to begin again in the Antarctic.

Notes to Chapter 7

1. Robert Daley, *Juan Trippe and His Pan American Empire* (New York: Random House, 1980).

2. L. Breitfuss, "The Arctic and the Aeroarctic," trans. by M. B. A. Anderson, International Arctic Congress [hereafter cited as IAC], RG85 v785 f5988, NAC.

3. Lincoln Ellsworth and Edward H. Smith, "Report of the Preliminary Results of the Aeroarctic Expedition with Graf Zeppelin, 1931," *Geographical Review* (January 1932): 61-82.

4. Breitfuss, "The Arctic and the Aeroarctic," p. 12.

5. U.S. Congress, House Document #133, "Exploring Arctic Regions by Airship," 70th Cong., 1st sess., January 4, 1928. Member countries: Bulgaria, Denmark, Germany, England, Estonia, Finland, France, Italy, Japan, Latvia, The Netherlands, Norway, Austria, Sweden, Switzerland, Spain, Czechoslovakia, Russia, The United States.

6. "International Society for the Exploration of the Arctic Regions by Means of the Airship: Problems and Methods of Work." IAC, 1928. Weather stations: Bear Island, Spitsbergen, Jan Mayen established by Norway; Novaya Zelya, Dickson Island at the mouth of the Yenissey (northeastern Siberia) established by Russia; Alaska established by the United States.

7. Proceedings of the Second Regular General Conference of the Aeroarctic, June 18, 1928, p. 14, IAC. *Annals of the International Geophysical Year* (Pergamon Press, 1959), pp. 205-381. The proposed equipment was described as "a picture telegraphy transmitter and receiver . . . [for] the transmission of pictures from the airship." IAC Memo.

8. U.S. Congress, House Document #133, Frank Kellogg, "International Society for the Exploration of the Arctic by Means of Airship," 70th Cong., 1st sess., May 1927.

9. O. S. Finnie memo, March 26, 1928, IAC. The press noted that American participation in the planning session at Leningrad would be the first time the U.S. had "participated side by side with a Russian Soviet delegation . . . and [if Canada participated] the first time Canada sent an official representative to Russia since it became the USSR."

10. Nansen to Office of Under Secretary of State for External Affairs, September 10, 1928. See clipping from Fort *Williams Times Journal* (March 9, 1929), IAC.

11. Special Meeting Northern Advisory Board, IAC. U.S. Congress, House Document #282, 72nd Cong., 1st. sess., 1931.

12. Nansen to Under Secretary of State for External Affairs. See also, Special Meeting Northern Advisory Board, IAC.

13. H. K. E. Kruger, "Polar Exploration and Polar Aviation," trans. by M. B. A. Anderson, p. 5, IAC.

14. Minutes of the Meeting of the Research Board of the "Aeroarctic," May 13-14, 1929, p. 10, IAC.

15. Memorandum, pp. 4-5; Bruns to Skelton, November 1930, IAC.

16. U.S. P.D. y4;F76/1 p. 75. U.S. Congress, House Committee on Foreign Affairs, Second Polar Year Program Hearings, 1932. U.S. Congress, House of Representatives, Report #2700, Secretary of State Henry Stimson, 71st Cong., 3rd sess., February 9, 1931.

17. U.S. Congress, Senate Document #16, 72nd Cong., 1st sess., December 10, 1931; U.S. Congress, Senate Report #162, 72nd Cong., 1st sess., 1931.

18. Ellsworth and Smith, "Graf Zeppelin," p. 65.

19. J. A. Fleming, "The Proposed Second International Polar Year, 1932-33," *Geographical Review* (January 1932): 131-34.

20. *Science* 70 (December 27, 1929): x.

21. *New York Times*, July 30, 1932, p. 2; July 31, 1932, sec. 7, p. 4.

22. *Science* (September 29, 1933): 277. During the period of participation, the U.S., through the War Department and Alaska Road Commission, spent $12,000 building a landing field at Fairbanks.

8

Conclusion

Between 1900 and 1932, countries engaged in arctic exploration hoped to gain political and economic advantages by sponsoring prestigious expeditions of heroic dimension and by establishing a legitimate presence in areas rich in natural resources or suitable for sea and air bases. A second goal, less widely publicized but equally important, was to study natural phenomena. The scientific knowledge gained from extensive studies of arctic geography, meteorology, oceanography, and terrestrial magnetism contributed to rapid developments in technology, especially in transportation and communication. In the contest that developed over reaching the North Pole, discovering new land, cataloging natural resources, and understanding the environment, relations between countries hoping to gain from arctic development reflected that competition.

The organization and methods used in exploration changed in the twentieth century, paralleling an increasing reliance on the latest developments in science and technology. After 1900, expeditions began to reflect a general interest in efficiency and professionalism although arctic exploration continued to attract men seeking adventure and glory. Traditionally, expedition leaders and their staffs had been men chosen for their ability in and knowledge of the arctic environment, but when the goals of expeditions became more technical, staffing changed to reflect those new goals. By World War I, the new expedition captains were men trained in science and technology; the engineer began to replace the explorer, and industrial modernization soon had its parallel in arctic studies and development. One example was Vilhjalmur Stefansson's Canadian Arctic Expedition which involved a complex organization, part of which was designed to gather scientific data. The controversy over that expedition was, in part, a classic conflict between nineteenth century individualism represented by Stefansson, and twentieth century professionalism represented by the expedition itself.

After World War I, when advances in aviation technology began to make air travel a realistic possibility, the United States, Canada, Russia, Norway, Germany, and Italy began to consider access to arctic regions necessary to the development of air routes between Asia and Europe. As airplanes and dirigible flights along northern latitudes significantly reduced the distance and travel time between countries, the political importance of the Arctic became more apparent. Countries then sought to expand their spheres of influence to include arctic territory potentially useful for bases along future air routes.[1] Competing interest in the Arctic became an important issue between the United States and Canada early in the 1920s as each country defined the region north of its continental borders to the North Pole as an area of political and economic importance. Canada was primarily concerned with establishing uncontested sovereignty over the North American archipelago. The United States, preferring to apply an Open Door policy to the general area, was reluctant to recognize a Canadian sphere of influence. However, because the Canadian claim was more acceptable than a *terra nullius* status that might allow expansion into the area by a non-American power, the United States adopted a position of nonrecognition rather than express outright objections. By 1930, despite nonrecognition by the United States, the Arctic was effectively divided into sectors extending around the Arctic Circle and encompassing an area from the subarctic to the North Pole.

Advances in aviation technology in the 1920s contributed to an unstable relationship between the United States and Canada. Airplane and dirigible flights corroborated the absence of any new land north of Alaska, ending competition between countries hoping to be the first to make new discoveries. However, because of the limited range of airplanes, small arctic islands along the path of these flights became important as possible air bases on future air routes. These islands then caused contention between the United States and Canada as each country attempted to claim jurisdiction for the purpose of development. By 1927, the potential value of the islands as intermediate bases declined with rapid improvements in engine and airplane construction and as airways were redirected along a more southerly route, the "Great Circle."[2] Also, as aircraft replaced ships and sledges in exploration, and air expeditions concentrated on transarctic flights after 1926, Canada felt less threatened by foreign expansion into arctic territory.[3] In this regard, arctic aviation helped reduce tensions temporarily between countries with historic interests in arctic territory and waterways. Conversely, arctic flights dramatically shortened the distance and travel time between countries in the northern hemisphere, vividly demonstrating national vulnerability should an adversary attack from a northern air route.

Continued arctic exploration and development demonstrated the closeness of countries rimming the North Polar area. Because of that closeness, countries would have to be considerably more careful to avoid conflicts as national interests converged in the North. Norway and Canada engaged in diplomatic disputes over eastern arctic islands but did reach a settlement in the early 1930s.[4] Although Canada continued to be suspicious of American expansion and regarded expeditions sponsored privately or by the United States government as an attempt to violate Canadian sovereignty, the Canadian government refrained from issuing any ultimatum and relied on legislation passed by Parliament to control expeditions. Surrounded by foreign presence, the United States in Alaska, Norway and Denmark in Greenland, and Russia in Herald and Wrangel islands, Canada accelerated its program of arctic development as a way to discourage any possible attempts by countries to move into the Canadian Arctic.

The United States carefully publicized its interests in arctic territory other than Alaska, notably Spitsbergen, Greenland, Ellesmere, and Wrangel Island. Ever mindful of national benefits from successful scientific experiments and economic development, the United States government cooperated fully with the press in publishing plans for expanding arctic exploration, especially expeditions promoted by the army and navy. Although Canada objected to American military expeditions, there were no plans to undermine Canadian sovereignty. The primary motivation for American arctic exploration appears to have been scientific and economic rather than strategic, but the United States refused to recognize and comply with Canadian statutes, exacerbating tensions between the two countries.

In the fifty years between the two International Polar Years, American explorers participated in extended surveys of weather conditions on

Ellesmere Island and Greenland, mapped the northern rim of Greenland, compiled extensive studies of the geography and geology of arctic islands, produced detailed studies of Eskimos, surveyed glaciers, and tested the performance of radio equipment and aircraft. Newspapers and magazines reported these achievements and data was made available to the American government by expedition commanders. When the scientific and geographic information aided in national objectives of promoting commerce and protecting territory and investments, the government responded by sponsoring or cooperating in arctic exploration. Expeditions in the 1920s not only furthered traditional American interest in trade and science but also encouraged the development of naval air power and established an American presence in arctic areas rich in mineral resources or astride commercial and defensive transportation routes between Europe and Asia.

Canadian explorers in this same period charted interisland waterways, discovered and mapped islands in the western Arctic Ocean, and took part in long-term scientific studies. Some of these activities were engaged in independently of exploration by other countries, but an acknowledged impetus to Canadian exploration and administration of northern islands was concern over encroachment by foreign powers. Some of the land involved was found to be rich in vital resources such as gold, silver, copper, coal, iron, and oil, but in the 1920s extraction of these minerals was difficult, if at all possible. Canadian claims to arctic islands were, in part, designed to protect natural resources, but were also meant to exclude foreign interests which might restrict Canadian geographic or economic development. Canadian nationalism, especially in the interwar years, grew out of many factors, but one that clearly provides a historical thread is the distinctive northern environment that has been described as being responsible for building a strong, self-reliant country.[5]

Arctic air expeditions in the 1920s produced valuable geographic reports such as those that ascertained that there were no undiscovered islands north of Alaska. However, the most notable contributions from these flights had less to do with arctic exploration in the historic sense of discovery than with testing aircraft and mapping air routes. In the United States, General "Billy" Mitchell's dramatic and extensive campaign to build a unified air force demonstrated clearly that arctic airways would be the commercial and defensive routes of the future.[6] Vilhjalmur

Stefansson stimulated Canadian northern development with his unrelenting campaign to open the Arctic for commercial enterprises and with his many publications describing the advantages of arctic airways. Stefansson and Mitchell agreed that the Arctic was important for the defense and economic growth of North America.[7] The proliferation of flights after 1925, including those of Byrd, Amundsen, and Wilkins, reinforced the idea that arctic air routes were a natural extension of national economic and strategic interests.[8]

It was evident by the end of the 1920s that aviation development had advanced to the point where aircraft would soon became crucial economic and strategic vehicles and the Arctic, as predicted earlier, would become a "Northern Mediterranean" between Europe, North America, and Asia. In the 1930s, the Arctic, once an area of both cooperation and contention between the United States and Canada, had become a target for private organizations and governments representing most of the industrialized countries of Europe, which hoped to benefit from access to natural resources and transportation routes, and to establish a presence that could be strategically valuable in developing long-range defense plans.

Tension between the United States and Canada declined in the 1930s as America turned to the Antarctic for exploration. Through the 1930s, Richard E. Byrd's antarctic expeditions attracted the attention of the press, and these new adventures rapidly replaced the Arctic as a news item. The public's imagination may have been captured by these new stories of exploration, but the economic and strategic importance of the Arctic, although minimally publicized, became even more evident to the government and to industry.[9]

Increased mining operations in Alaska and northern Canada and experimentation with air routes by private companies, such as Pan American Airways, contributed to the growing acceptance of the Arctic as a frontier for development.[10] By 1940, accurate information about arctic weather conditions and well-charted sea and air routes were available to the Allies, who realized the Arctic's potential as an area for military operations with the establishment of air fields in Greenland.[11]

As World War II began and military installations were rapidly constructed, it became clear that earlier predictions by explorers regarding the military importance of arctic regions had been correct.[12] The United States, Canada, and Great Britain engaged in submarine, ship, and air maneuvers in the North Atlantic from Spitsbergen to Iceland, Greenland, and Labrador, all following a pattern described between 1900 and 1932.[13]

Military planners, previously hesitant to consider the Arctic as more than an area of very tenuous importance because of the difficulties with weather and terrain, readily acknowledged the successful use of bases in both the eastern and western Arctic during World War II.[14] After 1945, developments in military technology and the emergence of Russia as a military and political adversary provided the impetus to continue to view the Arctic as a critical defensive region.[15]   By 1947, deteriorating relations with Russia led General Carl Spaatz, commanding general of the U.S. Army Air Force, to warn Congress that the Arctic would be the American defensive frontier if war were to occur between the United States and Russia.[16]   The perceived threat from Russia, increased experience in arctic operations, and cooperation between the United States and Canada during World War II culminated in the building of the Distant Early Warning radar line (DEW) which, along with the Pinetree Line near the Canadian-American border, formed the base of the North American Air Defense Command (NORAD).[17]

By 1958, American military strategists agreed that the Arctic had become the center of the world and as such had to be defended from a possible attack by the Soviets.[18] As part of this defense project, the United States established infantry, antiaircraft, and engineer units in Alaska. It used naval aircraft and ships to patrol the areas of the DEW stations, and employed Marine Corps units to guard the installations themselves.[19] By the end of the 1950s, the overriding characteristic of arctic activity was the establishment of defense facilities. The area from Greenland to Alaska had become part of a major strategic air route between Russia and the power centers of the United States.[20]

American arctic activity in the 1960s and 1970s represented years of careful planning by the government and private organizations.[21] New developments in polar technology in the 1970s, such as the construction of super icebreakers, aided in extracting and utilizing arctic resources. From the mid-1960s through the 1970s, arctic development shifted from military objectives to exploitation of minerals with strategic value: oil in Alaska; uranium and gold in Canada; nickel, gold, diamonds, and oil in Russia; coal in Norway; and in Greenland, cryolite, necessary in the production of aluminum.[22]

The Arctic, long a stage where epic quests had been enacted, became primarily a defense perimeter during the years of hostility between the United States and the Soviet Union. Curiosity about the gravitational characteristics of the magnetic North Pole that had attracted explorers and scientists alike over decades was no longer associated with adventure but was replaced with pragmatic studies concerning the effects of the gravitational field on the paths of long-range missiles.[23] By 1990, American and Soviet military bases ringing the Arctic could have been the next targets in a policy of arms reduction growing out of improved relations between the United States and the Soviet Union. This development could be viewed as the beginning of the end of the role of the Arctic as a critical part of the American defense system but the importance of oil and other minerals necessary for industrial and military systems could also mean a renewed interest in supporting military bases in Arctic areas for protection of oil fields. A north polar geographic projection has conclusively shown that the United States is fully integrated in a transcontinental system; the idea of a western hemisphere protected by two oceans is obsolete.

The spirit of adventure and driving curiosity that had been historic forces in the exploration of the Arctic have been replaced by military appraisals of national security and projects regarding the exploitation of strategic resources.[24] The airplane, indeed, ended the heroic age of exploration.

Notes to Chapter 8

1. An example of this situation occurred regarding Jan Mayen. In 1925, Habard Ekerold, member of the American Institute of Mining Engineers and a member of the Explorers Club, notified the State Department that he thought it prudent to consider the possibility that Jan Mayen might become important as a landing area when transpolar air routes were established. He believed it might be advantageous to the United States to exercise some control over the area. The State Department replied that the area was officially recognized as under Norwegian sovereignty and should any precautions be necessary, the American government would appeal to Norway for protection. Ekerold to State Dept., September 24, 1925, State Department Records, RG59 857.014, NA. For the importance of Greenland, see also Nancy Fogelson, "Greenland: Strategic

Base on a Northern Defense Line," in *The Journal of Military History* 53, 1 (January 1989): 51-64.

2. The Great Circle Route included the area from the Great Lakes to Labrador, Greenland, and then to Europe, following a latitude north of the steamship lanes.

3. Flights by Amundsen, Byrd, and Wilkins made no attempt to use Canadian territory for bases and, despite the rhetoric surrounding the flights, no claims were made to territory or waterways sighted from the aircraft.

4. The dispute between Canada and Norway over the Sverdrup Islands was settled in 1930 when the Canadian government paid a cash settlement to the Sverdrup family. R. A. J. Phillips, *Canada's North* (Toronto: MacMillan of Canada, 1967), p. 107.

5. Carl Berger, "The True North, Strong and Free," in *Nationalism in Canada*, ed. by Peter Russell (Toronto: McGraw Hill, 1966), pp. 3-26. John D. Hicks, *Republican Ascendency 1921-1933* (New York: Harper & Row, 1960), p. 164.

6. Blair Bolles, "Arctic Diplomacy," *Foreign Policy Reports* 24, 5 (June 1, 1948): 62. Mitchell has been credited with coining the phrase, "He who holds Alaska holds the world;" in congressional testimony, he so stated.

7. Ibid., pp. 59-60. Stefansson to Cory, March 19, 1923, Department of the Interior, RG85 v610 f2718, NAC. Stefansson related a conversation he had had with Mitchell. Stefansson believed there would be great commercial value for airplanes in 50 years, especially in Brazil, Siberia, mainland Canada, and polar regions, in that order. Mitchell agreed but felt that transpolar air commerce would be the most important.

8. William S. Carlson, *Lifelines Through the Arctic* (New York: Duell, Sloan & Pearce, 1962), p. 10.

9. Ibid., pp. 49-53. The following items illustrate the growing use of the Arctic for strategic purposes. In 1933, the Italian Fascist Italo Balbo, leader in the promotion of an Italian Air Force, led a squadron of Italian planes over Greenland on a Rome to Chicago flight. In 1935, William H. Hobbs, leader of the University of Michigan expeditions, appealed to the American government to secure access to Greenland in order to block an attempt by Germany to establish a presence there. Hobbs based his assumption of German interest on numerous reconnaissance flights made by Germany over Greenland. In 1939, as Germany began its move through Europe, a proposal was made in the Senate recommending purchase of Greenland, but the War Department consulted with other departments and declined to support the proposal. Fogelson, "Greenland."

10. Carlson, *Lifelines Through the Arctic*, p. 191. Walter S. Ross, *The Last Hero: Charles A. Lindbergh* (New York: Harper & Row, 1968), pp. 181-93. Matthew Josephson, *Empire of the Air: Juan Trippe and the Struggle for World Airways* (New York: Arno Press, 1972), pp. 6-8. Phillips, *Canada's North*, pp. 108-9.

11. J. Anker Nielson, "Our Hibernating Arctic," *Washington Post*, July 11, 1971, p. 3.

12. Bernt Balchen, *Come North With Me* (New York: E. P. Hutton & Co., 1958), p. 234. Nazi planes were sighted patrolling Greenland's east coast and Nazis in disguise were picked up off the coast. Bolles, "Arctic Diplomacy," p. 61. In 1939, the United States began its first serious attempt to fortify Alaska by building air stations at Sitka, Kodiak, and Dutch Harbor.

13. Jorgen Taagholt, "Greenland's Future Development: A Historical and Political Perspective," *Polar Record* 21, 130 (January 1982): 23-31. Elmer Plischke, "Trans-Polar Aviation and Jurisdiction Over Arctic Airspace," *The American Political Science Review* 37 (December 1943): 995-1013.

14. Balchen, *Come North With Me*, p. 71. Balchen's book and Carlson's *Lifelines Through the Arctic* provide detailed descriptions of the establishment of military bases in Alaska and Greenland.

15. Brian D. Smith, "U.S. Arctic Policy," *Oceans Policy Study* 1:1 (University of Virginia: Center for Ocean Law and Policy, 1978), pp. 11-14.

16. Bolles, "Arctic Diplomacy," p. 58. General H. H. Arnold also noted that the strategic center of a third world war would be the Arctic. Carlson, *Lifelines Through the Arctic*, p. 191.

17. Phillips, *Canada's North*, p. 111. The Canadian government required that all physical improvements including buildings be turned over to Canada when and if the stations were considered no longer useful. However, there was no expression of suspicion about U.S. encroachment. CIA, *Polar Regions Atlas* (Washington, D.C.: Government Printing Office, 1978), p. 31. The DEW line bases extend from Alaska through Canada to Greenland. Oscar Svarlien, "The Legal Status of the Arctic," *Proceedings of the American Society of International Law* (April 1958): 135. Department of Defense, *Continental Air Defense* (Washington, D.C.: Government Printing Office, 1955), pp. 2-4. Bolles, "Arctic Diplomacy," p. 60. Smith, "U.S. Arctic Policy," pp. 11-14.

18. Department of Defense, *A Hot Spot of Free World Defense* (Washington, D.C.: Government Printing Office, 1958), pp. 3-14.

19. Ibid., p. 4.

20. Robert W. Hoyton, "Polar Problems and International Law," *American Journal of International Law* 52, 4 (October 1958): 746. Smith, "U.S. Arctic Policy," p. 14.

21. John Hanessian, Jr., *Polar Area Series* (New York: American Universities Field Staff) 1, 3 (August 27, 1960): 1-3. R. MacDonald, ed., *The Arctic Frontier* (Toronto: University of Toronto Press, 1970), p. 51. National Security Council, National Security Decision Memorandum #114, December 22, 1971 (copy in author's files).

22. John Dyson, *The Hot Arctic* (Boston: Little Brown & Co., 1979), p. 82. *Cincinnati Enquirer*, December 21, 1980, p. I 9.

23. Edgar J. Dossman, ed., *The Arctic in Question* (Toronto: Oxford University Press,1976), pp. 1-11. Lisle A. Rose, "Recent Trends in U.S. Arctic Affairs," *Arctic* 35, 2 (June 1982): 241-42.

24. Carl G. Jacobsen, "Soviet-American Policy: New Strategic Uncertainties," *Current History* 81, 477 (October 1982): 305-308. Richard T. McCormack, "Export of Alaskan Oil," *Department of State Bulletin* 83, 2078 (September 1983): 57-59. "The Frozen War," *Newsweek* (January 23, 1984): 36-38.

Appendix A

List of American Members of the
*Aeroarctic Expedition**

Anthony, H. E., Director of American Museum of Natural History, New York City.

Austin, Louis W., Chief of Laboratory for Special Radio Transmission Research, U.S. Bureau of Standards, Washington.

Bauer, Louis A., Professor, Director of Department of Terrestrial Magnetism, Carnegie Institute, Washington.

Bowie, William, Chief of Division of Geodesy, U.S. Coast and Geodetic Survey, Washington.

Brooks, Charles F., Professor, Meteorology and Climatology, Clark University, Worcester, Massachusetts.

Eielson, Carl B., Polar explorer, honorary member of Aeroarctic, New York City.

Fergusson, S. P., Meteorologist, U.S. Weather Bureau, Washington.

Fleming, John A., Assistant Director, Department of Research in Terrestrial Magnetism, Carnegie Institute, Washington.

---

*Reprinted from IAC, RG85, NAC.

Graves, Ralph A., Assistant Editor, National Geographic Society, Washington.

Greely, A. W., General, U.S. Army, Washington.

Gregg, W. R., Senior Meteorologist, U.S. Weather Bureau, Washington.

Grosvenor, Gilbert H., President and Editor, National Geographic Society, Washington.

Hammer, Richard, Professor of Physics, University of Pittsburgh, Pennsylvania.

Hazard, Daniel L., Assistant Chief, Division of Terrestrial Magnetism and Seismology, U.S. Coast and Geodetic Survey, Washington.

Heck, N. H., Commander, Chief Division of Terrestrial Magnetism and Seismology, U.S. Coast and Geodetic Survey, Washington.

Hobbs, W. H., Professor, Director of Department of Geology, University of Michigan.

Humphreys, W. J., Meteorologist, U.S. Weather Bureau, Washington.

Jochelson, V. J., Professor, Research Associate Archeology, Carnegie Institute, Washington; American Museum of Natural History, New York City.

Joerg, W. J. G., Editor, Polar Series for American Geographical Society, New York City.

Jones, E. Lester, Director, U.S. Coast and Geodetic Survey, Washington.

Krijanowsky, N., Commander, American Geographical Society, New York City.

Lagorce, John O., Vice President and Associate Editor, National Geographic Society, Washington.

Mielberg, Ivan, Engineer, American Geographical Society, New York City.

Murphy, Robert C., Curator of Ornithology, American Museum of Natural History, New York City.

Nichols, A. G., Commander, late member of the Russian hydrographic Survey Expedition to the Polar Ocean, American Geographical Society, New York City.

Rosendahl, C. E., Commander, Airship *Los Angeles*, Lakehurst.

Rude, G. T., Commander Chief Division of Tides and Currents, U.S. Coast and Geodetic Survey, Washington.

Stefansson, V., Chief Canadian Polar Expedition 1913-1918, New York City.

Todd, W. E. C., Curator of Ornithology, Carnegie Museum, Pittsburgh.

Tolmachoff, I. P., Curator of Geology, Carnegie Museum, Pittsburgh.

Transche, N. A., Commander, late member of the Russian hydrographic Survey Expedition to the Polar Ocean, American Geographical Society, New York City.

Ward, Robert, Professor, Harvard University, Cambridge, Massachusetts.

Appendix B

*Aeroarctic Statement of Purpose**

In consideration of the far-reaching import of these problems, the Council of our Society have drawn up the following programme for the future investigation and permanent
control of the geophysical conditions of the Arctic regions.
As of course, it cannot be expected to have this ample
programme brought into execution at once. It ought to be
considered, rather, as the ideal end, indicating the line of our
efforts. It presents tasks of evident significance for any
nation, it comprises the research of geophysical agencies,
affecting the everyday life of all men. There may be hope for
results of both scientific and palpable practical importance.
Besides meteorological readings, the men in the stations will
naturally be able to execute other geophysical and biological
investigations of notable interest. Thus we surely may expect that researches of this kind, if only duly prepared and
competently conducted, will prove extremely fruitful.

Fridtjof Nansen

THE MAIN END:

The scientific investigation and permanent control of the Arctic by
means of explorations (voyages) and by the disembarking and support of
wireless stations.

---

*Reprinted from IAC, RG85, NAC.

To secure the accomplishment of this main end the Council have fixed on the following programme.

1. Continued extension of the international scientific organisation of the "Aeroarctic," especially formation of still missing national sections.

2. Formation of international, internal scientific committees for the treating of the different individual branches (Geography, Meteorology, Oceanography, Terrestrial Magnetism, Biology, Wireless, Atmospheric Electricity, Aerogeodetics, Technicalities) and for the setting up of the line of work for the scientific arctic stations.

3. Publication of a scientific Quarterly "Arktis," to start on April 1st 1928, with the object of demonstrating the importance of permanent research-work in the Arctic for Science and the world's commercial interests, further to discuss the methods applicable, finally for the publication of the results of such investigations and studies in the whole domain of polar research.

4. Issue of new large-scale Map of the Arctic Regions for the school-room, in several languages.

5. Organisation of the intended permanent control, comprising:

   a) Preparatory work:

   1. Execution of Airship expeditions, several ones if possible, for a minute investigation of the scientific conditions and technicalities, towards an unbroken control of the Arctic.

   2. Construction and testing of light wireless stations, fit for transportation by air-vehicles.

   3. Furtherance of a close cooperation of the subarctic stations extant.

   4. Improvements in the existing wireless service around the Arctic.

b) Achievement of the permanent control:

1. Establishment and support of fixed permanent wireless stations, remaining in daily connexion with the synoptic system of the Northern hemisphere, by seaship, airship or airplane.

2. Setting up of, and providing for, unfixed permanent wireless stations on the floating-ice of the innermost Arctics, by airship.

6. Creation of a financial basis of the running and intended work of the Society, by application to the governments of the countries of the Northern hemisphere and to the chief Institutions of traffic and commerce on land, sea and air, as well as the leading agricultural corporations.

The Acting Council of the "Aeroarctic"

Signed: Bauer, Berson, Bleistein, Bruns, Delcambre, de Elola, v. Ficker, Issatchenko, Krell, Nansen, Shaw

Appendix C

*Exploration Plans of the
International Society for the Exploration
of the Arctic Regions by Aircraft during the
Spring of 1930 with the Airship* Graf Zeppelin*

In the spring of 1930 there will be undertaken a systematically extended scientific exploration of the Arctic Regions by means of the airship "Graf Zeppelin," under the leadership of the doyen of Polar exploration work Professor Dr. Fridtjof Nansen, with the participation of a large staff of international scientists. The International Society for the Exploration of the Arctic Regions by aircraft (the Aeroarctic) includes groups of members in twenty different countries, U.S.A. among the number, comprising leading scientists in the domain of such sciences as are interested in the exploration of the earth. The Chairman of the American group of the Aeroarctic is Professor Louis A. Bauer, Director of the Department of Terrestrial Magnetism, Carnegie Institute. The American group is participating in this international exploration journey with many scientists. A representative of the American Press will go in the airship as correspondent. The visit of Professor Dr. Fridtjof Nansen in May 1928 to Washington and New York has greatly contributed thereto that the plans of the Aeroarctic have met with an active material assistance on the part of the American Government. Preparations for the expedition are now being urgently carried out.

The exploration work is based on the following plan: By the beginning of April 1930 the airship "Graf Zeppelin" will take off at Friedrichshafen for an approximately three-weeks' exploration journey in the Arctic Regions. She will start for Leningrad where the USSR Government will have by that time erected a mooring mast and where the

---

*Reprinted from IAC, RG 85, NAC.

expedition will complete its final preparations. Among other objects about forty polar dogs will board the airship at Leningrad. The flight will then take its course over Murmansk to Kaiser-Franz-Josef Land. Such parts of Kaiser-Franz-Josef Land over which the airship will fly will be subject to aerogeodetical measurements by means of stereographic photography. From there the flight of the airship will be continued near the Northern coast of Greenland, where the chief task of the expedition will begin. It is proposed to establish the exact limit between the deep sea and shallow sea, namely, the so-called shelfridge, with the help of soundings by echo apparatus. For this purpose a special apparatus is now being constructed, which will hang down from the airship at the end of a 100 m rope. As soon as the airship will meet with loads on its flight—and according to Sir Hubert Wilkins' report such are to be found at about every twenty miles—she will drop the apparatus into the water and sound the depths according to the usual methods of sounding by echo apparatus. In this way a great number of soundings may be carried out along the Canadian shelfridge. It will be possible to establish how far the as yet unknown shelfridge penetrates into the region between Alaska and the North Pole, and whether there is any possibility of hitherto undiscovered land to be found there. The airship will not follow a definitely outlined course, she will follow, during the soundings, the course which corresponds with the line of the shelfridge. After the expedition will have thoroughly sounded the Canadian shelfridge the airship will fly over Point Barrow to Nome. A mooring mast will also be erected at Nome by the American Government together with a storehouse for the exploitation material (hydrogen blue gas, benzine, etc.). The airship will remain at Nome for about five days and refill her stores of material. The crew will also have an opportunity of providing itself with all that might be necessary for the further journey. From there the airship will start on her flight. This will serve for an oceanographic and geographic exploration of the unknown parts of the Arctic between Point Barrow and the Pole. The airship will steer towards a point lying 85° northern latitude and 80° western longitude. The course will then lead towards the presumed Andreyev Land. On the first part of the journey up to about 83° n. lat. and 140° east long. Oceanographic series soundings will be carried out to a depth of about 1500 m. The airship will alight for this purpose on an open lead and anchor on its edge. She will remain so for a certain number of hours in order to enable the oceanographists to accomplish series measurements for determining the temperature and salt contents of the water at the various depths. This measurement is in Professor Nansen's opinion of particularly scientific importance because it will be sufficient to give the necessary information as to what connection exists between the water masses of this part of the Arctic and the water masses between the North Pole-Spitsbergen-Kaiser Franz-Josef-Land. It will be possible to draw very important conclusions concerning the currents in the enormous Polar basin. This knowledge will be of the utmost significance for the solution of a whole number of other questions. The airship will thereupon explore the regions between the Neo-Siberian Islands and Wrangel-Island. Should now land be discovered there, its limits will be determined and it will also be measured aerogeodetically. The airship will then fly back to Nome, where she will again remain for about five days to be put in order for the return flight to Leningrad. During this return flight the main task will be the measurement of the Asiatic shelfridge. Over and above this the extent of the Nikolas II Land which has hitherto only been partially explored on its eastern coast, will be definitely established and aerogeodetically measured. During the whole course of the expedition flight in the Arctic photographs of the ice will be taken at certain intervals. The nature of the ice allows important conclusions to be drawn in regard to the presence of currents, or the proximity of land, or the influence of tides, etc. To this end and for the purposes of the aerogeodetic land measurements the expedition will be provided with 16 km of film material. Besides this other scientific exploration work will be carried out, regarding terrestrial magnetism, aeroelectricity, biology and aerology. For such explorations also special apparati are being constructed. The Carnegie Institute in Washington has kindly placed its apparatus for terrestrial magnetism explorations at the disposal of our Society. The apparatus has already arrived at Friedrichshafen and will be erected in the airship "Graf Zeppelin" for preliminary testing. All the other scientific instruments and apparati will also be tested and improved during the trial flights of the "Graf Zeppelin." Lastly the airship will be provided with a complete set of Polar equipment, as naturally an accident might happen to even such a large and capable airship as she is. She will carry with her sufficient provisions to last for over one hundred days, polar kit, sledges, tents, dogs, several wireless short wave apparati, boats, rifles, munitions, etc. In accordance with a definitely established plan a wireless communication with all the wireless stations surrounding the Arctic regions will be organized.

During the whole flight which will lead over more than 10,000 km of unknown regions the airship will be in constant communication with the wireless stations of Spitsbergen, Point Barrow and Leningrad.

It will be possible by means of a short-wave apparatus to send wireless telegraph pictures of any important geographical discovery made during the expedition.

Such are the general features of the exploration plan that our Society is preparing to carry out. It is only the first step towards the achievement of the aims, for the propagation and attainment of which our international Society has been formed.

These airship journeys during 1930 will first of all serve to prove whether the airship is a practical means for arctic transport and communication. It has not been possible as yet to solve the numerous scientific problems of the Arctic with the hitherto known means of penetrating into the Arctic Regions, such as sea-ships, dog-sledges. It will certainly not be possible even with the airship. We hope, however, that we shall attain our object, which is a permanent systematicyears-long exploration of the Arctic, insofar, that we shall be able to create a network of permanent observation stations in the Arctic regions. These wireless observation stations will consist of five or six men, with wireless equipment, sufficient provisions for at least two years, and a good tent equipment which will enable them to carry on their scientific work even in winter. The personnel and materials for these stations will be brought to the necessary places by airships.

We hope that the international scientific world will man and equip these stations in a spirit of noble competition. Each of these stations will consist of men of one nationality. The scientists working at these stations will be relieved by others once a year by means of airships or if possible by airplanes.

A precise knowledge of the at present but scarcely known conditions in the Arctic, a daily observation of all occurrences by means of wireless, will be of the greatest advantage for weather forecasts, and for all magnetic, electric, oceanographical, biological and aerological conditions in the inhabited latitudes of the Northern hemisphere. Agriculture and all communications by land, by water or by air, will benefit greatly by such systematic permanent observation work in the Arctic regions.

(Captain Walter Bruns
Secretary General of the *Aeroarctic*)

Essay on Sources

Books on arctic exploration describing expeditions through the centuries provide the reader and researcher with a necessary overview of explorers, their goals, adventures, and accomplishments. Fortunately, there are numerous volumes covering this subject, some written by explorers, some by geographers, scientists, journalists, and historians. Only those materials dealing with the subject and time period covered in this study will be discussed.

The best written and most thoroughly researched overviews of arctic exploration are Lawrence P. Kirwan's *A History of Polar Exploration* (1960) and Jeannette Mirsky's *To the Arctic* (1970 edition). Each allows the reader to savor the excitement of arctic exploration, but the adventures are described against the broader spectrum of geographical discovery and the general history of the countries engaged in exploration. J. E. Nourse's *American Exploration in the Ice Zones* (1884) is a detailed account of American exploration in the nineteenth century. The episodes are compiled from government records and personal narratives and include discussion of the value of arctic exploration to the United States. John Caswell's *Arctic Frontiers* (1956) also concentrates on the nineteenth century. Based on narratives, solid use of government documents and records of scientific institutions, this work examines American arctic exploration in terms of contributions to scientific knowledge. Adventure is underplayed; the emphasis is on accomplishment. Leslie Neatby's *Conquest of the Last Frontier* (1960) is also an overview of nineteenth century arctic exploration, although a good section is devoted to Robert E. Peary's expeditions through 1909. This finely detailed account contains intriguing tidbits of information regarding personal characteristics of the explorers, especially Greely, Nansen, and Peary. Unfortunately, the work is not annotated. Lawrence M. Gould, in *The Polar Regions in Relation to Human Affairs* (1958), briefly discussed the impact of arctic and antarctic exploration on the general course of scientific inquiry. This is a small book of essays that directs the reader to an investigation of polar areas as a means of understanding natural history. Herman R. Friis, former director of the Polar and Scientific Archives at the National Archives, edited a valuable book, *U.S. Polar Exploration* (1970), containing information on the study of arctic and antarctic exploration based on materials in the National Archives. This partial list of general sources is most valuable in beginning any in-depth study of the Arctic.

After becoming familiar with arctic exploration, the reader can peruse individual narratives and biographies for a more thorough understanding of particular expeditions. Personal narratives of nineteenth century exploration can be found in most libraries. Books by Elisha Kent Kane, Isaac Israel Hayes, and Frederick Schwatka, the story of the *Jeannette,* Hall's narratives, and Greely's memoirs are readily available. For twentieth century accounts, Robert E. Peary's numerous volumes describing his expeditions vividly illustrate the transition period between nineteenth century heroic expeditions and twentieth century quests for scientific information. Peary's volumes, especially *Nearest the Pole* and *The North Pole* (1909), were published to raise funds to continue his expeditions and they attempt to justify each expedition in terms of scientific, geographic, and national accomplishments as well as provide the reader with exciting adventure stories. Matthew A. Henson, Peary's Black assistant, has generally been overlooked or inaccurately described as a servant. Peary depended on Henson's ability to lead the Eskimos and his skill in navigating across vast stretches of northern ice. Henson's autobiography, *A Negro Explorer at the North Pole* (1912), corroborates Peary's insistence that he did cross the North Pole area. Donald B. MacMillan's *How Peary Reached the Pole* (1934), *Four Years in the White North* (1918), and *Etah and Beyond* (1927) concentrate on the activities and discoveries made on each expedition. Descriptions are concise and the reader is struck by the absence of histrionics. These are literate tales of travel, filled with details concerning the natural environment. Peter Freuchen's *Arctic Adventure* (1935) describes his life in Greenland as an explorer who accompanied Knud Rasmussen on numerous forays across arctic territory. Freuchen describes encounters with Peary, MacMillan, and other explorers. There is a personal quality to this book that makes it stand out among the many narratives written about the period 1900 to 1930. Peary and MacMillan wrote with a fine literary style; Freuchen surpassed both. Knud Rasmussen's *Across Arctic America* (1927) is a detailed account of his study of arctic Eskimos from Greenland across arctic North America to Siberia. The study, like those of Freuchen and MacMillan, deals with descriptions of people and places and avoids the dramatic adventure tales so prevalent in earlier narratives. Vilhjalmur Stefansson's numerous books are a mixture of adventure, justification for his theories regarding arctic development, and descriptions of his accomplishments. In particular, *The Friendly Arctic* (1922), *The Adventure of Wrangel Island* (1928), and his autobiography, *Discovery* (1964), provide an understanding of his expeditions and his philosophy regarding utilization of arctic territory. Roald Amundsen's *My Life as an Explorer* (1927) and Lincoln Ellsworth's *Search* (1932) describe each author's compulsive attraction to exploration. Amundsen and Ellsworth's *Our Polar Flight* (1925), Richard E. Byrd's *Skyward* (1928), and George Hubert Wilkins' *Flying the Arctic* (1928) describe the first successful use of aircraft for arctic exploration. The books contain valuable information on aircraft performance, navigation, association with the aviation industry, and speculation on future development of arctic airways for commercial and military purposes. William S. Carlson's *Lifelines Through the Arctic* (1962) and Bernt Balchen's *Come North With Me* (1958) began with the 1920s and carry the story of air exploration and development of arctic air bases through World War II. These narratives form the core for an examination of changes in arctic exploration from ship and sledge to the use of aircraft.

A more in-depth study of American explorers and their expeditions is possible by examining private papers collected at various libraries and archives. The Robert E. Peary and Lincoln Ellsworth papers are at the Polar and Scientific Archives (National Archives) in Washington, D.C. The Peary collection is extensive and contains numerous items on his association with the international community of explorers as well as a section devoted to his interest in aviation. The Ellsworth collection is small, but the items deal primarily with his relationship with Amundsen and help in understanding international aspects of arctic exploration. The MacMillan and Bartlett collections are at Bowdoin College (Brunswick,

Maine). The MacMillan papers are the more extensive and include published as well as unpublished material. Numerous diaries and record books are part of the collection and enable the researcher to reconstruct MacMillan's major expeditions.

Archival material on Stefansson and Amundsen is available at the Public Archives of Canada (Ottawa) and is discussed more fully in relation to Canadian materials. The Explorers Club Library (New York City) contains a solid collection of narratives but access is limited, and the collection of private papers is not available to researchers. The library at the Council on Foreign Relations (New York City) contains numerous articles on the importance of the Arctic in international affairs. The library and archives at the American Museum of Natural History (New York City) has an extensive collection of expedition reports, especially on MacMillan's Crocker Land trip, and a small collection of private papers and correspondence with explorers. The Library of Congress (Washington, D.C.) houses the Adolphus W. Greely and William Mitchell papers as well as a collection of press clippings on explorers associated with the Navy. The Mitchell collection contains some interesting unpublished material on the Arctic as an American strategic frontier. The Carl Ben Eielson (Wilkins' associate) papers are located in the Bismarck, North Dakota, Historical Society. Copies of this small collection are available to researchers. The papers contain Eielson's diary of the 1928 flight from Point Barrow to Spitsbergen. The private papers of the three presidents involved with arctic exploration, Theodore Roosevelt, William Howard Taft, and Calvin Coolidge, are available on microfilm at the University of Cincinnati Library. References to specific explorers and expeditions are in each collection. The Taft and Coolidge papers contain a few items dealing specifically with the government's promotion of explorers and their expeditions.

The association of the American government with arctic exploration can be traced through various government documents and papers. State Department records (RG59) are arranged with a special serial number designation (800) for records relating to the Arctic from 1910 through the 1930s. The papers contain formal correspondence, reports, personal letters, memos, and hearings involving various expeditions. This material is arranged by region and requires careful cross-checking using names of explorers, regions explored, and territory in order to put together a logical progression of events. Additional official correspondence has been published in the *Foreign Relations of the United States* in volumes covering 1900 to 1930. Papers describing the navy's association with arctic exploration can be found in the Records of the U.S. Navy (RG80), particularly in two collections: Office of the Chief of Naval Operations and Planning Division, File SC111-99, and General Correspondence of the Navy Department File 29455 (on microfilm). Additional information can be found in the U.S. Navy Annual reports 1900-1930. The U.S. Naval War College in Newport, Rhode Island, has published a valuable report describing military concern about jurisdiction over polar areas. Some material on Richard Byrd can be found in the Library of Congress and at the Polar and Scientific Archives but no collection of papers has been put together. The Byrd Papers are at the Ohio State University Polar Research Center but, at the time of writing this study, are not open to researchers. Records of the army air force and its participation in arctic exploration can be found in RG18 at the National Archives. The amount of material is small but pertinent.

Congressional reports, documents, and records of appropriations round out the record of government participation in arctic exploration and can be found indexed in the *U.S. Serial Set, Congressional Globe*, and *Congressional Record*. The collection of *U.S. Treaties, Conventions, International Acts, Protocols and Agreements* from 1910-1930 contain copies of treaties dealing with arctic territory.

Additional information on U.S. government involvement in arctic affairs can be found in publications such as *A Hot Spot of Free World Defense* (1958) and *Continental Air Defense* (1955) by the Department of Defense. American foreign policy regarding the Arctic is discussed by Blair Bolles in "Arctic Diplomacy" in *Foreign Policy Reports* (1948) and Brian Smith in "United States Arctic Policy" in *Oceans Policy Study* (1978). An overview of polar research is available in a report published in 1970 by the National Research Council of the National Academy of Science and a field staff study of the polar area published in 1960 by American University. A discussion of aviation and the Arctic can be found in Grover Loening's *Our Wings Grow Faster* (1935), William Mitchell's *Winged Defense* (1925), H. H. Arnold's *Global Mission* (1949), and the U.S. Air Force Officers Training Corps' *Military Aspects of World Political Geography* (1954).

Unpublished papers of Canadians involved in arctic affairs can be found in the National Archives of Canada (Ottawa). The Loring Christie papers (MG30E44) are the most extensive and contain correspondence with the American government and numerous European and American explorers. The Rudolph M. Anderson papers (MG30B4) contain correspondence and reports relating to Stefansson and the Canadian Arctic Expedition (CAE). Additional material on Stefansson and the CAE can be found in a special collection filed under the John D. Craig papers (MG30B57). Robert A. Logan's report concerning development of the Canadian north for air bases can be found in MG30B68. Records of the Canadian Air Board (RG24), Department of External Affairs (RG25), Department of Marine (RG42), and the Department of National Defense (RG24) contain information illustrating the broad scope of Canadian interest in arctic territory. The most complete collection is that of the Northern Affairs Program (RG85) which contains a considerable amount of correspondence between the Canadian and American governments. Parliamentary debates in the House of Commons and Senate provide additional information on support for and conflict over arctic exploration.

Extensive coverage of arctic exploration appeared in the *New York Times*, *The Times*, London, and in periodicals such as *The Literary Digest*, *Nation*, *Science*, and *Scientific American*. *Foreign Affairs* and *U.S. Naval Institute Proceedings* published essays by government and naval personnel on the importance of arctic development. The *National Geographic Magazine* and the *Bulletin of the American Museum of Natural History* published full reports of expeditions sponsored by each institution. For additional reports of geographic studies, the *American Geographical Society Bulletin*, *Geographic Journal*, *Geographic Review*, *Journal of Geography*, and the *Annual Report of the Smithsonian Institute* regularly reported findings of twentieth century expeditions.

Biographies of explorers and secondary accounts of specific expeditions vary in merit. John E. Weem's study of Peary (1967) based on personal papers, Richard Diubaldo's examination of Stefansson and Canadian politics (1978), William R. Hunt's more balanced study of Stefansson, Edwin Hoyt's biography of Richard E. Byrd (1968), and Alfred Hurley's study of William Mitchell are most successful in putting the men and their accomplishments in a perspective of national and international activity. Additional biographies, especially those written before 1960, tend to concentrate on describing explorers as national heroes and are similar to the adventure tales produced by the explorers themselves.

Canadian arctic policy is discussed in Fred Alexander's *Canadians and Foreign Policy* (1960), Robert C. Brown's *Canada's National Policy 1883-1900* (1964), *The Arctic in Question* (1976) edited by Edgar J. Dossman, Richard Finnie's *Canada Moves North* (1944), *The Arctic Frontier* (1970) edited by R. MacDonald, R. A. J. Phillips' *Canada's North* (1967), and Morris Zaslow's *The Opening of the Canadian North 1870-1914* (1971). American policy regarding Alaska is examined in Thomas A. Bailey's *A Diplomatic History of the American People* (1969); the Central Intelligence Agency's *Polar Regions Atlas* (1978), John Dyson's *The Hot Arctic* (1979), and John Gaddis' *Russia, the Soviet Union, and the United States* (1978) regarding American interest in Siberia; Lawrence Gelfand's *The Inquiry* (1963) on the United States and Spitsbergen; and William H. Goetzman's *Exploration and Empire* (1967) on nineteenth century military expedition; Lt. Com. C. V. Glines' *Polar Aviation* (1964), Dudley W. Knox's *A History of the United States Navy* (1936), and Donald W. Mitchell's *A History of the Modern American Navy from 1883 Through Pearl Harbor* (1946) document the role of the American military in arctic exploration and development.

Recent studies of arctic exploration and development have been written primarily by Canadian, English, Scandinavian, and Russian authors. A few articles have appeared written by American military personnel, geographers, scientists, and lawyers, but few American historians have tackled the problem of putting American arctic exploration into an historical context. Paul A. Carter's *Little America* (1979) is one of the few studies authored recently by an American historian which deals with Richard Byrd's antarctic expeditions.

A full list of material used in preparation of this study follows.

Bibliography

Archival Materials

Air Board. Record Group 24. National Archives of Canada, Ottawa.

Anderson, Rudolph M. Private papers. MG 30 B40. National Archives of Canada, Ottawa.

Bartlett, Robert A. Private papers. Bowdoin College Library, Brunswick, Maine.

Christie, Loring. Private papers. MG30 E44. National Archives of Canada, Ottawa.

Coolidge, Calvin. Private papers. University of Cincinnati Microfilm Collection, Cincinnati, Ohio.

Craig, John D. Private papers. MG30 B57. National Archives of Canada, Ottawa.

Crocker Land Expedition. Private papers. American Museum of Natural History, New York City.

Department of External Affairs. Record Group 25. National Archives of Canada, Ottawa.

Department of the Interior. Record Group 85. National Archives of Canada, Ottawa.

Department of Marine. Record Group 42. National Archives of Canada, Ottawa.

Department of National Defense. Record Group 24. National Archives of Canada, Ottawa.

Eielson, Carl Ben. Private papers. Historical Society, Bismarck, North Dakota.

Ellsworth, Lincoln. Private papers. Center for Polar and Scientific Archives, National Archives, Washington, D.C.

Greely, Adolphus W. Private papers. Library of Congress, Washington, D.C.

International Arctic Congress. Record Group 85. National Archives of Canada, Ottawa.

Logan, Robert A. Private papers. MG30 B 68. National Archives of Canada, Ottawa.

MacMillan, Donald B. Private papers. Bowdoin College Library, Brunswick, Maine.

Mitchell, William. Private papers. Library of Congress, Washington, D.C.

National Archives, State Department Records. Record Group 59. Washington, D.C.

National Archives, U.S. Army Air Force. Record Group 18. Washington, D.C.

National Archives, U.S. Navy. Record Group 80. Washington, D.C.

Naval Historical Center Archives. General Board #438, Series #1284, Washington, D.C.

Northern Affairs Program. Record Group 85. National Archives of Canada, Ottawa.

Northwest Territories Council Minutes M-11. National Archives of Canada, Ottawa.

Peary, Robert E. Private papers. Center for Polar and Scientific Archives, National Archives, Washington, D.C.

Roosevelt, Theodore. Private papers. University of Cincinnati Microfilm Collection, Cincinnati, Ohio, 1873.

Taft, William Howard. Private papers. University of Cincinnati Micro-film Collection, Cincinnati, Ohio.

Government Publications

Canada. Department of Mines and Technical Surveys. *The Canadian Arctic*. Ottawa, 1951.

Canada. Parliament. *House of Commons Debates* 1900-30.

―――. *Senate Debate* 1900-30.

Committee on Naval Affairs, *Congressional Hearings*, March 4, 1910.

Congressional Globe (1850-56). Washington, D.C.: Government Print-ing Office.

Department of Defense. *Continental Air Defense*. Washington, D.C.: Government Printing Office, 1955.

―――. *A Hot Spot of Free World Defense*. Washington, D.C.: Govern-ment Printing Office, 1958.

Foreign Relations of the United States 1900-1930. Washington, D.C.: Government Printing Office.

Moore, Hon. Joseph Hampton. *Peary's Discovery of the North Pole*. House of Representatives, March 22, 1910.

National Security Council. *National Security Division Memorandum*, #144, December 22, 1971.

Office of U.S. Naval Intelligence. *The U.S. Navy in Peace Time*. Washington, D.C.: Government Printing Office, 1931.

Report of the Canadian American Expedition 1913-18. Ottawa, 1923.

Schrader, F. C. *Recent Work of the U.S. Geological Survey in Alaska*. Washington, D.C.: Government Printing Office, 1902.

U.S. Congress. *Congressional Record* 1800-1930, Washington, D.C.

―――. House of Representatives. Report #453. 46th Cong., 2nd sess., March 9, 1880.

―――. House Executive Document #56. 48th Cong., 1st sess., January 17, 1884.

————. House Resolution #149. Hearings before the Committee on Naval Affairs. 68th Cong., 1st sess., 1924.

————. House Document #133. Frank Kellogg, "International Society for the Exploration of the Arctic by Means of Airship." 70th Cong., 1st sess., May 1927.

————. House Document #133, "Exploring Arctic Regions by Airship," 70th Cong., 1st sess., January 4, 1928.

————. House Report #2700. 71st Cong., 3rd sess., February 9, 1931.

————. House Document #282. 72nd Cong., 1st sess., 1931.

————. House Committee on Foreign Affairs, Second Polar Year Program Hearings, 1932.

————. Senate. Senate Executive Document #8. 31st Cong., 1st sess., January 4, 1850.

————. Senate Report #94. Appropriations for the Lady Franklin Bay Station. 45th Cong., 2nd sess., February 13, 1878.

————. Senate Executive Document #111. 48th Cong., 1st sess., March 1884.

————. Senate Executive Document #132. 48th Cong., 1st sess., March 17, 1884.

————. Senate Document #424. 68th Cong., 1st sess., December 6, 1923.

————. Senate Document #16. 72nd Cong., 1st sess., December 10, 1931.

————. Senate Report #162. 72nd Cong., 1st sess., 1931.

U.S. Navy Annual Report, 1900-32. Washington, D.C.: Government Printing Office.

U.S. Navy War College. Jurisdiction Over Polar Areas. Newport, RI, October 29, 1937.

U.S. Treaties, Conventions, International Acts, Protocols, and Agreements 1910-1913. Washington, D.C.: Government Printing Office.

Books

Alexander, Fred. *Canadians and Foreign Policy*. Toronto: University of Toronto Press, 1960.

Allen, Everett S. *Arctic Odyssey: The Life of Rear Admiral Donald B. MacMillan*. New York: Dodd, Mead & Co., 1962.

Amedo, Luigi. *On the Polar Star in the Arctic Sea*. New York: Dodd, Mead & Co., 1903.

Amundsen, Roald. *My Life as an Explorer*. New York: Doubleday, Page & Co., 1927.

Amundsen, Roald, and Lincoln Ellsworth. *Our Polar Flight*. New York: Dodd, Mead & Co., 1925.

Andrews, Ben E. *The United States in Our Time*. New York: Charles Scribner's Sons, 1903.

Annals of the International Geophysical Year. London: Pergamon Press, 1959.

Armstrong, Terence, George Rogers, and Graham Rowley. *The Circumpolar North*. London: Methuen & Co., 1978.

Arnold, Henry H. *Global Mission*. New York: Harper & Bros., 1949.

Bailey, Thomas A. *A Diplomatic History of the American People*. New York: Merideth Corp., 1969.

Baker, J. N. L. *A History of Geographical Discoveries and Exploration*. Boston: Houghton Mifflin, Co., 1931.

Balchen, Bernt. *Come North With Me*. New York: E. P. Hutton & Co., 1958.

Beard, Charles A. *The Idea of National Interests*. New York: The MacMillan Co., 1934.

Berton, Pierre. *Arctic Grail*. New York, 1988.

Bertrand, Kenneth J. *United States Exploration in Antarctica*. New York: American Geographical Society, 1971.

Billington, Ray A. *The Far Western Frontier 1830-1860*. New York: Harper & Bros., 1956.

Bridgewater, William and Seymour Kurtz, eds. *The Columbia Encyclopedia*. New York: Columbia University Press, 1963.

Brown, Robert Craig. *Canada's National Policy 1883-1900: A Study in Canadian-American Relations*. Princeton, NJ: Princeton University Press, 1964.

Byrd, Richard E. *Skyward*. New York: G. P. Putnam's Sons, 1928.

Carlson, William S. *Lifelines Through the Arctic*. New York: Duell, Sloan & Pearce, 1962.

Carter, Paul A. *Little America: Town at the End of the World*. New York: Columbia University Press, 1979.

Caswell, John E. *Arctic Frontiers*. Norman, Okla.: University of Oklahoma Press, 1956.

Central Intelligence Agency. *Polar Regions Atlas*. Washington, D.C.: Government Printing Office, 1978.

Corner, George W. *Doctor Kane of the Arctic Seas*. Philadelphia: Temple University Press, 1972.

Croft, Andrew. *Epics of Twentieth Century Polar Exploration*. London: Adam & Charles Black, 1939.

Curti, Merle. *The Growth of American Thought*. New York: Harper & Row, 1964.

Daley, Robert. *Juan Trippe and His Pan American Empire*. New York: Random House, 1980.

Diubaldo, Richard J. *Stefansson and the Canadian Arctic*. Montreal: McGill-Green's University Press, 1978.

Dossman, Edgar J., ed. *The Arctic in Question*. Toronto: Oxford University Press, 1976.

Downs, Robert B. *In Search of New Horizons: Epic Tales of Travel and Exploration*. Chicago: American Library Association, 1978.

Dupree, A. Hunter. *Science in the Federal Government*. Cambridge, MA: Harvard University Press, 1957.

Dyson, John. *The Hot Arctic*. Boston: Little Brown & Co., 1979.

Ellsworth, Lincoln. *Search.* New York: Brewer, Warren & Putnam, 1932.

Finnie, Richard. *Canada Moves North.* New York: The MacMillan Co., 1944.

Fisher, Raymond H. *Bering's Voyages: Whither and Why.* Seattle: University of Washington Press, 1977.

Freuchen, Peter. *Arctic Adventure.* New York: Farrar & Rhinehart, 1935.

Friis, Herman R., and G. Bale Sehlby, eds. *U.S. Polar Exploration.* Athens: Ohio University Press, 1970.

Gaddis, John. *Russia, The Soviet Union and the United States.* New York: Wiley Co., 1978.

Gates, Thomas S., Jr. *The U.S. Navy and Its Influence Upon History.* New York: Newcomb Society in America, 1958.

Gelfand, Lawrence E. *The Inquiry.* New Haven, Conn.: Yale University Press, 1963.

Glines, Lt. Col. C. V. *Polar Aviation.* New York: Franklin Watts, Inc., 1964.

Goetzman, William H. *Exploration and Empire.* New York: Alfred A. Knopf, 1967.

Gould Lawrence M. *The Polar Regions in Relation to Human Affairs.* New York: American Geographical Society, 1958.

Grant, Shelag. *Sovereignty or Security? Government Policy in the Canadian North 1936-1950.* Vancourver: University of British Columbia Press, 1988.

Greely, Adolphus W. *Handbook of Arctic Discoveries.* Cambridge, Mass.: John Wilson & Son, 1895.

———. *Three Years of Arctic Service.* New York: Charles Scribner's Sons, 1886.

Grierson, John. *Challenge to the Poles: Highlights of Arctic and Antarctic Aviation.* London: G. T. Foulis, 1964.

Hanessian, John Jr. *Polar Area Series*. New York: American Universities Field Staff Report Series, 1960.

Heilprin, Angelo. *The Arctic Problem*. Philadelphia: 1893.

Henson, Matthew A. *A Negro Explorer at the North Pole*. New York: Frederick A. Stokes, 1912.

Holmes, Prescott. *The Story of Exploration and Adventure in Frozen Seas*. Philadelphia: Henry Altemus, 1896.

Hoyt, Edwin P. *The Last Frontier: The Adventures of Admiral Byrd*. New York: The John Day Co., 1968.

Hunt, William R. *Arctic Passage*. New York: Charles A. Scribner's Sons, 1975.

———. *Stef: A Biography of Vilhjalmur Stefansson*. Victoria: University of British Columbia Press, 1986.

Huntford, Roland. *Scott and Amundsen*. New York: G. P. Putnam's Sons, 1980.

Hurley, Alfred F. *Billy Mitchell: Crusader for Air Power*. Bloomington: Indiana University Press, 1964 (1975 edition).

Joerg, W. L. G. *Problems of Polar Research*. New York: American Geographical Society, 1928.

Josephson, Matthew. *Empire of the Air: Juan Trippe and the Struggle for World Airways*. New York: Arno Press, 1972.

Ketie, John Scott, and O. J. Howarth. *History of Geography*. London: G. P. Putnam's Sons, 1913.

Kimble, George, and Dorothy Good. *Geography of the Northlands*. New York: American Geographical Society, 1955.

Kirwan, Lawrence P. *A History of Polar Exploration*. New York: W. W. Norton & Co., 1960.

Knox, Dudley W. *A History of the United States Navy*. New York: Van Rees Press, 1936.

Lawson, Samuel E. *Stanford's Compendium of Geography and Travel: North America, Canada and Newfoundland*. London: Edward Stanford, 1897.

Leigh, William Francis. *Matthew Fontaine Maury: Scientist of the Sea*. New Brunswick, NJ: Rutgers University Press, 1963.

Leopold, Richard E. *The Growth of American Foreign Policy*. New York: Alfred A. Knopf, 1962.

Lindbergh, Anne Morrow. *North to the Orient*. New York: Harcourt Brace & Co., 1935.

Loening, Grover. *Our Wings Grow Faster*. New York: Doubleday, Doran & Co., 1935.

Loomis, Chauncy C. *Weird and Tragic Shores: The Story of Charles Francis Hall, Explorer*. New York: Alfred A. Knopf, 1971.

MacDonald, R., ed. *The Arctic Frontier*. Toronto: University of Toronto Press, 1970.

MacMillan, Donald B. *Etah and Beyond*. Boston: Houghton Mifflin Co., 1927.

———. *Four Years in the White North*. New York: Harper & Bros., 1918.

———. *How Peary Reached the Pole*. Boston: Houghton Mifflin Co., 1934.

MacMillan, Miriam. *Green Seas White Ice*. New York, 1948.

Marks, Frederick W., III. *Velvet on Iron: The Diplomacy of Theodore Roosevelt*. Lincoln: University of Nebraska Press, 1979.

Mathiasen, Therkel. *Report of the Fifth Thule Expedition*. Copenhagen, 1945.

McNeil, William H. *The Rise of the West*. Chicago: University of Chicago Press, 1963.

Mirsky, Jeannette. *Elisha Kent Kane and the Seafaring Frontier*. Boston: Little Brown & Co., 1954.

———. *To the Arctic*. Chicago: University of Chicago, Press, 1970.

Mitchell, Donald W. *A History of the Modern American Navy from 1883 Through Pearl Harbor*. New York: Alfred A. Knopf, 1946.

Mitchell, William. *Winged Defense*. New York: G. P. Putnam's Sons, 1925.

————. *General Greely: The Story of a Great American.* New York: G. P. Putnam's Sons, 1936.

Morrison, William R. *Showing the Flag: The Mounted Police and Canadian Sovereignty in the North 1894-1925.* Vancouver: University of Brtish Columbia, 1985.

Morton, W. L. *The Canadian Identity.* Madison: University of Wisconsin Press, 1972.

Murphy, Charles J. V. *Struggle; The Life of Commander Byrd.* New York: Frederick A. Stokes Co., 1928.

National Research Council: Committee on Polar Research. *Polar Research: A Survey.* Washington, D.C.: National Academy of Sciences, 1970.

Neatby, Leslie H. *Conquest of the Last Frontier.* New York: H. Wolff, 1960.

Nordenskjold, Otto, and Ludwig Mecking. *The Geography of the Polar Regions.* New York: American Geographical Society, 1928.

Nourse, J. E. *American Exploration in the Ice Zones.* Boston: B. B. Russell, 1884.

Osherenko, Gail and Young, Oran R. *The Age of the Arctic: Hot Conflicts and Cold Realities.* Cambridge, 1989.

Patterson, Thomas. *American Foreign Policy.* 1983.

Payer, Julius. *New Lands Within the Arctic Circle.* London: MacMillan Co., 1876.

Peary, Robert E. *The North Pole.* New York: Frederick A. Strokes, Co., 1909.

Penlington, Norman. *The Alaskan Boundary Dispute: A Critical Appraisal.* New York: McGraw Hill, 1972.

Phillips, R. A. J. *Canada's North.* Toronto: MacMillan of Canada, 1967

Rasmussen, Kund. *Across Arctic America: Narrative of the Fifth Thule Expedition.* New York: G.P. Putnam's Sons, 1927.

Reingold, Nathan. *Science in Nineteenth Century America.* New York: Hill & Wang, 1964.

Robertson, James Oliver. *American Myth American Reality.* New York: Hill & Wang, 1980.

Robeson, George M. *Hall's Polaris Expedition Report to the President of the United States,* 1873.

Robinson, Bradley. *Dark Companion.* New York: Robert M. McBride, Co., 1947.

Ronne, Finn. *Antarctica My Destiny.* New York: Hastings House, 1979.

Ross, Walter S. *The Last Hero: Charles A. Lindbergh.* New York: Harper & Row, 1968.

Sater, John E. *The Arctic Basin.* Washington, D.C.: Arctic Institute of North America, 1968.

Schley, Winfield S., and J. R. Soley. *The Rescue of Greely.* New York: Charles Scribner's Sons, 1885.

Schulzinger, Robert. *American Diplomacy in the Twentieth Century.* New York: Oxford University Press, 1984.

Shannon, David A. *Twentieth Century America: The Twenties.* Chicago: Rand McNally, 1974.

Sherwood, Morgan R. *Exploration of Alaska 1865-1900.* New Haven, Conn.: Yale University Press, 1965.

Signh, Elen C. *The Spitsbergen (Svalbard) Questions: United States Foreign Policy, 1907-1935.* New York: Columbia University Press, 1980.

Smedal, Gustav. *Acquisition of Sovereignty Over Polar Areas.* Oslo: I Kommisjon Has Jacob Dybwad, 1931.

Stefansson, Vilhjalmur. *Discovery.* New York: McGraw Hill, 1964.

———. *The Adventure of Wrangel Island.* New York: The MacMillan Co., 1925.

———. *The Friendly Arctic: The Story of Five Years in Polar Regions.* New York: The MacMillan Co., 1922.

———. *The Northward Course of Empire.* New York: The MacMillan Co., 1924.

Stefansson, Vilhjalmur, ed. *Arctic Encyclopedia*. Microfilm. Ann Arbor, Mich.: 1974.

Storey, Noah. *The Oxford Companion to Canadian History and Literature*. Toronto: Oxford University Press, 1967.

Sundman, Per Olaf. *The Flight of the Eagle*. New York: Pantheon Books, 1970.

Thomas, Lowell. *Sir Hubert Wilkins*. New York: McGraw Hill, 1961.

Thonger, Charles. *Canada's Alaskan Dismemberment*. Ontario: Charles Thonger, 1904.

Turner, Frederick Jackson.*The Frontier in American History*. New York: Holt Rinehart & Winston, 1962.

U.S. Air Force Officers Training Corps. *Military Aspects of World Political Geography*. Montgomery, Ala.: U.S. Air University, September 1954.

Van Deusen, Glyndon S. *William Henry Seward*. New York: Oxford University Press, 1967.

Victor, Paul Emile. *Man and the Conquest of the Poles*. London: Hamish Hamilton Ltd., 1964.

Wector, Dixon. *The Hero in America: A Chronicle of Hero Worship*. New York: Charles Scribner's Sons, 1941.

Weems, John Edward. *Peary: The Explorer and the Man*. Boston: Houghton Mifflin Co., 1967.

Westermeyer, William E. and Kurt M. Shushterich, eds. *United States Arctic Interests: The 1980s and 1990s*. New York: Springer-Verlag, 1984.

Who Was Who In American History—The Military. Chicago: Marquis' Who's Who, 1975.

Williams, Archibald. *Conquering the Air*. New York: Thomas Nelson & Sons, 1930.

Wilson, Derek. *The World Encompassed: Drake's Great Voyage*. New York: Harper & Row, 1977.

Wolfe, Tom. *The Right Stuff*. New York: Farrar, Strauss, Giroux, 1979.

Wilkins, George Hubert. *Flying the Arctic*. New York: G.P. Putnam's Sons, 1928.

Wright, John Kirtland. *Geography in the Making: The American Geographical Society 1851-1951*. New York: American Geographical Society, 1952.

Zaslow, Morris. *The Northward Expansion of Canada 1914-1967*. Toronto, 1988.

—————. *The Opening of the Canadian North 1870-1914*. Toronto: McClelland & Stewart Ltd., 1971.

Periodical Articles

"A Flying Explorer's Two Weeks Afoot the Arctic Ice," *Literary Digest* (May 28, 1927).

"A New Polar Expedition," *Scientific American* 86 (February 15, 1902).

"American Arctic Exploration in the Early Days," *Outlook* 130 (March 8, 1922).

"Amundsen's Heroic Backer," *Literary Digest* (August 8, 1925).

"Amundsen's Poleward Flight," *Review of Reviews* (August 25, 1925).

"Amundsen's Splendid Failure," *Literary Digest* (July 4, 1925).

"Analysis of the Commerce of the United States With Various Countries of the World," *The Journal of Geography* (September 1906).

"Arctic Exploration by Aircraft," *Scientific American* (March 1924).

"Arctic Explorations," *American Geographical Society Bulletin* 34 (1902).

"Arctic Flight of the Graf Zeppelin," *Science* 70 (December 27, 1929).

"Back from the Arctic," *Outlook* (October 1, 1924).

Baker, Ray Stannard. "Robert E. Peary and His Campaign for the Pole," *McClure* 18 (February 1902).

Baldwin, Evelyn B. "How I Hope to Reach the North Pole," *McClure* 17 (September 1901).

Bolles, Blair. "Arctic Diplomacy," *Foreign Policy Reports* 24, 5 (June 1, 1948).

"Canada's Arctic Claims" *Literary Digest* 85 (June 20, 1925).

"Crowding the North Pole," *Literary Digest* (May 22, 1926).

Danehower, Lt. John W. "The Polar Question," *U.S. Naval Institute Proceedings* 11: 11, 4 (1885).

Dickey, Philip S. "The Liberty Engine 1918-42," *Smithsonian Annals of Flight* 3 (1968).

Dinwoodie, D. H. "Arctic Controversy: The 1925 Byrd-MacMillan Expedition Example," *The Canadian Historical Review* (March 1972).

"Dissolution of the American Section," *Science* (September 29, 1933).

Diubaldo, Richard J. "Wrangling Over Wrangel Island," *The Canadian Historical Review* 48 (1967).

"Dixmude's Lesson to Shenandoah," *Literary Digest* (January 12, 1924).

Ellsworth, Lincoln, and Edward H. Smith. "Report of the Preliminary Results of the Aeroarctic Expedition with Graf Zeppelin, 1931," *Geographical Review* (January 1932).

Fiala, Anthony. "Fighting the Polar Ice," *Bookman* 24 (January 1907).

Finnie, Richard. "Farewell Voyages: Bernier and the Arctic," *Beaver* (Summer 1974).

Fleming, J. A. "The Proposed Second International Polar Year 1932-33," *Geographical Review* (January 1932).

Fleming, Mary A. "Russia and Siberia," *Bulletin of the American Bureau of Geography* 2, 1 (March 1901).

Fogelson, Nancy. "Greenland: Strategic Base on a Northern Defense Line," *The Journal of Military History* 53, 1 (January 1989).

———. "Robert E. Peary and America's Exploration in the Arctic 1886-1910," *Fram: The Journal of Polar Studies* 2 (1985).

———. "The Tip of the Iceberg: The United States and International Rivalry for the Arctic 1900-25," *Diplomatic History* 9, 2 (Spring 1985).

"From New York to Nome and Siberia by Air," *Literary Digest* 66 (September 11, 1920).

Gould, Lawrence M. "Strategy and Politics in the Polar Areas," *American Academy of Political Science* (January 1948).

Greely, Adolphus W. "Amundsen's Expedition and the Northwest Passage," *Century* 73 (February 1907).

———. U.S. Army, "Scientific Results of the Norwegian Polar Expedition 1893-96," *Popular Science Monthly* 57 (August 1900).

Green, Com. Fitzhugh. "Across the Pole by Planes," *U.S. Naval Institute Proceedings* (March 1924).

———. "Over the Top of the World," *Literary Digest* 135 (December 1923).

———. "The Navy and the North Pole," *U.S. Naval Institute Proceedings* (March 1924).

Henrikson, Alan K. "The Map as an 'Idea': The Role of Cartographic Imagery During the Second World War," *The American Cartographer* 2, 1 (1975).

Howgate, Henry W. "Polar Colonization: The Preliminary Arctic Expedition, 1877," *History: North Pole* 349 (1879).

———. "The North Pole: An Abstract of Arctic Legislation in the Congress of the United States," *History: North Pole* (1879).

Hoyton, Robert D. "Polar Problems and International Law," *American Journal of International Law* 52, 4 (October 1958).

Jacobsen, Carl G. "Soviet-American Policy: New Strategic Uncertainties," *Current History* 81, 477 (October 1982).

Johnson, V. Kenneth. "Canada's Title to the Arctic Islands," *Canadian Historical Review* 14 (1933).

Kumlien, Ludwig. "Natural History of Arctic America: The Howgate Polar Expedition 1877-78," *Smithsonian Institute Bulletin* 23 (1879).

Lairt, Agnes C. "The Sky—Way to the North," *The Independent* (June 11, 1921).

Lakhtine, L. "Rights Over the Arctic," *American Journal of International Law* (1930).

LeBourdais, D. M. "The Aerial Attack on the Arctic," *The Nation* 118 (1924).

———. "When America Looks North," *Outlook* 135 (November 1923).

"Lincoln Ellsworth at the North Pole," *Yale Review* (July 1927).

McGrath, R. T. "For the Conquest of the Pole," *Review of Reviews* 32 (1905).

Miller, David Hunter. "Political Rights in the Arctic," *Foreign Affairs* 4 (1925).

Nansen, Fridtjof. "On North Polar Problems," *Geographical Journal* (July-December 1907).

———. "To the North Pole by Airship," *Forum* 75 (1926).

New York Times 1900-32.

Nielson, J. Anker. "Our Hibernating Arctic," *Washington Post*, July 11, 1971, pp. 2-3.

"Our Most Important Neighbor," *Review of Reviews* 32 (1905).

"Over the Top by Air," *The Independent* (June 5, 1926).

"Peary's Latest Work in the Arctic" *McClure* 14 (January 1900).

Peary, Robert E. "My Plans for Reaching the Pole," *Harpers Weekly* 48 (July 9, 1904).

"Picking up MacMillan by Radio," *Literary Digest* (November 24, 1923).

Plischke, Elmer. "Trans-Arctic Aviation," *Economic Quarterly* (July 1943).

———. "Trans-Polar Aviation and Jurisdiction Over Arctic Airspace," *The American Political Science Review* 37 (December 1943).

"Polar Expedition of Joseph E. Bernier," *Current Literature* 32 (April 1902).

"Polar Perils Await the *Shenandoah*," *Current Opinion* (March 31, 1924).

Preuss, Lawrence. "The Dispute Between Denmark and Norway Over Sovereignty of East Greenland," *American Journal of International Law* 26 (1932).

"Radio in the Frozen North," *Scientific American* (December 1923).

Rose, Lisle A. "Recent Trends in U.S. Arctic Affairs," *Arctic* 35, 2 (June 1982).

"Seeking the North Pole," *Journal of Geography* 4 (1905).

"Shall We Have an Aerial Route by Way of the North Pole," *Literary Digest* (March 3, 1923).

Smith, Brian D. "United States Arctic Policy," (University of Virginia Center for Oceans Law and Policy) in *Oceans Policy Study* 1:1 (January 1978).

Smith, Gordon W. *Canada's Arctic Archipelago: 100 Years of Canadian Jurisdiction.* Pamphlet, Northern Affairs Program: Ottawa, 1980.

Smith, Philip S. "A Survey of Oil in Alaska," *Science* (February 19, 1926).

"Star Trip of the Star's Daughter," *Literary Digest* (December 29, 1923).

Stefansson, Vilhjalmur. "Arctic Air Routes to the Orient," *Forum* (December 1924).

———. "The Arctic as an Air Route of the Future," *National Geographic Magazine* (August 1922).

———. "U.S. in Relation to Greenland," *Arctic Encyclopedia* (1974) microfilm reel #27.

———. "U.S. Weather Bureau," *Arctic Encyclopedia* (1974) microfilm reel #10.

Stafford, Marie Peary. "Peary's Ideas About U.S. Rights in Greenland," *Arctic Encyclopedia*, 1974, Reel #27.

"Sverdrup's Arctic Work," *American Geographical Society Bulletin* 34 (1902).

Svarlien, Oscar. "The Legal Status of the Arctic," *Proceedings of the American Society of International Law* (April 1958).

Taagholt, Jorgen. "Greenland's Future Development: A Historical and Political Perspective," *Polar Record* 21, 130 (January 1982).

Taylor, C.J. "First International Polar Year," *Arctic* 34, 4 (December 1981).

"The Baldwin-Ziegler Polar Expedition," *Harpers Weekly* 45 (June 22, 1901).

"The Byrd Flight to the North Pole," *Aviation* (May 24, 1926).

"The Crocker Land Expedition," *American Geographic Society Bulletin* 45 (1913).

"The Discovery of the North Pole," *National Geographic Magazine* 21 (1910).

"The First Hop Over the Earth's Roof," *Literary Digest* 97 (May 5, 1928).

"The Frozen War," *Newsweek* (January 23, 1984).

"The Northwest Passage at Last Accomplished," *Journal of Geography* (January 1906).

"The Only Way to Reach the Pole," *McClure* (February 1900).

"The Race for the Pole," *Current Literature* (June 1901).

"The Submarine Polar Expedition," *Current Literature* (June 1901).

The Times (London) 1900-32.

"The Tragic Crusoes of Wrangel Island," *Literary Digest* 79 (December 8, 1923).

"The Ziegler Polar Expedition," *American Geographical Society Bulletin* 35 (1903).

"To Annex the Arctic By Air," *Literary Digest* (February 23, 1924).

"To Seek the Unknown in the Arctic," *National Geographic Magazine* (June 1925).

"United States Arctic Colonization and Exploration in 1881," Reprint from the *Kansas City Review of Science and Industry* (August 1881).

Webster, E. G. "The Economic Development of the Soviet Arctic and Subarctic," *The Slavonic and Eastern European Review* (December 1950).

Westervelt, Col. G. C. and H. B. Sanford. "Possibilities of Transpolar Flight," *U.S. Naval Institute Proceedings* (May 1920).

Wilkins, George Hubert. "The Flight from Alaska to Spitsbergen," *Geographical Review* (October 1928).

———. "Flights North of Point Barrow," *Geographical Journal* (February 1928).

Additional periodicals referred to in the text may be found in cited collections.

Dissertations

Mattson, Margaret S. "The Growth of Canadian Civil Commercial Aviation 1918-30." Ph.D. dissertation, University of Western Ontario, 1979.

Smith, Gordon W. "The Historical and Legal Background of Canada's Arctic Claims." Ph.D. dissertation, Columbia University, 1952.

Miscellaneous

Browne, R. H. C. *The Canadian Polar Expedition or Will Canada Claim Her Own*. Pamphlet, University of Toronto, 1901.

Logan, Robert A. Letter with author, November 1981.

MacMillan, Miriam. Telephone interview with author, Brunswick, Maine, 17 July 1981.

Index

Nancy Fogelson received her B.S. degree in child development from the University of Connecticut in 1954. She received her first M.A. degree in education from Western Reserve University (Cleveland, Ohio) in 1959, a second M.A. degree in 1975 and her Ph.D. in 1983, both from the University of Cincinnati (Ohio) and both in history—the former in American history and the latter in American and Eastern European history. Her interest in diplomacy and international relations is reflected by the focus of the articles she has written for scholarly journals and by her professional memberships. Fogelson currently teaches American and European history at the high school and college levels.